DISCOVER THESE "BEST BETS

- **Arizona State University** boasts ...
beaches, an active nightlife, a bus...
country, *and* alumni that includ...
Democratic Party Chairman and ....ciary of Commerce,
Ron Brown.

- **Berea College** has *NO tuition,* a long tradition of civil rights activity,
and a long list of prominent African-American graduates.

- **Carnegie Mellon University,** an absolute heaven for computer ad-
dicts, is a smart choice for competitive students heading for a high
tech future.

- **Howard University,** the "Black Harvard," has graduated a majority
of this country's African-American health care professionals—*a great
college!*

- **Marlboro College,** small and unique, is organized as a community
which stresses personal growth, one-on-one interaction with the faculty, plus a sensational internship program that spans the globe from
Uganda to Tasmania.

- **Oberlin College** offers a solid education in an atmosphere where
social and moral responsibility count and such graduates as Carl
Rowan become part of a great legacy.

- **University of Pittsburgh** has the Kuntu Repertory Theatre, and
Kuntu Writing Workshop—and 100 African-American faculty members in a school truly committed to an interracial campus.

YOU'LL FIND THE PERFECT COLLEGE FOR YOUR NEEDS WITH

THE 100 BEST COLLEGES FOR AFRICAN-AMERICAN STUDENTS

ERLENE B. WILSON was a TV reporter and producer in Baltimore and
an associate editor for *Glamour* magazine, where she wrote an advice
column for college women. She co-founded Creative Planners, a
college marketing firm that published and distributed an activities
calendar for Black students. She now specializes in writing and producing literature about colleges. She lives in Randallstown, Maryland.

THE 100

BEST COLLEGES FOR
AFRICAN-AMERICAN
STUDENTS

Erlene B. Wilson

A PLUME BOOK

PLUME
Published by the Penguin Group
Penguin Books USA Inc., 375 Hudson Street,
New York, New York 10014, U.S.A.
Penguin Books Ltd, 27 Wrights Lane,
London W8 5TZ, England
Penguin Books Australia Ltd, Ringwood,
Victoria, Australia
Penguin Books Canada Ltd, 10 Alcorn Avenue,
Toronto, Ontario, Canada M4V 3B2
Penguin Books (N.Z.) Ltd, 182–190 Wairau Road,
Auckland 10, New Zealand

Penguin Books Ltd, Registered Offices:
Harmondsworth, Middlesex, England

First published by Plume, an imprint of Dutton Signet,
a division of Penguin Books USA Inc.

First Printing, September, 1993
10 9 8 7 6 5 4 3

 REGISTERED TRADEMARK—MARCA REGISTRADA

Library of Congress Cataloging in Publication Data:
Wilson, Erlene B.
    The 100 best colleges for African-American students / Erlene B.
Wilson.
        p.   cm.
    ISBN 0-452-27020-0
    1. Universities and colleges—United States—Directories.   2. Afro-
Americans—Education (Higher)—Directories.   I. Title.   II. Title:
One hundred best colleges for African-American students.
    L901.W58   1993
378.73—dc20   93-2941
                                                                         CIP

Printed in the United States of America
Set in New Baskerville
Designed by Leonard Telesca

TO PAT LEAKE,
forever with me . . .

ACKNOWLEDGMENTS

So many people had a hand in making this book possible, but none have been more important to me than my loving, supportive family and friends, who were patient with me as I sequestered myself for long periods to do the research and writing. Through it all, they were understanding and always cheered me on. My heartfelt thanks go especially to my son, Charlie, who was ever careful not to bother Mommy as she tried to write; to my mother, Esther, who was always there to bail me out when I needed a baby-sitter, an ear, or anything else; to the Douyons, Karen, Guy, Maisha and Angel, whom I leaned on heavily for the past three years as I tried to put my life back together, especially my loving sister, Karen; to Uncle "D," my towering hero, and Aunt Hattie, a mother's mother—both are the best second parents anyone could ever hope to have; and to my love, Bob, whose support, love, friendship and understanding are rare gems that I cherish. To Stephanie, who started it all—thanks for being a real friend. To my special sister in the spirit, friend and partner Jai, whose hard work and tenacity I could not have done without—sister, we did it! My thanks to the Ragin family matriarch, Aunt Lillie, and to the Jersey crew, Reg, Brenda, David, Gail and Dwight; also to Sheryl Lee, Leslie and Lynda—my friends through time; to John and Vicki; to legal eagle Andrea Johnson; to my agent, Madeleine; and many thanks to Nikki Giovanni for her generosity and inspiration—I will always be grateful.

I also want to extend special thanks to the many college and university staff members and faculty, administrators and students who indulged my requests for information few had ever asked for in the past. It is my hope that we will continue to move forward with the promise to create a better world for future generations.

Finally, to all young people—stay the course, keep your eyes on the prize and follow your dreams!

CONTENTS

x / Contents

FOREWORD

By Nikki Giovanni

Poet, Professor of English,
Virginia Polytechnic Institute and State University

The first pioneers who were Black came to America as explorers. Though exploring is a pioneering adventure, they were simply considered men who sailed toward the unknown seeking riches, dreams . . . something different. History has ignored them, tried to wipe them out because the people who could have told their story didn't realize there was a story to tell.

The Africans who came to this shore in the second decade of the seventeenth century weren't considered pioneers either. No one sang sagas of their journey, no one would be on shore to welcome them home. They came in chains on ships that would never take them back. "I'm going to fly away . . . one of these days . . . I'm going to fly away." They were the true pioneers. We talk, in American history, about the wagons moving westward, but we see no miniseries on the Middle Passage; we get no weekly sitcom called *My Night in the Galley*. The songs that were ultimately sung were sung by us about us. But the true pioneers were those whose hearts, hands and souls made this land come alive. Black pioneers cultivated the land and black songs cultivated the spirit.

You would think Frederick Douglass and Harriet Tubman were just about the only Black people who were abolitionists, every other person of color being so very content just to be a slave or to be some sort of "freed man." Not. The slaves who had to stay and the slaves who were able to leave were pioneers not only of Black freedom but of the American ideal.

The Harlem Renaissance brought us another pioneer, the artistic pioneer. For the first time, the masses of Black American people could not only create something but could sign their names to it. It could be a poem, a play, a novel, a dance, a piece of music, sculpture or the food on the table. In the 1920s, for the first time, a "signature" was meaningful to Blacks because we owned ourselves.

Throughout these centuries Black Americans have been breaking open doors that others would close, opening lands others stumbled through, finding emotional strength to carry on when a lesser people would have capitulated. Emmett Till found the strength to put his socks on before he was carried out to be brutally murdered; his mother found the strength to open his casket. Rosa Parks found the strength to stay seated; Martin Luther King found the words to define a movement.

But if there has been one overwhelming effort made by Blacks since our American sojourn, it has been the pursuit of education. The laws that were made against our reading, voting, holding certain jobs, living in certain areas were made not because we were incapable. You don't have to legislate against incapability. No one tells an infant, "You can't walk"; you tell that to a toddler. No one tells a six-year-old, "You can't drive"; you tell that to a fifteen-year-old. No one tells a man or a woman, "You can't read," unless there is the knowledge that if that person becomes educated he or she will no longer be a slave; will no longer sharecrop land; will no longer tolerate injustice.

Those of you looking now at colleges are pioneers, too. History may not record your struggles but they will be there and you, like your ancestors, will have to find a way to overcome. Education, higher education, graduate education, professional school, all these different ways of learning more and more will set you more and more apart . . . will make you stand out and become a target. But as you climb the educational ladder your ancestors hope you will "Walk together, Children . . . and don't you get weary." Every pioneer looks at a horizon and sometimes that horizon can look so far away that it seems safer and easier to go back. Your ancestors are whispering: "Don't let nobody turn you 'round."

College is a great, though difficult, adventure. Those of you who find your way there, like our ancestors on stormy seas, like our foreparents forging their way on the Underground Railroad, like your grandparents working against legal segregation, like your parents sitting in, kneeling in, praying in, in the sixties, know that once again Black Americans are being called to be our best selves. Knowledge is power. May that force be with you.

PREFACE

African-American students on predominantly white college campuses are challenged in ways that other students do not experience. Besides being intellectually ready to achieve academic excellence, African-American students at these schools must be self-confident, self-aware, ambitious and driven by the mind-set of a crusader on a mission. Indeed, these are the qualities African-American students must possess to succeed in our schizophrenic higher education system, which is both tolerant and intolerant of cultural and racial differences. At the same time, African-Americans have before them unprecedented educational and social opportunities in a college and university system that is the envy of the world.

The increasing pressure to attain parity for African-American students on U.S. campuses, as well as the recognition that minorities are an untapped source of good students in a time of decreasing enrollments, have prompted many colleges and universities to make generous offers of academic waivers and financial aid to African-Americans. It's up to you, the student, to look past these generous offers and find the combination of school, environment and academics that is right for you. For many of you the right school will be a predominantly white one; for others, one that is predominantly African-American.

In deciding which school to attend, you must consider first your own personality, background, family values and career goals. Your personal needs are far more important in choosing a school than academics or ability to pay. With the right match of student to school, these details can be worked out satisfactorily for both parties. Still, if you choose a predominantly white campus, you'll find that college offers no respite from the real-life problems of racism and intolerance. For you, campus life will not be the insular experience you might have found at a predominantly African-American college.

Selecting a school will probably be among the most difficult decisions you will make as a student. Although parents, school officials and others may offer advice on what is "best," in the end you, the student, will find that the best choice is the one college or university that is right for you.

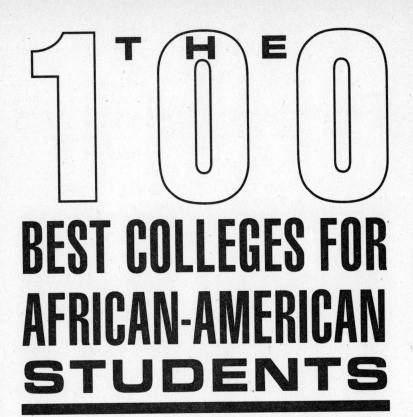

THE 100

BEST COLLEGES FOR AFRICAN-AMERICAN STUDENTS

INTRODUCTION

How the Colleges and Universities Were Selected

My initial concerns about this project centered around how to select 100 colleges and universities to profile out of more than 3,000 across this nation. Rather than reinventing the wheel, I mailed a detailed survey to institutions that had already achieved top ranking for academics and educational value in publications like *U.S. News & World Report* and *Money* magazine.

The survey included questions on the number of African-American students, faculty and administrators at the institution; on scholarship and other aid programs available to minorities; on admission requirements for African-American students, particularly standardized test scores; on provisions for remedial training and on the availability of counseling and tutoring services. I also asked for information on the institutions' success in graduating African-American students, and the percentage who went on to graduate and professional schools.

Each institution was asked to assign a student representative to respond to questions regarding campus life for African-American students. The survey inquired about social, professional and cultural organizations for African-Americans on campus, and requested reports on any racially motivated incidents, as well as the administration's handling of them.

The profiles included in this book represent 100 schools that found this project important enough to expend a great deal of time, energy and resources in completing the survey. They encompass colleges and universities at all points on the higher education spectrum, from Ivy League and liberal arts schools to predominantly African-American ones, in all parts of the country. The cooperation and support of committed administrators, students and staff made this project possible, and I am thankful to have had the opportunity to work with these professionals.

Student responses were especially important in providing an accurate view of life at both predominantly white and predominantly African-American colleges and universities. I am particularly grateful to the following students, who contributed their special insights:

ALABAMA
Fachia Penn

ARIZONA
Erica R. Wade

CALIFORNIA
Joli Williams
Toni Long
Kafi Watlington MacLeod

DISTRICT OF COLUMBIA
Kimberley H. Spight

FLORIDA
Kevin Cameron
Ricardo A. Whitted

GEORGIA
Jamal A. Chappelle

ILLINOIS
Lorraine Burrell
Keith Johnson
Lonnie Smith

INDIANA
Tina Rochelle Buchanan
Ann Hlabangana

Nicole Y. Oglesby
Tymika Robinson
Derrick Talbert

IOWA
Robert Easterling
Jason Edwards
Sara M. Madsen

KANSAS
Anita D. Shelton

KENTUCKY
Donna Kennedy

LOUISIANA
Alicia Kaigler

MAINE
Anni Taussig

MARYLAND
Douala Dennis
Hope M. Griffin
Nina Grimes
Ronda M. King
Nicole McFadden

MASSACHUSETTS
Craig Cobb

MINNESOTA
Troy Matson
Dennis Williams

MISSISSIPPI
De Teena R. Bender
Keeley A. H. McNeal

NEW YORK
Fritz François
LaPhillia Lockhart
Caitlin Enright Sen
Damon Williams

NORTH CAROLINA
Kedrick Lowery

NORTH DAKOTA
Olga Jamed

OHIO
Sofrina Hinton
Gale S. Nelson
Karla Scoon

OKLAHOMA
LaRonda Brown

OREGON
Karen Edwards

PENNSYLVANIA
Aletha Akers
Peter Anderson
Deborah Cousins
Mary Green
Cicely Horsham-Braithwaite

SOUTH CAROLINA
Jill Dowdy
Joseph J. Mungo

TENNESSEE
Linda Brewer

TEXAS
Kimberly Bell
Cassandra Lyons

VERMONT
Monique Mikell

VIRGINIA
Curtis C. Anderson II
Troy E. Drafton
Cynthia Murray

WASHINGTON
Darice R. Johnson
Adenike Long

WYOMING
Stephanie R. Gusters

The Realities of College Life for African-American Students

In researching this book, I made some surprising discoveries about campus life for African-American students in this country. For one thing, African-American students are spread out at colleges and universities all across this country. African-American students can be found at small, remote colleges like Cornell College in Mount Vernon, Iowa; prestigious schools like Hampden-Sydney in Virginia; big city and state universities like the University of Pittsburgh and University of Michigan, and Ivy League institutions like Yale, as well as at historically African-American schools like Spelman College and Howard University—institutions that produce the largest numbers of African-American college graduates.

The majority of the more than 1 million African-American college students attend predominantly white institutions, and competition for these students is fierce! There seems, at last, to be a recognition of the value of African-American students and an appreciation for the fact that, given the support and understanding afforded majority students, these students can and do succeed. Some schools do a better job than others in creating an environment conducive to success for African-American students, whether that means remediation and counseling programs, the presence of African-American professors and staff, relevant social and cultural activities, or support of African-American student and professional organizations. A correlation plainly exists between these efforts and the number of students enrolled at a particular college or university. However, despite their best efforts, few institutions have been able to enroll 10 percent or more African-American students. The average enrollment is about 5 percent, and schools with more African-American students are generally in large urban centers like Atlanta or New York City and appeal to older students, working women or graduate students. While the reasons for such low numbers are unexplained, the fact is that without special efforts by predominantly white institutions to recruit African-Americans, the numbers will continue to fall.

For now, you should know that many colleges and universities are attempting to attract African-Americans to their schools, some with offers of money and special programs that you may find difficult to resist. The important thing to keep in mind is that the selection of a college or university should be based on a number of factors, including the academic program a college offers; its campus environment for African-Americans; the existence of such support systems as counseling, tutoring, remedial and study-skill building; the interest and support of faculty and staff; social and cultural activities, and the overall climate of racial under-standing and tolerance. It's the last, after all, that drives many students to predominantly African-American colleges and universities.

This trend is likely to continue as African-American students seek an environment where race is not an issue. Colleges and universities that are sincere about helping African-American stu-dents succeed on their campuses will have to do more to meet this challenge and continue their efforts to see to it that all students are treated with fairness and respect. Indications are that schools are working hard to achieve this goal; many have instituted written policies that articulate their intolerance of racism, discrimination and acts of violence. Many, too, have established specific guide-lines and procedures for handling grievances filed against stu-dents, faculty or staff.

Though I'm sure I have not addressed every question and concern you may have about a college or university, I believe that each profile in this guide paints a picture, albeit with broad strokes, of each campus and covers the basic program offerings and support systems available to African-American students. I implore you, if you're interested in a school, to write to the admis-sions office for brochures and catalogs and to ask admissions officers any questions not answered in your research.

You and your parents also should spend some time at any colleges or universities in which you're seriously interested. No amount of reading or research will take the place of the firsthand knowledge that can be culled from a visit. Most colleges have an established procedure for such visits, and many will let you stay overnight on campus. This is the ideal situation. But even if you can't stay overnight, explore all aspects of the campus: sit in on a class, see the dormitories, sample the food, browse through the library and student center and, of course, speak with the admis-sions and financial aid staff and students. Be sure your decision-making is not achieved in a void, without conferring with your parents. After all, they want you to succeed and deserve to have some voice, though the final decision should be left to you.

If I could offer one piece of advice to potential college students, it would be this: Decide what it is you want from a college experience; look past the obvious (every school puts on a good face to get you interested); and bear in mind that selecting a college is the first step in making responsible decisions that will shape your life.

Good luck!

Your College and Your Future

Choosing the college you'll attend is one of the most important decisions you'll ever make. The college you attend will not only determine the kind of education you receive, but will influence your future earning power and the degree of success you may have in a chosen career. In fact, few experiences will have as great an impact on your view of the world and your ideas about what you can achieve.

African-American students face a special challenge as they grapple with concerns about how to fit in academically and socially on a predominantly white campus or whether they can obtain a good education at a less prestigious college or university. For many African-American students, attending college is their first experience of coping in the "white world." Nervous about educational and cultural differences, they often feel isolated from the rest of the student body and intimidated by campuses whose academic and social activities are devoid of any signs of African-American culture. As if that were not enough, African-American students now face a resurgence of racial intolerance at many schools nationwide.

These incidents are of great concern to students, parents and campus administrators and have many students rethinking whether they want to deal with the pressure of attending a majority college. While these are valid concerns, it's important to place them in proper perspective and recognize that each campus is different and should be judged accordingly.

As an African-American student, remember that while the American educational system is not perfect, it does provide invaluable opportunities to succeed in life. U.S. higher education is unmatched in the world, with more than 3,000 colleges and universities encompassing more academic programs and more various environments than most students can imagine. Schools offer everything from a beach view in sunny California to breathtaking vistas of snow-capped mountains in Alaska. You can study under Pulitzer prize winners and Nobel prize laureates at nationally renowned universities or follow in the footsteps of America's most famous men and women of color at one of the several hundred predominantly and historically Black colleges around the country.

Each year thousands of students from abroad flock to this country to obtain a college education which, even with rising costs, is a bargain compared to the educational opportunities available in their own countries.

More important, the higher education system in the United States offers students choice—something which we often take for granted but which does not exist in many places in the world. It's no wonder that many world leaders come here to be educated! The point is that the choice is yours when it comes to a good education. If you have the qualifications and are willing to work hard, you can get into a good school and get the money to pay for it. Whatever you envision for yourself, there's a college that fits your dream. Before considering a college, ask yourself a few questions:

• Are you prepared for life on a predominantly white campus? This may not be a problem if you've grown up in an interracial environment and know what to expect. But if you have never studied or worked among students of other races, you may be uncomfortable at a predominantly white college. It's for this reason that many African-American students attend predominantly and historically Black colleges. Some students blossom at predominantly Black schools. In fact, Black colleges and universities account for the majority of African-American college graduates in this country—something you may want to keep in mind as you make your selection. But bear in mind also that attending a predominantly African-American college will not save you from experiencing racism, and that in some cases it just delays the inevitable. Whether you face it in college or in the work environment, you will eventually have to learn how to function in the white world.

• What is your work style? Do you flourish in large institutions or urban environments with lots of people and activities? If so, you'll probably have no problem fitting in at a large university like UCLA, the University of Chicago or Columbia University. If crowds make you nervous and you don't have an outgoing personality, a liberal arts college or predominantly Black college where you can gets lots of one-on-one contact may be more suitable for you.

• Do you want to use your college experience to live in a different environment? Think about this carefully before you stake something as important as your college career on a living experiment. Often students who want to escape the fast pace, crime and noise of city life think they will find utopia in the country. African-American students on predominantly white rural campuses are often dismayed to find that along with this peace and solitude comes isolation and boredom. They're also surprised to discover that many urban problems (crime and drugs) exist in the country, too.

• What do you plan to do when you finish college? Will you go on to graduate school and eventually into a doctoral program? Is medical school, law school or other professional training in your plans? Or are you planning to get a job right out of college? Whatever your plans, find out the college's reputation in helping other students achieve what you want to do. Find out how many graduates get accepted into graduate degree programs and what percentage are African-American. Ask about the college's job placement service, the kinds of companies that recruit on campus each year and the number of African-American students who landed jobs. Inquire about alumni and the success they've had after graduation. The college admissions officer, job placement officer or minority affairs officer can provide this information.

Your College Search

Knowing what to look for in a college is great, but you'll still have to find one that's right for you. This book can help by providing information on the number of African-American students, faculty members and administrators on a campus; and on campus organizations as well as activities, cultural centers and course offerings that focus on African-American culture and history. This book should be only one of the many resources and strategies you use in your college search. Be sure to ask your high school counselor for assistance. Many have insights into the way particular colleges and universities make their admissions decisions. Counselors should know the reputations of various colleges for admitting and graduating African-American students and can help direct you to schools for which you are best qualified. But be aware that a counselor's knowledge of certain schools may be limited. Even the best-intentioned counselor can steer a student wrong. Here again, it's up to you to decide what's in your best interest and to seek information from a variety of sources.

You can obtain information about a college and talk with a representative of the admissions staff at one of the many college fairs that travel the country each year. Ask your high school counselor about the college fairs coming to your area. You can also contact your state's council on higher education to get the schedule and to obtain information on colleges and universities in your state. State education councils are also an excellent place to find out about sources of financial aid. And, don't overlook the colleges themselves; write to them for information and be sure to ask about special admissions and financial aid programs for African-Americans. Fraternities and sororities, too, are a good source of information and often organize tours for high school students of predominantly and historically Black colleges and universities. Contact your local chapter for information on these tours. The college alumni association often has an African-American chapter whose members serve as recruiters; these alumni have a wealth of information about the campus and how African-American students can expect to be treated. Ask the college admissions office whether such an organization is active on campus and how you can contact a representative.

When you begin your college selection process, start with a wish list of fifteen or twenty schools. Write down each school and beside it make two columns—one for the school's advantages and the other for its disadvantages. In the advantages column you may write things like "has the major I want," "campus is beautiful and near the beach," "my best friend is going to this school," "the social life is great," "a large majority of students are African-American." The disadvantages column might list things like "too far from home," "too few African-American students," "campus too large (or too small)," "insufficient academic program." Complete this exercise for each school (you'll probably only be able to place two colleges on a sheet of paper). From this you can cull a list of three to five colleges to visit and apply to.

Be sure to include on your list one or two schools to which you're assured admission. These may be community colleges, state universities or other schools to which an applicant with your academic background and SAT scores is all but guaranteed entrance. Pick schools you're comfortable with; you may wind up enrolled at one of these if your other choices fall through.

Many students find more opportunities in their home state or want to attend a school near home. To obtain information about these colleges and universities, write to the council on higher education in your state for a list. Also inquire about state-sponsored financial aid opportunities, particularly for minority students.

Finally, don't overlook friends and family members for recommendations and suggestions. They can offer insight into life at a predominantly Black college or how they coped with being a minority student at a predominantly white school. But take what they have to say with a grain of salt. Today's college campuses are different from those of the 1960s and 1970s. For one thing, there's far more competition for admission into prestigious schools and for jobs once students graduate. Today's students are also more conservative than the socially idealistic students of that era.

Campuses have also changed with the stronger push toward ethnic and cultural diversity. Predominantly white campuses are making special efforts to recruit African-American and other minority students and faculty. And, in an unexpected turn of events, states like Tennessee and Mississippi are mandating that to receive state funding, predominantly Black colleges must recruit more white students and faculty.

Your Application

Filling out college applications can be frustrating and time-consuming, but it's not a task to be taken lightly. Your application is the first impression a college admissions officer will have of you, so take great care in completing it. Ask yourself what kind of idea you want the admissions officer to get about you. Be accurate and thorough and include all of the information requested, including high school grades, references and recommendations, college admission test scores and a well-written essay. Be sure to include the fact that you are African-American in your correspondence, as most schools have admissions information specifically designed for minority students.

Indicate, too, whether you want your application to be considered for Early Decision or Early Action admissions. Early Decision commits you to attending the college if you are accepted and bars you from accepting admission at another school. Although you'll get an early response from your first-choice college (and sometimes be favored for admission), applying under Early Decision is only advisable if you're positive about your college choice. Early Action, on the other hand, does not commit you to attending the college if you're accepted; however, you may be less likely to be favored by colleges under this plan. These admissions programs are generally used by highly selective colleges and Ivy League universities, and the competition is stiff to get in early. If you're looking to get into one of these schools, it's a good idea to apply to six or seven other colleges as well. Otherwise, you'll generally need to apply to only three or four colleges.

Be sure, however, that your list contains at least one school you're assured of getting into. This may mean including at least one predominantly Black college. These schools tend to be less selective. State colleges and universities as well as community colleges are usually safe bets and favor students from their own state. Beyond that, be sure you have the minimal qualifications to apply to each of the schools on your list.

Here are some other tips to help you get through the process:

Decide what you want from your college experience. You don't have to attend an Ivy League college to obtain a good education. Nor do you have to attend a predominantly Black college to feel a part of college life. Properly matching your college to your requirements will improve your chances of achieving your life goals. If you want to attend graduate school, find out how successful other African-American students have been in getting into graduate programs, and at what schools. If you plan to move directly into the job market, find out what companies hire African-American graduates and at what job levels and salaries.

Start early. Your junior year of high school is a good time to start seriously looking at colleges. This will give you enough time to research several colleges and still meet the spring application deadlines. Include in your search at least one college you know you can get into, such as a predominantly Black college, a state college or community college. But be sure it's one that you'll be happy with, since you may end up there if you're turned down by your first choice.

Take the standardized tests. These tests are administered to prospective college students as a way of equalizing the basis on which a student's academic ability is judged. The tests used most often are the Scholastic Aptitude Test (SAT) of the College Board Admissions Testing Program, which is administered through the Educational Testing Service in Princeton, New Jersey, and the ACT Student Assessment administered by the American College Testing Program in Iowa City, Iowa. Each test is given several times during the year at various sites across the country. The SAT has two parts, verbal and mathematical, each scored on a scale from 200 to 800. The ACT score is reported as a composite average. Although there is some controversy over the fairness of these tests and whether coaching improves scores, don't hold your breath waiting for the tests to be abolished. For now, they're mandatory, so do your best to get a good score. For more information and registration materials on these tests write to (SAT) College Board Admissions Testing Program, Box 592, Princeton, NJ 08541, and ACT Registration, P.O. Box 414, Iowa City, IA 52243.

By now you've probably taken the PSAT/NMSQT, the Preliminary Scholastic Aptitude Test for the National Merit Scholarship Program. This test is identical to the SAT and is administered to high school sophomores and juniors to give them an idea of how they may score on college entrance exams. It also serves as the qualifying exam for the National Merit Scholarship program. Students who score high may qualify for a scholarship worth $2,000 or more per year based on demonstrated need.

Visit the college before you enroll. Visiting the colleges you're interested in attending may save you from being miserable once you're there. Try to spend at least a day on the campus, use the facilities and get permission to sit in on a few classes. If at all possible, go without your parents. College administrators and faculty are likely to respond differently when you're with your parents than when you're just another student on campus. Besides, spending a day on campus alone will give you a good idea of what you can expect as a student. A number of colleges have special summer orientation programs that give minority students an opportunity to spend a weekend or several days on the campus, sampling college life firsthand. Inquire whether the schools you're applying to have such programs.

Get up-to-date information about the college and its programs. Colleges and universities are constantly changing their focus and course offerings to keep pace with economic and student demand. Therefore, it's important to obtain recent catalogs and other information on the school and to talk with the admissions office before you apply. A simple postcard to the admissions office will get you on the mailing list to receive viewbooks, brochures, applications and more. When you write, be sure to inquire about admissions and retention programs for African-American students, how many are enrolled and the percentage who graduate. Also ask which programs are most popular and why.

Write a clear and concise college admissions essay. This is the most important part of your application. A well-thought-out and clearly written essay will tell an admissions officer more about you than admissions tests and letters of recommendation. A good essay is natural, straightforward and easy to follow. Write in your own style, using language (grammatically correct) that you're comfortable with. Writing in a scholarly or high falutin manner is not impressive; it's not appreciated by admissions officers and may do more harm than good. Be honest and be yourself. If you're having trouble constructing a good essay, get help. A number of good books have been written on the subject, and you may be able to get help from your high school teachers or guidance counselors.

Financing Your Education

A major concern of parents and students today is the rising cost of a college education, and most people expect tuitions and fees to continue to climb steadily into the next decade. The current rise in college costs is being fueled by a slow-growing American economy, inflation, and a diminishing college-age population. This post–baby-boom phenomenon has institutions scrambling to make up lost revenues by increasing the cost of tuition and class size, and instituting other cost-saving methods. Even so, experts estimate that many colleges and universities will not survive and that students' choices will eventually be diminished by several hundred colleges and universities nationwide.

The decreased number of traditional college-bound white students has forced institutions to focus more attention on recruiting minorities and nontraditional "older" students—primarily women looking to return to the work force. In some cases the result has been a boon to African-American students, who are being accepted into colleges and universities that in the past gave little consideration to the numbers of minority students they enrolled. Today, as I mentioned earlier, many institutions place a great deal of emphasis on the recruitment of minorities—particularly African-American students—and have developed special recruitment, financial aid and academic programs designed to attract these students. Such "enrollment loading" has been a mixed blessing, particularly in cases where admission standards are lowered and there are no remedial or support programs to help these students adapt. As a result, some students who might have succeeded at institutions more specifically designed to meet their needs, such as public colleges, predominantly Black colleges or two-year schools, have lost an opportunity for a good education. Given the sheer number of colleges and universities across the country that offer appropriate programs, African-American students do not have to make such sacrifices.

Starting your college search by looking for money is putting the cart before the horse. The first step is to find the college that's right for you—*then* work on getting money to pay for it! It's not unusual for the college to which you apply to help you finance your education. More than 70 percent of African-American students receive some type of financial aid, and more than 50 percent of all college students receive aid. Usually only the most well-heeled students pay for all of their college education, and even some of them receive aid.

Colleges fully expect to help you finance your education, but they also expect that you or your parents will help foot the bill according to what you or they can afford. This is what colleges refer to as "need," or the difference between what college costs and what you can afford to pay. "Need" is the basis on which financial aid packages are awarded. These packages can take many forms: grants (money that does not have to be paid back); loans (money that must be paid back with interest); college work-study (an opportunity to earn money for your education); and other forms like outright scholarship money, which usually does not have to be repaid.

To qualify for financial aid you must complete one or more financial aid application forms, depending on the school and type of aid you seek. The standard forms used for this purpose are the Financial Aid Form (FAF), which is generally accepted by schools that require the SAT for admission. The Family Financial Statement (FFS) form is generally used by schools that accept the ACT for admission. In addition, individual colleges, grant providers and, in some cases, state departments of higher education have their own form. Each must be carefully completed and submitted to the school or grant provider by a certain deadline.

The college financial aid officer reviews your application and uses a formula developed by the school to establish your financial need. The financial aid package which the officer puts together usually consists of a combination of grants, loans and other financing such as scholarships or work-study allotments. The type of aid you receive can also be influenced by your own situation. You may, for example, qualify for academic or athletic scholarships, as well as special aid designated for minority students.

Typically, students apply for financial aid through the federal government, which offers five major student financial aid programs: Pell Grants (formerly BEOG); Supplemental Educational Opportunity Grants (SEOG); College Work-Study (CWS); Perkins Loans (formerly National Direct Student Loans); and Guaranteed Student Loans (GSL), PLUS Loans, and Supplemental Loans for Students (SLS). Undergraduates may receive aid from all three types of programs: grants, work-study, and loans.

You can apply for any of the federal financial aid programs using the FAF and FFS. The deadline for applying for such aid is May 1, but it's advisable to apply as soon after January 1 as possible. It takes about four weeks for your application to be processed, and you may have to confirm and correct information and return it for reprocessing, which takes an additional two to three weeks. You may also have to provide proof that the information in your application is correct. Each of these processes slows down your application approval, and *if you miss the deadline you'll lose out on student aid!*

Once you've applied for aid, you will receive a SAR form (Student Aid Report), which will explain your eligibility for federal student aid. This form is to be submitted to the financial aid officer and included in your financial aid award package. The amount of federal student aid you receive will vary depending on the cost of your education and what the government defines as the difference between that cost and your family's contribution. If you qualify for federal student aid, be aware that it's not guaranteed from one year to the next. You must reapply each year.

You may qualify for one or all of the federal student aid programs. Here are descriptions of the programs and the general requirements for eligibility:

Pell Grant. These are awards of money to help undergraduate students pay for education after high school. The Pell Grant is often used as a "foundation" of financial aid to which other kinds of aid can be added. The U.S. Department of Education uses a standard formula, passed into law by Congress, to evaluate your Pell Grant application. This formula produces a figure called the Student Aid Index number, which determines your eligibility and will appear on your Student Aid Report (SAR). The actual amount you receive will depend on available funds, your Student Aid Index number and whether you're a full or part-time student. To obtain a free booklet that describes the formula in detail, write to Formula Book, Department K-9, Pueblo, CO 81009-0015, or to the Federal Student Aid Information Center, P. O. Box 84, Washington, D.C. 20044.

Supplemental Education Opportunity Grants (SEOG). The SEOG is an award of money to help undergraduates who have exceptional financial need pay for their education after high school. You can apply for the SEOG through your college financial aid office.

College Work-Study (CWS). This program gives you an opportunity to work—usually at an on-campus job—to earn money for your education. Students are paid at least the federal minimum wage, but sometimes more, depending on the type of job. The college sets an amount that you can earn according to your financial need and the amount of money you receive from other financial aid programs.

Perkins Loans. These are low-interest loans to help undergraduate and graduate students pay for their education. The program is administered through participating schools, which set the deadlines and determine the amount of the loan depending on your need and other sources of aid you're receiving.

Guaranteed Student Loans (GSL). The GSL program provides low-interest loans through a private lender such as a bank, credit union or savings and loan association. These loans are insured by a state guarantee agency and reinsured by the federal government. Under this loan program you can only borrow the cost of education at your school minus any other financial aid you may receive. The financial aid office can give you a GSL application, or you can obtain one from a lender or your state guarantee agency. Once you complete your portion of the application, your school financial aid office will have to certify your enrollment, your academic standing, the cost of your education, any other financial aid you're receiving and your financial need. You should begin looking for a lender as soon as you're accepted by your school, as it takes between four and six weeks to approve a loan.

PLUS Loans/Supplemental Loans for Students (SLS). PLUS loans allow your parents to borrow money for your education; SLS loans are for student borrowers. Both kinds of loans are made by private lenders such as banks, credit unions or savings and loan associations. You can apply for these loans in the same way you apply for GSL loans. The difference is that you don't have to show need to obtain a loan, although you may have to submit to a credit check.

For information on any of the federal financial aid programs outlined here, write to the Federal Student Aid Information Center, P. O. Box 84, Washington, D.C. 20044.

The federal government is the largest provider of financial aid funding to students; however, there are numerous other sources of aid. You might want to explore some of the following resources:

• Your state council on higher education has information about financial aid programs offered to residents.

• If you're interested in becoming a teacher, you may qualify for the Paul Douglas Teacher Scholarship Program, which provides up to $5,000 a year to high school students who graduate in the top 10 percent of their class and meet other criteria. Your state council on higher education can tell you how to apply for this program.

• Your high school counselor or state council on higher education can tell you about the Robert C. Byrd Honors Scholarship Program and the National Science Scholars Program (NSSP). The Byrd Program awards $1,500 to students who demonstrate outstanding academic achievement, and the NSSP Program awards up to $5,000 to students who demonstrate excellence in the physical, life or computer sciences; mathematics, or engineering.

• Your public library has information on state and private sources of financial aid. Many have applications on hand for your use. Also ask for help in researching financial aid in the library's directories.

• Your parent's employer or labor union may have a program to help finance your education. The personnel office can usually provide this information.

• If you've chosen a historically Black college, the United Negro College Fund, 500 62nd Street, New York, NY 10021, can supply information about the financial aid programs at its member schools.

• Many African-American sororities and fraternities, such as Delta Sigma Theta, offer scholarships to young people through their local chapters. Contact the chapter in your area for information on financial aid and other programs for college-bound students. Check the yellow pages under "Associations" or "Organizations" for a local chapter, or use the *Directory of Associations* in the reference section of your library.

• Numerous civic organizations and foundations provide funds for college. Some major ones to investigate are religious organizations, the YMCA, 4-H clubs, chambers of commerce, the Girl Scouts and Boy Scouts, the Jaycees, Kiwanis and local PTAs.

• If you're a veteran, you may qualify for financial assistance. Check with your local Veterans Affairs office to see whether you qualify.

• Be sure to look into professional associations, especially those in fields which you have an interest in studying—journalism, psychology, medicine, law, computer science, education or engineering, to name a few. Many of these organizations are listed in the U.S. Department of Labor's *Occupational Outlook Handbook* and can also be found in directories of associations in your local library. To obtain a copy of the handbook, write to VGM Career Horizons, 4255 West Touhy Avenue, Lincolnwood, IL 60646-1975.

Scholarship Opportunities for African-Americans

A fair amount of student financial aid comes from the colleges and universities themselves and from the federal government. However, students can also find money for college through a wide variety of scholarship programs. Many scholarships come from professional and trade organizations in such fields as business, medicine, journalism, the sciences and the arts. These organizations award scholarships as a means of bringing new talent into the field and, in the case of African-Americans, of specifically encouraging and supporting young aspirants. If you've decided on a career field, you'd be wise to look to its professional and trade organizations for financial assistance. Your local library can help you find these organizations. Service organizations and private foundations also provide scholarships to students, usually on the basis of merit and overall academic excellence.

Following is a list of scholarship programs available specifically for African-American students. A brief description is provided of the scholarship, criteria and application information. This list is but a small sampling of the types of scholarship opportunities available to African-Americans. You're encouraged to investigate others using the reference sources at your local library (including *The Foundation Directory*), and using your contacts in church groups, fraternities and sororities and community organizations.

Keep in mind that there's a great deal of competition for these scholarships and that any information you can provide to set yourself apart from other applicants will give you an edge. If you do community or charitable work, tutor, participate in a theater group, design crafts, or speak a language, besides English, mention it in your letter of application. Groups that award scholarships are interested in helping young people not only achieve academic excellence but develop into well-rounded individuals.

AICPA Scholarships for Minority Undergraduate Accounting Majors, Ms. Sharon L. Donahue, Manager, Minority Recruitment, American Institute of Certified Public Accountants, 1211 Avenue of the Americas, New York, NY 10036. African-American and other minority students majoring in accounting are eligible to receive awards of up to $1,500 per year through this program, which is underwritten by the AICPA, public accounting firms, corporations, individual CPAs and others. You must have certification of your coursework and academic standing from your college financial aid officer; you must be a U.S. citizen or have a permanent resident's visa.

American Institute of Architects' Minority/Disadvantaged Scholarship Program, Director, Education Programs, American Institute of Architects, 1735 New York Avenue, N.W., Washington, D.C. 20006. The AIA offers scholarships to African-American and other disadvantaged students. You must be nominated by an individual or organization. The deadline for nominations is December 1.

Arts Recognition and Talent Search, Arts Office, 300 N.E. 2nd Avenue, Miami, FL 33132. Sponsored by the National Science Foundation for Advancement in the Arts, the Arts Recognition and Talent Search (ARTS) is designed to identify, recognize and encourage young people who have demonstrated excellence in dance, music, theater, visual arts and writing. Participants in the Talent Search become eligible for apprenticeships and cash awards ranging from $500 to $3,000. African-Americans and other minorities are encouraged to participate in the program.

Cox Newspaper Minority Scholarship Program, Cox Newspapers, P. O. Box 4689, Atlanta, GA 30302. African-American students who attend Georgia State University or an undergraduate Atlanta University Center school (Atlanta Clark, Morehouse, Spelman College) and maintain a B average may be eligible for this scholarship program.

Financial Aid Unscrambled: A Guide for Minority Engineering Students. National Action Council for Minorities in Engineering, Inc., 3

West 35th Street, New York, NY 10001. This handbook helps you understand how to complete financial aid applications and contains a list of financial aid opportunities for full-time minority students interested in engineering or science- and mathematics-based majors.

Garrett Park Press, P. O. Box 190, Garrett Park, MD 20896. Garrett Park Press produces a series of booklets on financial aid opportunities for minorities. Each booklet costs $4 and the complete set can be purchased for $20:

- Financial Aid for Minority Students: Awards Open to Students with Any Major.
- Financial Aid for Minority Students in Business and Law.
- Financial Aid for Minority Students in Education.
- Financial Aid for Minority Students in Engineering and Science.
- Financial Aid for Minority Students in Health Fields.
- Financial Aid for Minority Students in Journalism/Mass Communications.

Geoscience Scholarships for Ethnic Minorities, AGI Minority Scholarships, American Geological Institute, 4220 King Street, Alexandria, VA 22302-1507. African-American students majoring in geoscience may be eligible to receive scholarships through this program, which is designed to increase the participation of minority ethnic groups in the geosciences. To qualify, you must major in geology, geophysics, geochemistry, hydrology, meteorology, oceanography, planetary geology or earth science education.

Herbert Lehman Foundation. This Foundation awards $1,000 per year to an African-American high school graduate attending a public college in the South. Ask your college financial aid officer about this grant if you are planning to attend a Southern public college.

Minority Editing Intern Program for College Seniors, Dow Jones Newspaper Fund, Inc., P. O. Box 300, Princeton, NJ 08543-0300. Targeted at college seniors, this program provides a student with a paid summer internship on a daily newspaper and a $1,000 scholarship for use in graduate studies in the fall after the internship. The deadline for applying is November 15.

Minority Journalism Career Guide, Dow Jones Newspaper Fund, P. O. Box 300, Princeton, NJ 08543-0300. This guide provides information on careers in journalism, as well as opportunities for scholarships, fellowships, internships and special training for minorities.

Music Assistance Fund, New York Philharmonic, Avery Fisher Hall, Broadway at 65th Street, New York, NY 10023. This fund provides financial assistance to minority students who play orchestral instruments and want to attend a recognized conservatory, university school of music or summer institute. You must audition to qualify (pianists needn't audition). Recipients can receive awards from $500 to $2,500 per academic year depending on financial need and talent.

NAACP Afro Academic, Cultural, Technological and Scientific Olympics Scholarships (ACT-SO); contact your local NAACP branch. This program provides scholarships to African-American students who are winners in its local competitions, usually held in June. There are twenty-four categories, including the performing arts, humanities, visual arts and sciences, and awards range from $500 to $1,000.

NAACP–Roy Wilkins Scholarships, NAACP Youth and College Division, 4805 Mt. Hope Drive, Baltimore, MD 21212-3297. This program awards scholarships up to $1,000 to needy African-American students in their senior year of high school or first year of college.

National Association of Black Journalists Scholarship Program, Box 17212, Washington, D.C. 20041. African-Americans majoring in journalism and enrolled in a four-year accredited college or university may apply for this $2,500 award. You must write a 500- to 800-word article on a Black journalist and submit three other samples of your work.

National Achievement Scholarship Program for Outstanding Negro Students, One Rotary Center, 1560 Sherman Avenue, Evanston, IL 60201.

African-American students compete for college undergraduate scholarships underwritten by corporations, foundations, colleges and individuals. To enter the competition, you must take the Preliminary Scholastic Aptitude Test/National Merit Scholarship Qualifying Test (PSAT/NMSQT) in high school and meet other published eligibility requirements.

National Presbyterian College Scholarships, Vocation Agency, Presbyterian Church (U.S.A.), 475 Riverside Drive, Room 430, New York, NY 10015. If you belong to the Presbyterian Church and are an entering freshman at a participating church-affiliated college, you may qualify for one of 175 awards ranging from $500 to $2,000. To obtain an application, write to the above address after September 1. The deadline for submitting applications is December 1.

Rhodes Scholarships, Office of the American Secretary, Rhodes Scholarship Trust, Pomona College, Claremont, CA 91711. This prestigious scholarship program entitles the recipient to a minimum of two years' study at Oxford University in England. Each year thirty-two American students are selected as Rhodes scholars based on merit and without regard to race or gender. Candidates must be U.S. citizens, unmarried and between the ages of eighteen and twenty-three, inclusive, by October 1 of the year of the application.

Jackie Robinson Foundation, Jackie Robinson Scholarship Program, 80-90 Eighth Avenue, New York, NY 10011. This foundation provides scholarships to minority high school seniors who have demonstrated academic excellence, have financial need and have "leadership potential." You must already have been accepted at a college or university. Applications are available beginning November 1. The deadline is March 30.

Sachs Foundation Scholarship, Sachs Foundation, 101 North Cascade Avenue, Suite 430, Colorado Springs, CO 80903. Established for African-American students who live in Colorado, the Sachs Foundation provides approximately sixty grants each year for four years to high school graduates with good academic records. Applications are available after January 1; and the deadline is March 1.

United Negro College Fund Scholarship Programs, UNCF, 500 East 62nd Street, New York, NY 10021. The UNCF offers a number of scholarship opportunities for African-American students who attend member colleges and universities:

Citicorp Fellowship Program. You must show financial need, have a 3.5 GPA, demonstrate leadership ability, and be recommended by the school administration.

Michael Jackson Scholarship Program. You must demonstrate financial need, have a 3.0 GPA, be recommended by the school administration and submit an autobiographical essay.

Annenberg General Foundation. You must show financial need, have a 3.5 GPA and submit recommendations from the school administration.

UNCF/Toyota Scholarship Program. You must demonstrate financial need and have a 3.0 GPA.

General Motors Engineering Excellence Awards. These awards are available to college sophomores who attend UNCF member colleges and have a 3.5 GPA.

Paying for Your Education through the Military

In addition to the government's Federal Student Aid program, the U.S. military offers an extensive financial aid package to potential college students through a variety of programs. African-American students have no doubt seen or heard some of the countless radio and television advertisements pitching the military as a career choice and source of financial aid for college. Many of these advertisements are specifically targeted at the African-American community, and we are responding; statistics indicate that a growing number of African-Americans enroll in military education programs each year. The military's intense recruitment and retention efforts have made it an attractive option for many African-Americans who want to obtain a good education or a marketable skill after high school. Some of the programs not only pay for educational costs but provide an income as well.

If these offers seem too good to be true, consider the price. When the military pays for your education it requires you to perform active military service for no less than two years. During peacetime, this may look like a good deal. If war breaks out, the military option may not seem as sweet. During the Persian Gulf War large numbers of African-American soldiers were called into action, and we heard time and again that they'd never thought they would have to go to war; that they played soldier to make extra money or to get a college education. If you decide in favor of the military option, be sure you understand what you're getting into. Here are some of the educational programs the military offers to college-bound students:

Air Force ROTC. Through this program a student can obtain a two- to four-year, fully paid scholarship covering tuition, fees, expenses and a $100 nontaxable allowance each month, as well as earn an officer's commission in the Air Force. Scholarships are awarded on a competitive basis and are open to men and women. For applications (DD Form 1893) for four-year scholarships, write for the brochure "Scholarship Applicant Booklet," Air Force ROTC, Selections Division, Maxwell AFB, Alabama 36112. The deadline for submitting these applications is December 1. If you're interested in two- or three-year scholarships, write to the Professor of Aerospace at the college to which you're applying, or write to Air Force ROTC, Recruiting Division, Maxwell AFB, Alabama 36112.

U.S. Coast Guard Academy. The Coast Guard also provides an opportunity for a student to obtain a four-year college education and become commissioned as an ensign in the Coast Guard through an annual nationwide competition based on the SAT or ACT test. For more information on the program, write to Director of Admissions, U.S. Coast Guard Academy, New London, CT 06320. To qualify, submit your application before December 15.

U.S. Marine Corps. The Marine Corps sponsors a number of educational programs, including the following opportunities to obtain a college degree:

Marine Corps Enlisted Commissioning Education Program (MECEP). This program is for enlisted Marines and gives them an opportunity to obtain a four-year college degree as full-time students and become commissioned officers.

College Degree Program (CDP). This program provides selected Marine officers an opportunity to complete their baccalaureate degrees by attending a college or university as full-time students for up to two years.

Marine Corps Tuition Assistance Program. This is a financial assistance program for Marines who want to take college courses during their off-duty time toward a degree or other post-secondary education. The Marine Corps may pay 75 to 100 percent of the cost of tuition for approved college courses, depending on the status of the applicant.

Naval ROTC. The Navy offers students an opportunity to earn a commission as ensign, U.S. Navy, or second lieutenant, U.S. Marine Corps, by successfully completing the NROTC Navy–Marine Corps Scholarship Program at one of the sixty-five colleges and universities nationwide that offer the program. Students may receive two-year or four-year scholarships which cover full tuition, fees, books, uniforms, and a $100 nontaxable allowance each month (for up to forty months). To obtain an application for the four-year scholarship program, contact your local Navy or Marine Corps recruiting station or your high school guidance counselor, or write to NROTC units and the Commander, Navy Recruiting Command (Code 314), 4015 Wilson Boulevard, Arlington, VA 22203. Be sure to apply between March 1 and December 1 of the year before your college enrollment. Two-year scholarship program applicants can obtain information in the same way but must enter one of the sixty-five host institutions with junior status at the time of enrollment in the program.

New Mexico Military Institute Regent Scholarship, North Hill, Roswell, New Mexico 88201. Scholarship awards of $300, $500 and $1,000 are available through this program to the New Mexico Military Institute. The scholarships are conditional on attending NMMI and entering the Advanced Course of Senior Army ROTC leading to a commission as second lieutenant in the two years at the institute.

Scholarships and Grants vs. Loans

Obviously, not every African-American student will qualify for a scholarship or grant, and even those who receive such aid may need additional money to pay for school. To fill this gap, many students will have to apply to one of the student loan programs described in this section. These loans are usually fairly easy to obtain from a bank or other lending institution because the federal government guarantees their repayment should you default. The problem with taking out student loans, of course, is that you have to repay them once you complete your education. Recently many students have found repayment a problem because they have not found jobs after college. The result is an enormous increase in the number of student loan defaults. In 1992 it is estimated that student loan defaults cost the American taxpayer more than $3.4 billion. Unchecked, the situation will worsen as more students apply for the loans and fewer are able to pay them back because they cannot find work after college.

Complicating the problem is an inefficient system of managing the loan programs which has failed to monitor both the lenders and borrowers. Some charge that the Department of Education has been remiss in devising a system of tracking students who default. Even those who attempt to pay off loans may run into problems because of lenders who, rather than make an effort to recover payment, are quick to place the loan in default because the federal government will pay off the debt.

All of this has left the taxpayer holding the bag, but change is inevitable. Judging from the current political and economic climate, which favors cost-cutting and greater accountability for money spent by the government, the student loan program is primed for a major shakeup. In an effort to clean up its act, the Department of Education has already started to implement rules that limit lending to schools with high rates of default and has begun collecting some outstanding loans through the Internal Revenue Service, which turns over the income tax refund checks of former students who have defaulted. The IRS now also reports those in default to credit bureaus, which sends up a red flag to potential lenders of credit, jeopardizing the chances of obtaining a home, car or credit card. If you're applying for a student loan, here are some of the things you should consider to protect yourself:

- Talk with your college financial aid officer or contact the U.S. Department of Education about college loan programs and the rules for repayment.
- Find out whether your bank or lender sells its student loans to a secondary party such as Sallie Mae (Student Loan Marketing Association). It is better to deal with the original lender so that you can communicate directly if you have problems or want to make special payment arrangements.
- If you have questions about student loans, call the Department of Education at 1-800-433-3243 or write to Department of Education, Office of Postsecondary Education, 400 Maryland Avenue, S.W., Washington, D.C. 20202.

Other Ways to Finance Your Education

If obtaining a college education through the traditional routes seems out of reach for you, there are other ways to get a degree. With vision and tenacity many people do it the old-fashioned way—they work for it!

With today's depressed economy, working still may be the most realistic way to pay for a college education, though it may take years to complete a degree. Single women who are the heads of their households, children from large families, and children from poor families who want to go to college often have to work to help support the household. Such circumstances are clear obstacles to obtaining a college degree, but they need not stop you from going to college.

Recognizing the constraints of many potential students, some community and public colleges now offer evening and weekend programs. Increasingly, too, employers are developing cooperative relationships with local colleges and universities to provide training and other job skills to their employees. These institutions are happy to oblige and have begun to design curriculums that will provide employers a more qualified work force. The local community or public colleges in your state can provide information on programs that may meet your specific needs and tell you whether financial assistance is available.

Community Colleges

A typical route to a full-time college degree for many African-American students is through the community college system. Community colleges are a viable option, particularly for students who don't have good grades. Community colleges and other two-year institutions tend to be less expensive than traditional institutions, and their admissions policies are often less restrictive. At the same time, they offer good academic training and provide disadvantaged students an opportunity to obtain the remedial skills needed to qualify for admission to a four-year institution.

Although community colleges generally help students become job-ready, many students use the experience as a stepping stone to higher education. The more ambitious student may even go on from these humble beginnings to obtain a doctoral degree. Generally, a college or university has a policy on the admission of transfer students into its bachelor's degree program. Many welcome transfers from their local community college and have established recruitment programs to smooth the way for these students. Others have programs that provide associate degrees and transfer the students through an internal process. To learn more about the transfer policies of schools in your area, contact your local college admissions office.

Making It As a College Athlete

It's no secret that many colleges and universities provide full scholarships, awards of cash and other perks to athletes who show promise in helping to build a winning sports team. For many African-Americans, such an opportunity is the dream of a lifetime. For all the financial support they receive, however, student athletes are expected to devote the majority of their time to playing and practicing sports. These demands often conflict with academics, and the latter may take a back seat. Even the best-intentioned student will find it challenging to spend sixty or more hours playing sports and still attend classes, complete assignments and just explore "being a student." But college athletes need to recognize the importance of giving some time to academics. Failure to do so may result in a student's leaving the campus without either a sports career or a college education. Unfortunately, this situation occurs disproportionately among African-American athletes and will continue to do so unless the students take charge of the situation.

If you're a student athlete, you'd be well advised to keep in mind that a college education—more than sports—is the key to opportunity. Your chances of finding meaningful work are greatly increased with a college degree. The odds of becoming a superstar athlete like Michael Jordan or Magic Johnson are small, but you can achieve star status in any field that you apply yourself to academically—and that's the true measure of success.

Your Future

The process of selecting a college is difficult enough, and it may seem premature to consider what you want to do after graduation. But giving some thought to your future now can help smooth the way to fulfilling your career goals. If you plan to do postgraduate work, for example, take note of the colleges and universities that have good records in helping African-American students obtain entry into top graduate schools. If you plan to go to work right after college, you'll want to select a school with a strong undergraduate program and a good reputation with major companies in your field. Whatever your future plans, take some time now to make a personal assessment of your interests, skills, work style, and talents so that you can begin to establish a broad range of career interests. From there you can begin the process of determining which careers offer the best opportunities and fit comfortably into your life. Here are some questions you can ask yourself that will help narrow your focus of career possibilities, either now, as you begin your college career, or after you graduate:

- What kind of work interests you? Is the corporate world exciting to you? Or is a job in government or the nonprofit sector more appealing?

- What skills do you have? Do you write well, speak well? Are you artistic, sports-minded? Do you have a healthy curiosity?
- What talents do you have—music, sports, writing, arts and crafts, organizing, fund-raising? Once you begin thinking about them you'll probably discover you have many talents.
- Which of your talents do you most enjoy using?
- What kind of environment do you like working in? Do you enjoy the outdoors, or do you thrive on the hustle and bustle of working in a big city? Is a job in a large company with hundreds of employees what you envision for yourself? Or is a small company where everyone knows your name more your style?
- What kind of income do you expect? What importance do you place on having power and authority in your job?

These are just some of the questions you may want to ask yourself as you think about your career goals or set out to find a job after graduation. Reviewing your answers will give you a profile of yourself and what is important to you, and will help you identify career fields and jobs that you may find satisfying and rewarding.

Where the Jobs Are

Today's job market offers myriad opportunities, particularly in technology, the sciences and information-based fields. Despite the slow economy, there continues to be high demand for qualified applicants in selected fields, and experts predict that the demand will continue to grow at least through the next decade. Discovering what jobs are available in high-growth fields is one of the greatest challenges to young people today, and students are well advised to use a number of strategies to settle on suitable job and career interests.

Talking with college job placement counselors and professors and reading career guides is a good start. Keeping up with current events and new developments in industry is also a good way to learn about different jobs. To obtain information on specific careers, you might also take some of these suggestions:

- Talk to teachers, parents, friends, relatives—ask them what they think you'd be good at.
- Give some thought to what your dream job would be. Then go about finding out how to get it.
- Investigate published resources such as the *Occupational Outlook Handbook* compiled by the U.S. Department of Labor and published by VGM Career Horizons; *The College Board's Guide to Jobs and Career Planning;* and one of the best-known guides, *What Color Is Your Parachute?* by Richard N. Bolles (Ten Speed Press). Your local library should have these books, as well as numerous other career and job-hunting books.
- Read newspapers, magazines and biographies to learn what kinds of jobs people have.
- When you meet someone who has an interesting job, ask him or her about the day-to-day aspects of the work and how to get into the field.

Job-hunting is no easy task, and few people look forward to it. Let's face it, selling yourself is like selling anything else. It requires discipline, tenacity and the ability to swallow a healthy portion of rejection. No matter how well qualified, it takes the typical job-seeker about three months to find a suitable job. One of the real challenges of job-hunting is to remain encouraged and to keep your self-confidence. Knowing where the jobs are will make this task more palatable.

As we move toward the year 2000, service-oriented and high-tech jobs are becoming increasingly important. Coupled with the change to a more global economy, this has had the effect of creating jobs that did not exist before. Following is a list of some of the current "hot career fields" in which job prospects are good.

Health Care. From physicians to health insurers, this field continues to grow, creating an increasing demand for care providers. Jobs that show the greatest growth potential include physician, physician assistant (PA), nurse, nurse-practitioner, pharmacist, veterinarian, dentist, physical therapist, health care manager and optometrist.

Business. Jobs in accounting, marketing, management consulting, sales, finance, insurance, advertising, public relations, job placement and banking are most often recommended.

Technology. It's no surprise that this field, which includes engineering and computer science, is leading the way in new job development. As we move into the twenty-first century, the importance of technology will only increase job prospects in this field. Some jobs that are hot include software engineer; electrical, environmental, aeronautical and civil engineer; computer analyst and network manager.

Sciences. As the demand for better medical treatments and environmentally sound products increases, so will the need for those who create them: chemists, biologists and medical researchers.

Education. A desire to improve our educational system has fueled renewed interest in careers as teachers, principals, superintendents, day care and special education instructors and college professors. Depending on academic achievement, location and the health of the community in which they serve, these professionals can command above-average salaries.

Law. The law is still where the money is, and it will remain there, but in more specialized areas such as environmental, bankruptcy, employment and labor law; paralegal work and legal assisting; and lobbying.

Other notable fields. These include architecture, human resource management, journalism, manufacturing, psychology and sociology.

Preparing Now for Success in Your Career Field

One of the best ways to prepare for a job and career is to know the talents and abilities you bring to the work force. Although you may not be ready to look for a job, there are some things you can do now as a student to increase your chances of success once you graduate.

• Make it a priority to do well in school. Study hard, earn good grades and take advantage of opportunities to improve your skills and expand your horizons.

• Get involved in campus activities such as the student government, professional organizations and sports. Take on a leader's role wherever possible.

• Develop good relationships with faculty members and administrators. Plan to meet regularly with key faculty and administrators to discuss classwork, seek advice and keep them informed of your progress. Remember, your college life is practice for the real world, and the key to success in a career often is the result of personal relationships that you build with employers and coworkers along the way.

• Begin to develop additional talents and abilities through internships, summer and part-time jobs, study abroad, hobbies, sports, volunteering and the like. Each of these activities will help you develop qualifications that extend beyond the educational requirements and acquire experience that may be needed for a particular job.

• Finally, keep in mind that your college major often will have little to do with the job you find and love! Unless you're going after specific professional training in medicine, law or certain other fields, you may find that skills, training and exposure to opportunity are what you need most to be successful at a particular job, no matter what your major was in college.

As the saying goes, "nothing succeeds like success," and success is a goal for which every student should strive. African-American students should know that success is not measured by what school you attend, but by what you learn and how you use it in life. Here are some words of wisdom from African-Americans who have achieved success in a variety of fields.

Ronald E. Goldsberry, General Sales and Marketing Manager
Ford Parts and Service Division
Dearborn, Michigan

Central State University, Wilberforce, Ohio, a predominantly African-American university

"Central State University is a small historically Black state college where I received a B.S. degree in chemistry. I later received advanced degrees from Stanford University (M.B.A.) and Michigan State University (Ph.D.).

"In retrospect, attending a small, predominantly black school provided me the environment to mature socially and helped me to develop the self-confidence I needed to reach my academic potential. I learned how to live and succeed among people with differences in culture, income, religion, sex, capabilities and aspirations. I developed an intangible capability—'street sense'—which has served me well throughout my career. My professors, recognizing my capability and talent, shaped, sheltered, influenced, disciplined, motivated and taught me as though I were their child. It was this careful and personal development that gave me a strong self-confidence, a sense of self-respect, and prepared me to succeed at furthering my education, prospering in business, and finally, enjoying Life!"

Ron James
Vice President and Chief Executive Officer—Minnesota
U S West Communications, Inc.
Minneapolis, Minnesota

Doane College, Crete, Nebraska, a small private liberal arts college

"Having grown up in the all-Black community of Port Arthur, Texas, where the business leaders, preachers, teachers, coaches, barbers, bus drivers and shopkeepers all looked just like me, I came to know the richness of my cultural and racial roots.

"Doane College provided a stark racial contrast from my adolescent years. With only 7 percent of the population minority, I now found myself having to adapt to a white world. Doane provided me with an opportunity to participate in a community that reflects the work world; and because it was small, I got to know my fellow students, faculty and administration well. During my time at Doane I captained a football team during a thirty-nine-game winning streak, met my wife, Renee, and graduated in three and a half years.

"My college experience was rich and full of good memories, and it gave me the opportunity to grow academically, emotionally and mentally."

Judy A. Johnson, Director, Profit Management Systems
IBM Corporation, Mid-Atlantic Area
Washington, D.C.

Hampton Institute, Hampton, Virginia, a small historically African-American college

"Hampton was very nurturing. It helped me to build leadership skills through participation in a sorority and other campus organizations and also taught me how to relate to people with varied backgrounds. Here I met people from all over the world and realized there are ways to bridge differences without changing who you are."

Jennifer Lawson
Executive Vice President
National Programming and Promotion Services
Public Broadcasting Service (PBS)
Alexandria, Virginia

Tuskegee University, Tuskegee, Alabama, a historically African-American college, and Columbia University, New York, New York.

"I found my years at Tuskegee University immensely rewarding, especially its rich history of African-American leadership and innovation—Booker T. Washington's theories on political, social and economic development for African-Americans; George Washington Carver's scientific studies; Alma Lomax's civil rights work and the legends of the World War II heroes, the Tuskegee airmen.

"The faculty was supportive of my special interests and provided a flexible curriculum to match my pursuits. The emphasis on hard work and the expectation of quality and excellence reaffirmed values given me by my family and community.

"As a graduate student in film studies at Columbia University, I felt the emphasis the faculty placed on meeting stringent standards of quality quickly caused a deep bond to form among all of us as students, despite any differences of race, class and culture.

"Filmmaking requires a team, and Columbia provided a supportive atmosphere in which students reached out to each other for help. I have affectionate memories of the many long hours and late nights of hard work that I shared with my fellow classmates whose cultural backgrounds included, among others, Pakistani, Peruvian, African-American, Irish-American, Greek-American and Jewish. Many of us made films about our families and the horrors experienced by many ethnic groups throughout history. These and similar experiences at Columbia served to remind me that my people have not been the only ones to have suffered injustice."

Stephanie Stokes Oliver
Editor
Essence Magazine
New York, New York

Howard University, Washington, D.C., a historically African-American college.

"Attending Howard University, the largest historically Black college in the country, had a great influence on my life because for the first time I found a peer group of Black students on my academic level with similar goals and aspirations. In my integrated, multicultural high school in Seattle, Washington, I was often one of only a few Blacks in my honors classes; at Howard, it was gratifying and stimulating to have a whole school full of like-minded, striving classmates.

"It was the excellent education I received at Howard that opened many doors for me in the predominantly white publishing world, including an editorial position at *Glamour* magazine that preceded my position at *Essence.* This positive experience at Howard gave me a strong impression of Black institutions that contributed several years later to my decision to work at a Black corporation."

Richard Wesley, TV Producer/Screenwriter/Playwright
20th Century Fox
Beverly Hills, California

Howard University, Washington, D.C., a historically African-American college

"My experience at Howard was the first time, outside of church, that I was ever in an institution in this country controlled exclusively by African-Americans. I had never thought such a thing possible.

"I was able to grow, develop and enjoy a higher level of self-esteem and self-confidence in an atmosphere where the expectations are so high and the pride and love shown in me were so pervasive. I owe Howard University so much, and will never forget the wonderful time I had there."

African-American Leaders and the Colleges They Attended

Arizona State University
Ron Brown, U.S. Secretary of Commerce
Reggie Jackson, baseball star

Berea College
Dr. Carter G. Woodson, founder, Black History Month

Boston University
Edward Brooke, first African-American U.S. Senator (Massachusetts)
Barbara Jordan, professor, LBJ School of Public Service, U of Texas-Austin, member, Watergate Committee

Bowdoin College
Oliver Otis Howard, founder, Howard University
John Brown Russwurn, second African-American college graduate in U.S.

California State University—Fresno
Lee Brown, former police commissioner, New York City
Shirley Anne Williams, Emmy-winning author

Columbia University
Langston Hughes, poet
Paul Robeson, actor, singer, civil rights activist
Franklin Thomas, President, Ford Foundation
Mario Van Peebles, actor and filmmaker

Creighton University
Clarence Shields, team physician, L.A. Rams football team
Paul Silas, former NBA player (Boston)
J. Clay Smith, former dean, Howard University Law School

Drake University
Wendell Hill, Dean, Howard University School of Pharmacy
Felix Wright, football player, Minnesota Vikings

Georgia State University
Lt. Gen. Henry Doctor, former inspector general, U.S. Army

Haverford College
Juan Williams, journalist, author, *Eyes On the Prize*

Howard University
Debbie Allen, producer, actress, dancer
Ed Bradley, journalist, CBS News
David Dinkins, Mayor, New York City
Michael Espy, U.S. Secretary of Agriculture
Roberta Flack, singer
Sharon Pratt Kelly, Mayor, Washington, D.C.
Thurgood Marshall, first African-American U.S. Supreme Court Judge
Toni Morrison, award-winning author
Stephanie Stokes Oliver, editor, *Essence* magazine
Richard Wesley, TV producer, screenwriter, playwright
Douglas Wilder, Governor, State of Virginia

Illinois State University
Donald McHenry, former U.S. ambassador, United Nations

Illinois Wesleyan University
Barrington Coleman, tenor soloist
Frankie Faison, actor

Iowa State University
George Washington Carver, botanist, educator

Michigan State University
Ernest Green, member "Little Rock 9"
Earvin "Magic" Johnson, former NBA star, Los Angeles Lakers
Craig Polite, psychologist, author
Bubba Smith, former football player, actor

Morgan State University
Earl Graves, Editor/Publisher, *Black Enterprise* magazine
Zora Neale Hurston, author, poet
Kweisi Mfume, U.S. Congressman (Maryland)
Deniece Williams, singer
Samm Art Williams, TV Producer, *Fresh Prince of Bel Air*

Morehouse College
Lerone Bennett, Executive Editor, *Ebony* and *Jet* magazines
Julian Bond, journalist, former state senator
Maynard Jackson, Mayor, Atlanta, Georgia
Dr. Martin Luther King, Jr.
Rev. Martin Luther King, Sr.
Spike Lee, filmmaker
Edwin Moses, Olympic gold medalist

New York University
Louis Gossett, Jr., actor
Constance Baker Motley, judge, civil rights lawyer
Charles Rangel, U.S. Congressman (New York)

Oberlin College
Avery Brooks, actor, professor
Johnetta B. Cole, President, Spelman College
Carl Rowan, syndicated columnist
Niara Sudarkasa, President, Lincoln University

Ohio University
Clarence Page, columnist, *Chicago Tribune*

Seattle University
Elgin Baylor, former NBA star
Quincy Jones, composer, arranger, producer

Spelman College
Marian Wright Edelman, Founder/Director, Children's Defense Fund
Varnette Honeywood, artist
Dr. Deborah Prothrow-Stith, Assistant Dean, Harvard School of Public Health; author

Stanford University
Dr. Mae Jemison, first African-American female astronaut

State University of New York—Purchase College
Wesley Snipes, actor

Swarthmore College
Mary Schmidt Campbell, Dean, New York University Tisch School of the Arts
Christopher F. Edley, Jr., professor of law, Harvard University
Dr. Sara Lawrence Lightfoot, professor, Harvard School of Education

Tuskegee University
Robert Beck, author (pseudonym "Iceberg Slim")

Ralph Ellison, author
Dr. Betty Shabazz, widow of Malcolm X, Director, Institutional Advancement and Public Affairs, Medgar Evers College, NY
Lionel Richie, singer, writer, producer

University of New Mexico
Robin Cole, Player, Pittsburgh Steelers
Ed Lewis, Publisher, *Essence* magazine
John Lewis, musician, Modern Jazz Quartet

University of Oklahoma
Wayman Tisdale, former NBA player
Derrick Minter, Dancer, Alvin Ailey Dance Company

University of South Carolina
George Rogers, Heisman Trophy winner
Frank L. Matthews, Co-Publisher, *Blacks In Higher Education*

University of Virginia
Ralph Sampson, former NBA player

Virginia Polytechnic Institute
Dell Curry, NBA player, Charlotte Hornets

Yale University
Anita Hill, professor of law, University of Oklahoma
Clarence Thomas, U.S. Supreme Court Justice

College and University Profiles by State

Each of the profiles of the schools in this book contains data about student enrollments; financial aid opportunities, programs and activities for African-American students. In some cases, the information is not complete for a school, and there are a number of reasons it is not included. While the schools represented in this book made attempts to comply, in some cases the information requested was not recorded by racial designation or the school was not willing to release it. In many cases, the request did not apply to the school. The following key will provide some guidance in reading the data profiles for each school.

N/A — not available at this school
N/R — not reported or released

Samford University
800 Lakeshore Drive
Birmingham, Alabama 35229
205-870-2901

Type: **Private liberal arts, affiliated with Alabama Baptist Convention**
Overall campus environment: **Caring/religious/conservative**
Total enrollment: **4,198**
African-American students: **238**
Graduate students: **1,054**
African-American graduate students: **49**
Percentage of applications accepted: **96%**
Average SAT/ACT score: **1028/23.9**
Average SAT/ACT African-Americans: **N/R**
Special admissions programs: **N/R**
Percentage of African-American graduates: **22%**
Percentage receiving financial aid: **80%**
Average amount of award: **$4,560**
Percentage in ROTC programs: **N/R**
Number of faculty: **198**
Number of African-American faculty: **1**
Student/faculty ratio: **25 to 1**
Tuition: **$7,064**
Scholarship programs: **N/A**
Academic programs: **College of Arts and Sciences; Schools of Business, Education, Music, Nursing, Pharmacy, Divinity, Law**
Most popular majors: **Business, Education, Pharmacy**
Prominent African-American faculty: **N/R**
Prominent African-American graduates: **N/R**

African-American student organizations/activities: **National African-American Sorority and Fraternity being established** Administrative services and programs: **Sound Off About Samford (SOAS)**

Founded in the 1800s, Samford University is currently the leading privately supported, fully accredited university in Alabama. A liberal arts school affiliated with the Alabama Baptist Convention, Samford provides students with undergraduate and graduate-level training in a Christian environment. Although all students are welcome, it's important to know that the university requires participation in religious activities. Attendance at church or Convocation, as it is referred to by the school, is mandatory, as well as the completion of religion courses known as "convo units."

Samford University offers a sound academic program in the liberal arts as well as professional and graduate programs in law, pharmacy, divinity, music, business and education. Samford prides itself on being a teaching rather than a research university, and its faculty spend a great deal of time getting to know the students. This personal approach is one reason many students cite for attending Samford, along with a desire to learn in an environment underpinned by religious values. "At Samford I am not a number," exclaimed one African-American student. "I am an individual and being treated as such makes asking questions and talking with professors much easier. I couldn't ask for a more caring institution. My father died recently and faculty and administrators reached out to me, sending me flowers, sympathy letters, and each of my instructors pulled me aside to talk or pray with me."

Samford points to this sense of caring as its focus in recruiting and retaining African-American students. There is currently an attempt to establish a national African-American fraternity and sorority on campus. However, the university's philosophy of inclusion encourages all students to participate equally and fully in all campus activities and programs. While the one "racial incident" reported was merely a name-calling between two students, the administration has a formal procedure by which students can register complaints. SOAS—Sound Off About Samford—provides students a forum for complaints as well as an opportunity to offer solutions. Students receive a response to their complaints within thirty days. Additionally, open forums and luncheons with administrators are held regularly, and faculty and administration maintain an "open door" policy. Students are also invited to serve on a number of administrative committees that make decisions about academic and campus life.

Students under twenty-two years of age who are unmarried and live beyond commuting distance are required to live on campus. Dormitories are single-sex, with two students per room. Students are expected to live by values consistent with Samford's Christian character. African-American students may find this philosophy of fairness and goodwill beneficial. "The social atmosphere at Samford is great," said one student. "I am not pressured to socialize with 'only' African-American students, and race does not play a role in my selection of friends. I believe the reason I have not encountered any racism here is due to the spiritual atmosphere that Samford provides."

If learning from caring faculty in an environment of strong religious values is what you seek, you should consider Samford University.

Tuskegee University
Tuskegee, Alabama 36088
205-727-8116

Type: **Private technical/professional, predominantly African-American**
Overall campus environment: **Good**
Total enrollment: **3,702**
African-American students: **3,278**
Graduate students: **177**
African-American graduate students: **105**
Percentage of applications accepted: **67%**
Average SAT Score: **750–900**
Average ACT: **15–18**
Special admissions programs: **N/A**
Percentage of African-American graduates: **62%**
Percentage receiving financial aid: **92%**

Average amount of award: **N/R**
Percentage in ROTC programs: **N/R**
Number of faculty: **249**
Number of African-American faculty: **130**
Student/faculty ratio: **13 to 1**
Tuition: **$6,535**
Scholarship programs: **N/A**
Academic programs: **College of Arts and Sciences; Schools of Business, Education, Engineering and Architecture, Agriculture and Home Economics, Nursing and Allied Health, Veterinary Medicine**
Prominent African-American faculty: **N/A**
Prominent African-American graduates: **Robert Beck, writer (pseudonym "Iceberg Slim"); Ralph Ellison, author,** *The Invisible Man***; General Daniel "Chappie" James, first Black four-star Air Force General; Lionel Ritchie, singer, writer, producer; Dr. Betty Shabazz, widow of Malcolm X, Director Institutional Advancement and Public Affairs, Medgar Evers College, NY**
African-American student organizations: **Student Union, Greek organizations, majority of student organizations**
Administrative services and programs: **N/A**

Founded in the late 1800s by Booker T. Washington, Tuskegee University (formerly Tuskegee Institute) still provides African-American students with a high-quality education and training in technical and professional fields. A private, predominantly African-American school, Tuskegee currently attracts students of all racial and ethnic backgrounds. The student body comes from forty-seven states and thirty-two countries. Tuskegee consists of seven schools and one college which provide liberal arts, technical and preprofessional training to more than 4,000 students. The university also offers graduate programs in a number of fields.

Long known for its technical programs, Tuskegee provides a strong foundation for careers in medicine, dentistry and a number of other professional careers. Its biology and chemistry programs are highly rated, and many of its graduates have been accepted at leading dental and other professional schools. The university's computer science program is one of its fastest-growing programs, and students can take advantage of internships thanks to relationships with large corporations such as IBM, AT&T and TRW. In fact, these companies and others look to Tuskegee to provide them with qualified candidates for jobs on their staffs. The university also offers opportunities for students to participate in research through the Carver Research Foundation, which funds laboratories and state-of-the-art equipment. Additionally, students may qualify for graduate work through the Minority Access to Research Careers Program.

One of Tuskegee's most attractive features, besides its historical reputation as one of the nation's finest predominantly African-American institutions, is its excellent faculty. The university boasts that 73 percent of its faculty hold Ph.D.'s or the highest degree in their fields, and many publish or conduct research. Many are graduates of prestigious institutions such as Harvard, Vanderbilt, Stanford, Cal Tech and Brown University. Most are African-American.

Tuskegee University is in the small town of Tuskegee, Alabama, which has a population of about 14,000. Students report that they are involved with the local community, attending church services and participating in social and volunteer activities. However, most rely on campus activities and fraternities and sororities for their social life. Greek organizations are very popular on campus and sponsor many of the parties and other social events. Some believe that there's too much partying at times and not enough attention paid to academics by many students.

Overall, most students are pleased with their experience at Tuskegee and note that living on a predominantly African-American campus provides a degree of nurturing and support that may not be available at predominantly white schools. Although most of the students here are either from Alabama or elsewhere in the South, the university does attract students from the Northeast and abroad. However, if you're considering Tuskegee you need to be prepared for life in a small, Southern, rural town and an academic environment that is adequate but not especially challenging.

Alaska Pacific University
4101 University Drive
Anchorage, Alaska 99508
907-561-1266

Type: **Private liberal arts, affiliated with Methodist Church**
Overall campus environment: **Multicultural**
Total enrollment: **681**
African-American students: **34**
Graduate students: **207**
African-American graduate students: **10**
Percentage of applications accepted: **67%**
Average SAT score: **800 SAT 18 ACT**
Average SAT African-Americans: **N/R**
ROTC program: **N/A**
Number of faculty: **100**
Number of African-American faculty: **0**
Student/Faculty Ratio: **12 to 1**
Tuition: **$6,800**
Scholarship programs: **Religious-affiliated and academic scholarships**
Academic programs: **Business and Management, Communications, Comparative Literature, Conservation and Regulation, Dramatic Arts, Elementary Education, Fine Arts, Foreign Languages, Hotel/Motel and Restaurant Management, Human Resources, Intercultural Communications, Labor/Industrial Relations, Management, Science, Music, Natural Resources, Social Sciences, Transportation and Travel Marketing, Visual and Performing Arts, Wildlife Management**
Most popular majors: **Education, Psychology, Management**
Prominent African-American graduates: **N/A**
African-American student organizations/activities: **Black History Month**
Administrative services and programs: **International Student Organization, Students for Social Unity, Students Against Racism**

There's a running joke among African-Americans that no matter where you go in the world you'll find a person of African descent.

And so it is that in Alaska there is a community of African-Americans. They came to work on the pipeline, were born here or followed their sense of adventure.

Clearly, you need to think carefully about going to college in Alaska, where 32 degrees is considered warm weather. Alaska is for those who love the outdoors, the cold and roughing it. If you're interested in wildlife, natural resources, forestry and the like, you'll find Alaska fascinating and breathtaking. While many people still think of Alaska as a no-man's-land, it's no longer isolated from the rest of the nation. Its major city, Anchorage, is a booming metropolis and the home of Alaska Pacific University, a small liberal arts institution with about 700 students, 5 percent of whom are African-American.

Founded by the United Methodist Church, Alaska Pacific is among the best liberal arts schools in the country. Still sustained by the Methodists, Alaska Pacific offers undergraduate, graduate and associate degree programs. The school is particularly proud of its multicultural environment; students hail from nineteen states and eighteen countries. Most of the university's offerings are in line with today's economic needs, the administration reports that business, education, management, the sciences and technology majors are among the most popular. The university has a philosophy of integrating education with real-life experience and the world of work; many nontraditional adult students are enrolled in Alaska Pacific in search of training that will get them better jobs.

It's no surprise that Alaska Pacific draws its students primarily from Alaska, although about 14 percent come from out of state and foreign countries. The largest minority are Eskimos and other Pacific Islanders, but a large number of other racial and cultural groups are represented as well, and the university's programs and services reflect the needs of all groups.

Alaska Pacific is not very competitive, and students who apply are generally accepted, particularly if they are residents of Alaska. To help marginal students, the administration schedules review and skill-building courses. Although there are no organizations specifically for African-Americans, the university encourages students to participate in all student organizations regardless of their racial origin. It also supports several minority student organizations, including the International Student Organization and Native American Student Organization, as well as groups whose purpose is to promote social and cultural unity. At Alaska Pacific, multiculturalism is a philosophy that works, primarily because of the university's cultural and racial mix and the administration's strong support of all students.

Alaska Pacific does not offer some of the features of a more traditional college, such as a solid sports program (sports here are very limited) or a job placement office. However, if you're looking for adventure or have a particular interest in Alaska, you'll find a culturally diverse campus.

Arizona State University
Tempe, Arizona
602-965-5078

Type: **4–5 year public**
Overall campus environment: **Cordial**
Total enrollment: **42,952**
African-American students: **763**
Graduate students: **10,925**
African-American graduate students: **237**
Percentage of applications accepted: **75%**
Average SAT Score: **970 SAT/22 ACT**
Average SAT score African-Americans: **N/R**
Special admissions programs: **N/A**
Percentage of African-American graduates: **10.8%**
Percentage receiving financial aid: **87%**
Average amount of award: **$900 (per semester)**
Percentage in ROTC programs: **Less than 1%**
Number of faculty: **1,877**
Number of African-American faculty: **22**
Student/faculty ratio: **22 to 1**
Tuition: **$3,467 per semester**
Scholarship programs: **ABC (Alliance of Black Community) Scholarship (for Arizona residents), Maroon and Gold Scholarship**
Academic programs: **Colleges of Engineering, Public Programs, Business, Architecture**
Most popular majors: **Business, Engineering, Architecture, Journalism, Communications, Sciences**

Prominent African-American graduates: **Ron Brown, U.S. Secretary of Commerce; Reggie Jackson, baseball star**
Prominent African-American faculty: **N/A**
African-American student organizations/activities: **STARS (Students Taking Action to Reach Success); Black Career Fair; Kappa Alpha Psi, Omega Psi Phi, Alpha Phi Alpha, Phi Beta Sigma, Alpha Kappa Alpha, Delta Sigma Theta**
Administrative services and programs: **Minority Assistance Program (MAP), Multicultural Board, African-American Coalition, Umoja Hall (planned), Black Caucus, Leadership 2000**

With more than 42,000 students on campus, you could easily feel lost and out of place at Arizona State University. This feeling of isolation can be overwhelming if you're one of the handful of African-American students at this predominantly white school. ASU's administration understands this and has taken great pains to help African-American students feel a part of university life, establishing myriad programs, cultural resources and systems of academic and career support. The most popular program is STARS (Students Taking Action to Reach Success), which is aimed at helping African-American students adjust to campus life and successfully complete their academic training. One of the program's goals is to improve the university's dismal record for graduating African-American students—currently a mere 10 percent of the students it enrolls. Also in the works is the Umoja Hall, a cultural center that will give students an opportunity to explore their African-American heritage and contributions to the building of this country.

ASU has the expected trappings of a large university: a sprawling campus; numerous student organizations (more than 300) including several African-American fraternities and sororities, and plenty of red tape. Yet students still feel "connected and in touch" with each other and the administration. Because of their small number, African-American students, faculty and administrators have formed a close-knit, supportive group. This cooperation was recently demonstrated when students led a peaceful march in support of increased hiring and retention of African-American faculty and administrators. ASU's president responded by setting up formal discussions to work toward a solution with all concerned parties, including students. In addition, there are continuing efforts to improve racial relations on campus through student, faculty and administrative participation in organizations such as the Black Caucus and Leadership 2000. One activity that seems to bring all groups together is sports. ASU's reputation for football is well known, and games are well attended. The university's state-of-the-art student recreation complex makes available more than sixty sport, dance and exercise activities. The intramural program boasts more than 15,000 student participants in thirty-five sports for both men and women.

Perhaps one of the strongest attractions of ASU besides the picture-postcard weather (the sun always shines here), nearby man-made beaches and active nightlife is the university's solid reputation for academics. The most popular programs are in business, engineering, architecture, journalism, communications and the sciences; all offer outstanding faculty and resources. ASU's business program is ranked fourth in the country and places a large number of its graduates with the Big Eight accounting firms, as well as with companies such as IBM, Intel, US West Communications and Motorola. African-American graduates of ASU are much sought-after, too. A special career development program called SOLID helps prepare them for internships and permanent placements once they graduate. The university sponsors a Black Career Fair to facilitate student job placements.

African-American students who select ASU will find an increasingly competitive university with a real commitment to integrating minorities into campus life and supporting African-American academic, social, career and fraternal organizations. "One of the major assets of ASU," wrote one student, "is its receptivity to the needs of university students." ASU students will also find they follow a long line of African-American graduates who have gone on to become prominent in their fields.

California State University—Fresno
Cedar and Shaw Avenues
Fresno, California 93740
209-278-2795

Type: **4-year public**
Overall campus environment: **Good**

Total enrollment: **19,824**
African-American students: **744**
Graduate students: **3,929**
African-American graduate students: **94**
Percentage of applications accepted: **72%**
Average ACT score: **18.5**
Average ACT African-Americans: **N/A**
Percentage in ROTC programs: **2% Army/10% Air Force**
Number of faculty: **816**
Number of African-American faculty: **30**
Student/faculty ratio: **18 to 1**
Tuition: **Resident $1,114**
Scholarship programs: **Young Black Scholars Grants**
Academic programs: **Agriculture, Industrial Technology, Business, Education, Engineering, Arts and Humanities, Natural Sciences, Social Sciences, Health and Social Work, etc.**
Most popular majors: **Business, Education, Health and Social Work, Natural Sciences**
Prominent African-American graduates: **Lee Brown, former commissioner, New York City Police Department; Ezunial Burts, Executive Director, Port of Los Angeles; Shirley Anne Williams, Emmy-winning author**
Prominent African-American faculty: **N/A**
African-American student organizations/activities: **Alpha Kappa Alpha, Alpha Phi Alpha, African Student Union,** *Uhuru Na Umoja* **newspaper, African-American Educators Society, African-American History Month**
Administrative services and programs: **Educational Opportunity Program, Summer Bridge, Upward Bound, Outreach Office**

This large university offers African-American students—especially residents of the state of California—a number of academic, financial and cultural opportunities. A four-year public university, California State University—Fresno admits nearly 10 percent of its nearly 20,000 students through special programs. About 6 percent of those admitted in this way help to achieve the university's goal of creating a better racial balance in the student population. These special admissions programs are limited to economically disadvantaged California residents who demonstrate the academic ability and motivation to succeed in college. CSU—Fresno provides considerable tutoring, counseling and financial support, including generous scholarships and grants. The university offers more than sixty undergraduate majors and forty-two master's degree programs in a variety of fields including business, industrial technology, education, engineering, arts and humanities, health and the natural and social sciences. The university provides a well-rounded educational experience in a multicultural environment that is academically challenging, yet not as competitive as some. CSU accepts the top 33 percent of high school graduates as well as a large number of community college and transfer students. This is not to say that the university has sacrificed its academic standards to create a more culturally diverse institution. To the contrary, the prestige of university faculty is one of the reasons students cite for attending CSU—Fresno as well as special programs on topics such as "Man and the Natural Environment" and enology (the science of wine making).

African-American students reap the benefit of a number of programs designed to help them succeed at CSU, such as the Educational Opportunity Program, Summer Bridge and Upward Bound, which provide counseling and tutoring. The administration is sensitive to the concerns of African-American and other minority students and recognizes the importance of promoting harmony among all racial groups. To that end it has established a Commission on Human Relations and has held several conferences on racial harmony in the academic environment. It is also supportive of African-American faculty, student organizations and cultural events, including the African-American Staff Educators Society, African-American Studies Program and African-American History Month.

As for the campus environment, social and cultural outlets include black fraternities and sororities and the African Student Union, and the student newspaper, *Uhuru Na Umoja*. While many students live on campus, housing is available off campus near the university. Tuition for residents of California is just over $1,000 for the year—almost a gift compared to other states. A student from out of state spends in one year what a California resident pays for the entire four—one reason that almost 90 percent of students at CSU—Fresno are residents of the state. CSU—Fresno offers a number of unique programs and a campus environment in which many African-American students will be comfortable and flourish, and if you're a resident, the price is right.

Claremont McKenna College
890 Columbia Avenue
Claremont, California 91711
714-621-8088

Type: **Private liberal arts**
Overall campus environment: **Cordial/conservative**
Total enrollment: **850**
African-American students: **40**
Graduate students: **0**
Percentage of applications accepted: **35%**
Average SAT score: **1170–1270**
Average SAT African-Americans: **N/R**
Special admissions programs: **N/R**
Percentage receiving financial aid: **60%**
Average amount of award: **$8,700**
Percentage in ROTC programs: **N/R**
Number of faculty: **92**
Number of African-American faculty: **2**
Student/faculty ratio: **10 to 1**
Tuition: **$15,620**
Scholarship programs: **CMC Scholarships**
Academic programs: **Accounting, Biology, Chemistry, Computers and Information Systems, Economics, Environment, Economics and Politics, Ethics, Government, International Relations, Legal Studies, Literature, Management Engineering, Management, Mathematics, Military Science, Modern Languages, Philosophy and Religion, Physics, Politics, Philosophy and Economics, Psychology, Science and Management**
Most popular majors: **Political Science, Economics, Business**
Prominent African-American faculty: **N/A**
Prominent African-American graduates: **N/A**
African-American student organizations/activities: **Black Student Union, Black Christian Fellowship, Gospel Choir**

Administrative services and programs: **Office of Black Student Affairs**

Claremont McKenna College is one of the Claremont consortium of five colleges, which are located within the same compound thirty-five miles east of Los Angeles and share facilities and services including a computer system, laboratories, auditoriums, a student newspaper and library system.

CMC began as a men's college and became coed in 1976, but still maintains a 2 to 1 ratio of men to women. CMC continues to provide excellent programs in political science, economics and business, its strongest and most popular majors. The academic program at CMC is very demanding, and its twelve-point grading system guarantees that every A received is well earned. Students are serious about doing well here. It's not unusual, for example, to find a number of students studying on weekends.

One student who was accustomed to excelling in high school got a rude awakening in his first literature class. "When I got back my first paper, I was devastated. A B-minus! I kept asking myself what I'd gotten myself into." This same student now counsels other students and advises them, "Whatever happens on the first paper, don't take it to heart. If you had a good high school academic experience, you'll be okay."

Of all the Claremont colleges, CMC is probably the most conservative. There is an active Republican student group on campus and a strong emphasis on preparing for a career in politics, business or public affairs.

The number of African-American students here is very small; combined with Hispanics, they represent only about 11 percent of the student body. However, students are usually able to make the adjustment to campus life here with the help of the Office of Black Student Affairs, which provides academic advising, tutoring and counseling.

Major advantages of the small size of CMC and its consortium environment are the friendly relationships among faculty and administration, as well as the exposure to a variety of programs, services and facilities. "In an environment as close-knit as Claremont, you really get to know your professors," a student wrote. "You can talk with them about anything, and you get to know them as people."

Although CMC's number of students of color remains small, there is commitment to increasing diversity on campus through a strong financial aid program as well as increased support of social and cultural programs. The administration encourages all students to get involved in all aspects of campus life. "CMC has given me a great education along with a great social life," a student wrote. "I play intramural sports and varsity football, and recently served as my dorm's president."

If you like the intimacy of a small school with all of the advantages of a medium-sized university; excellent facilities, extensive resources and a greater choice of courses and extra curricular activities than can be found at comparable colleges, Claremont McKenna is worth investigating.

Harvey Mudd College
Kingston Hall
Claremont, California 91711-9961
714-621-8011

Type: **Private technical**
Overall campus environment: **Academically challenging**
Total enrollment: **568**
African-American students: **17**
Graduate students: **6**
African-American graduate students: **N/R**
Percentage of applications accepted: **54%**
Average SAT score: **1270–1470**
Average SAT score African-Americans: **N/R**
Special admissions programs: **N/R**
Percentage of African-American graduates: **80%**
Percentage receiving financial aid: **75%**
Average amount of award: **$8,000**
Percentage in ROTC programs: **N/R**
Number of faculty: **68**
Number of African-American faculty: **N/R**
Student/faculty ratio: **9 to 1**
Tuition: **$13,870**
Scholarship programs: **Financial aid provided to all qualified students**

Academic programs: **Engineering, Physical Sciences, Mathematics**
Most popular majors: **Engineering, Environmental Design**
Prominent African-American faculty: **N/R**
Prominent African-American graduates: **N/R**
African-American student organizations/activities: **Office of Black Student Affairs, Black Family Weekend, Black History Month**
Administrative services and programs: **Student Affairs Office**

Harvey Mudd College is the smallest of the Claremont Colleges, a consortium of five colleges which are located within the same compound and share facilities and services, and is one of the most selective colleges in the country. With an enrollment just more than 500, HMC admits only top-ranking students (150 freshmen each year). The college looks for students who are serious about their education.

HMC is well known for its strong programs in math, engineering and the sciences, including computer science. But the college's emphasis on technical fields does not prevent it from providing students with a strong base in the liberal arts. In fact, HMC students take about a third of their coursework in the humanities and social sciences—a rare requirement for a technical college. The administration supports the view that students should receive a broad-based technical education, providing a foundation for a variety of professional goals. Graduates have become doctors, engineers, teachers, architects, businesspeople, government officials, musicians, congresspeople and research scientists.

The college's small size means students can get into the majors they want and take the classes they need to complete their coursework. "The biggest selling point I saw for HMC was the class and school size," said one student. "Rarely after the freshman year are you in classes larger than twenty people." Students report that faculty—all of whom have doctoral degrees—are excellent, and although the academic program is demanding, students find professors helpful and willing to work with those who make the effort. "The curriculum at HMC is very rigorous," said one student, "so I really appreciate the assistance that is readily offered by the professors."

HMC's percentage of African-American students is small—about 3 percent. As with the rest of the college, most are male. However, students of color report that the intimate atmosphere of the campus and the resources shared with the four other Claremont Colleges help them adjust to campus life. The Office of Black Student Affairs (OBSA) sponsors a number of activities and programs, including the freshman/sophomore retreat, leadership training programs, Black Family Weekend and a series of speakers of interest to African-American students. A member of OBSA sits on the college committee to represent students.

The administration at HMC provides additional academic student support through its academic affairs and student affairs offices, which offer counseling, tutoring, peer advising, faculty advocacy and alumni mentoring. It's not unusual for alumni to remain involved with the college and become counselors and career mentors. In fact, many alumni assist students in finding summer jobs and full-time positions after graduation.

All of these efforts are a result of the connection many alumni and students feel to the college. The unique experience students have on the HMC campus, from its student-directed Honor Code to its Pass/No Credit grading system and high academic standards, give students a sense of belonging to a special group as well as the responsibility to pass on what they have received to others.

African-American students will find the diversity of the Claremont schools an attractive feature of Harvey Mudd, although female students may find the predominantly male environment challenging. If you're looking for a small college with a strong technical program, you won't be disappointed with Harvey Mudd College. But you'll need to be prepared to work hard.

**Pitzer College
Claremont, California
714-621-8129**

Type: **4-Year liberal arts**
Overall campus environment: **Nontraditional, culturally supportive**
Total enrollment: **750**
African-American students: **50**

Graduate students: **0**
African-American graduate students: **0**
Percentage of applications accepted: **55%**
Average SAT score: **1150**
Average SAT African-Americans: **980**
Special admissions programs: **N/R**
Percentage of African-American graduates: **70–80%**
Percentage receiving financial aid: **80%**
Average amount of award: **$16,200**
Percentage in ROTC programs: **N/R**
Number of faculty: **80**
Number of African-American faculty: **4**
Student/faculty ratio: **10 to 1**
Tuition: **$17,170**
Scholarship programs: **Need-based grants**
Academic programs: **34 "fields of concentration" with emphasis on social and behavioral sciences**
Most popular majors: **Psychology, English, Political Studies, Sociology, Anthropology**
Prominent African-American graduates: **N/R**
Prominent African-American faculty: **N/R**
African-American student organizations/activities: **Black Student Union, Gospel Choir, Black Christian Fellowship, Model United Nations, Pan African Student Association**
Administrative services and programs: **Office of Black Student Affairs**

Founded in 1963, Pitzer is one of the Claremont Colleges in Southern California, 35 miles east of Los Angeles. As part of the Claremont consortium, Pitzer enjoys a reciprocal arrangement that allows students to take up to one-third of their courses at any of the other four Claremont colleges. Pitzer is truly a melting pot of students of various socioeconomic backgrounds and cultural and ethnic heritages. This is a distinction that the college holds in high esteem and works to maintain. Six percent of its students are African-American; 8 percent are Hispanic; 7 percent are Asian-American; 5 percent are from foreign countries. Pitzer's philosophy of cultural diversity is, according to its administration, "not something that is merely tolerated." It is actually lived on campus, and it's hoped that this culturally diverse experience will help students question their assumptions. Students are told up front that "they are likely to run into someone who disagrees with them at Pitzer and if they are going to college to have their ideas confirmed, they should look elsewhere." One African-American student reported, "Pitzer values diversity, so most of the time I feel comfortable on campus. When I feel isolated, I have the opportunity to network with other black students at the Office of Black Student Affairs or at the Pan-African Student Association."

A small liberal arts college whose focus is the study of the social and behavioral sciences, Pitzer encourages students to take an active role in their education. This is a college for the "independent-thinking student" who feels comfortable designing his or her own program of study, with the help of faculty. Students can choose a traditional liberal arts program or a nontraditional course of study; conduct independent research; develop the skills for critical thinking; explore mathematical and other formal systems to learn to think in the abstract; and learn to express their ideas through writing and speech. At the core of Pitzer's program is a strong emphasis on interdisciplinary education and an understanding of different cultures.

Pitzer's small size is another attraction for African-American and other minority students. There are only 750 students and 80 faculty members on campus, which allows for a fair amount of interaction between students and teachers. The average class size is about eighteen students, and classes are often taught seminar-style. For an African-American student, the 10 to 1 student-to-faculty ratio may ease the adjustment to life on a predominantly white campus. One student wrote, "I find that administrators and faculty are kind and helpful and that they are student-oriented." This close interaction is also critical in helping students design their coursework from the thirty-four "fields of concentration" that Pitzer offers in traditional and nontraditional majors, including anthropology (one of the most popular majors), Chicano studies, film and video studies, folklore, human biology, linguistics, management engineering, organizational studies, psychobiology, science and management, and science, technology and society. Because of Pitzer's commitment to intercultural understanding, the college strongly recommends that students participate in its off-campus study programs in the United States and in such countries as Argentina, Brazil, Morocco, Spain and Zimbabwe.

If you're looking for an opportunity to acquire a strong liberal arts education in a culturally diverse environment, Pitzer may be the college for you. As one senior said, "Pitzer's perfect for a student interested in being on the cutting edge of new theories and multicultural issues."

Pomona College
333 North College Way
Claremont, California 91711
714-621-8134

Type: **Private liberal arts**
Overall campus environment: **Cordial**
Total enrollment: **1,327**
African-American students: **66**
Graduate students: **Zero**
Percentage of applications accepted: **39%**
Average SAT score: **1240–1430**
Average SAT African-Americans: **N/R**
Special admissions programs: **N/R**
Percentage of African-American graduates: **85–90%**
Percentage receiving financial aid: **86%**
Average amount of award: **$20,313**
Percentage in ROTC programs: **N/R**
Number of faculty: **150**
Number of African-American faculty: **5**
Student/faculty ratio: **9 to 1**
Tuition: **$14,800**
Scholarship programs: **College Scholarships and need-based grants**
Academic programs: **American Studies, Anthropology, Art, Asian Studies, Astronomy, Biology, Black Studies, Chemistry, Chicano Studies, Classics, Computer Science, Dance, Economics, Education, English, Film Studies, Geology, Government, History, International Relations, Linguistics, Mathematics, Military Science, Modern Languages and**

Literatures, **Molecular Biology, Music, Philosophy, Politics and Economics, Physical Education, Physics, Psychology, Religion, Science, Technology and Society, Sociology, Theater, Public Policy Analysis, Women's Studies**
Most popular majors: **Biology, Economics, English**
Prominent African-American faculty: **N/R**
Prominent African-American graduates: **Willie Benton Boone, M.D., Professor of Ophthalmology, University of California—Irvine; Larry Carroll, television anchor, KCAL-TV, Los Angeles; George C. Wolfe, playwright;**
African-American student organizations/activities: **Black Christian Fellowship, Pan-African Students Association, Gospel Choir**
Administrative services and programs: **Office of Black Student Affairs**

Pomona College is the oldest and largest of the Claremont Colleges, a consortium of five institutions that are autonomous but whose programs, facilities and services are shared. Former Pomona College president James A. Blaisdell patterned the Claremont Colleges Consortium after the small colleges that make up England's Oxford and Cambridge universities. It was Blaisdell's belief that the values of the small college should be preserved and not be lost in the mire of big university status that threatened the continuation of Pomona as a small college in the 1920s.

Today Pomona is one of the top liberal arts colleges in the country and highly rated by many publications for the quality and dollar value of its academic programs. Pomona benefits from the libraries, theaters and other facilities of the consortium, including Bridges Auditorium, which features a variety of artists and entertainers; medical and counseling centers; the Office of Black Student Affairs, and a center for religious activities. Students benefit, too, from the more than 150 public events presented on these campuses each month, including art exhibits, plays, lectures, seminars, films and concerts. They can also participate in more than 280 clubs and organizations. Pomona students can eat at any of the nine dining facilities of the consortium.

Pomona's own attractions include campus-wide computer facilities, observatory with forty-inch telescope, a student-run radio station, and $15-million athletic facility with tennis, squash, handball and racquetball courts and a weight room. Construction of a $9.6-million theater complex and new administration building is under way.

One of Pomona's drawing cards is its excellent faculty and small class size. All of the faculty above the rank of instructor hold doctoral degrees, and the average class has fourteen students. Students get to work closely with professors and to participate in research and publishing projects. During one recent school year, for example, more than 150 faculty members presented papers on which students collaborated at more than fifty conferences in the United States and abroad.

The strong liberal arts program offers students more than thirty majors, including Black Studies, as well as study abroad opportunities in Africa, China, Europe, Japan and the former Soviet Union. Pomona also has a variety of internship opportunities, independent study programs and a 3-2 (three years of undergraduate and two years of graduate study) engineering cooperative effort with California Institute of Technology and Washington University in St. Louis. African-American students can also take advantage of exchange programs with the predominantly African-American Fisk University and Spelman College.

Though all of the colleges in the consortium have a strategy to increase the number of students of color, Pomona is probably the most diverse. African-Americans make up about 5 percent of the student body, with Asians and Latinos representing approximately 25 percent. A number of support groups exist to help students adjust to campus life, as well as a number of African-American organizations. However, the administration strongly encourages all students to work together and not segregate themselves along racial lines. "Pomona not only offers but encourages student involvement in a number of organizations and leadership positions on campus," says a student from Texas. "With such encouragement from faculty and administration, there is nothing a person of color cannot do and succeed at at Pomona."

Still, many students complain that there are not enough organizations and activities for African-American students. Some say that Pomona's laid-back environment may not be suited for all students, especially if they're looking for a "party school." Most of the social life for African-Americans revolves around the Office of Black Student Affairs and the social cliques that develop in residence halls (more than 95 percent of students live in dorms). There is also a very active Black Christian Fellowship and a Gospel Choir, and students get involved in religious and other activities in the Claremont Black community.

Pomona offers any student a great education and an opportunity to work on exciting projects and gain exposure to a wide variety of people and ideas. Any student seeking a top liberal arts education on the West Coast should consider this school.

Scripps College
1030 Columbia Avenue
Claremont, California 91711
714-621-8149

Type: **Private women's**
Overall campus environment: **Good**
Total enrollment: **627**
African-American students: **18**
Graduate students: **Zero**
Percentage of applications accepted: **67%**
Average SAT score: **1154**
Average SAT African-Americans: **N/R**
Special admissions programs: **N/R**
Percentage receiving financial aid: **67%**
Average amount of award: **$15,497**
Percentage in ROTC Programs: **N/R**
Number of faculty: **60**
Number of African-American faculty: **N/R**
Student/faculty ratio: **10 to 1**
Tuition: **$13,824**
Scholarship programs: **College scholarships and need-based grants**
Academic programs: **Arts, Asian Studies, Area and Ethnic Studies, Humanities, Language and Literature, Life Sciences, Psychology, Multi/Interdisciplinary Studies, Philosophy, Religion**
Most popular majors: **Art, English, Pre-Med, Social Science**
African-American student organizations/activities: **Black Student Affairs Center**

Administrative services and programs: **Office of Black Student Affairs**

Scripps is one of the smaller Claremont Colleges and is distinguished by its population of female students. A private liberal arts college, Scripps mirrors the atmosphere of Harvey Mudd College because of its close-knit student body and faculty. However, Scripps also has many unique qualities, such as its ability to attract more than half of its diverse student body from outside California. About 20 percent of the students are minority.

The college has a good reputation in the liberal arts, especially its humanities department, which students rate excellent. Students are encouraged to read, discuss and explore ideas and events from a variety of perspectives. They are also challenged to draw on their knowledge of subjects such as art, literature, economics and science. Says one student, "I was inspired by Scripps' academic focus. I wanted to be challenged and encouraged, and I liked the fact that it was a women's college and my goals would be treated seriously." "I am planning to work in the field of public affairs," said one student. "At Scripps, I gained the skills necessary to fulfill my dream of changing people's attitudes toward minorities."

Scripps is traditionally a predominantly white, middle-class college, but recent changes have shifted more attention to recruiting African-Americans and other minorities. There are also increased efforts to help African-American students adjust to campus life and to address issues such as divestment in South Africa. Scripps is attempting to reinvent itself and change its image from a traditionally "preppy" college to one that is more liberal and tolerant.

The fact that they can develop a close working relationship with the faculty is a primary reason that students believe the school and its students are successful. "I've found that faculty members at the Claremont Colleges, in general, are always there when you need them," a student said. "Many of my professors have become more like friends than instructors."

You should know, however, that the college's traditional emphasis on the humanities is undergoing some changes that have resulted in fairly strong departments of economics, psychology and international relations. Even with the curriculum changes,

Scripps still does not offer any math courses; students may take these at one of the other Claremont colleges. Scripps students also join students from Claremont McKenna College and Pitzer College in taking sciences courses at the Joint Science Center, which reportedly offers an excellent program.

Scripps is known for its lively social events. It's common for male students from the other Claremont colleges to date women from Scripps. The college puts a strong emphasis on feminism and the study of women's issues; some students say they feel as if these issues are being "shoved down their throats."

Overall, students will find that Scripps provides a good broad-based education and that life here is fairly laid-back. With the changes that the college is currently making, things can only get better.

**Stanford University
Old Union, Rm. 232
Stanford, California 94305-3005
415-723-2091**

Type: **Private**
Overall campus environment: **Competitive/culturally diverse**
Total enrollment: **13,549**
African-American students: **789**
Graduate students: **7,022**
African-American graduate students: **265**
Percentage of applications accepted: **22%**
Average SAT score: **1000–1600**
Average SAT/African-Americans: **N/R**
Special admissions programs: **Special consideration for African-Americans, Mexican-Americans, Native Americans and children of Stanford graduates**
Percentage of African-American graduates: **40%**
Percentage receiving financial aid: **60%**
Average amount of award: **$7,644**
Percentage in ROTC programs: **N/R**
Number of faculty: **1,406**
Number of African-American faculty: **30**
Student/faculty ratio: **10 to 1**

Tuition: **$16,536**
Scholarship programs: **University scholarships, merit-based scholarships**
Academic programs: **Humanities, Social Sciences, Engineering, Natural Sciences and Mathematics, Earth Sciences, interdisciplinary programs including African and Afro-American Studies**
Most popular majors: **Economics, Human Biology, Biological Sciences, English, Engineering**
Prominent African-American faculty: **James Lowell Gibbs, Jr., founder, African and Afro-American Studies Program, and first recipient of Martin Luther King, Jr., Centennial Professorship**
Prominent African-American graduates: **Dr. Mae Jemison, first African-American female astronaut**
African-American student organizations/activities: **Black Student Union, Black Pre-Law Society, Black Pre-Business Society, Black Pre-Medical Organization, Society of Black Scientists and Engineers, Caribbean Students Association, Stanford Gospel Choir, Kuumba Dance Ensemble, Ujamaa Students Association, Black Leadership Council, Stanford Black Alumni Club, Blacks in Transition, African/Black Student Statewide Alliance, *The Real News* newspaper, African-American Fraternal and Sororal Association, Alpha Phi Alpha, Delta Sigma Theta, Kappa Alpha Psi, Omega Phi Psi, Alpha Kappa Alpha Black Liberation Month, Nia Project, Soul Food Dinner, Stanford Black Music Association**
Administrative services and programs: **Undergraduate Scholars Program, Imaani, Martin Luther King, Jr., Papers Project, Stanford/Howard University Exchange Program, Library Research on African-Americans, Black Recruitment and Orientation Committee, Ujamaa House, Committee on Black Performing Arts, Black Community Services Center, Residence Deans, African-American Donor Task Force**

Stanford University is one of the preeminent universities in the country. Admission is highly competitive. The administration assiduously seeks out students who in high school have excelled at a rigorous program of English, foreign languages, mathematics and the sciences. The importance of this level of academic achievement goes to the heart of Stanford's established goals as set forth by Senator Leland Stanford, who with his wife founded the university in 1885 in memory of their son, who was of college age when he died. It was their goal to establish a university that would afford students a broad liberal education that would be useful in life.

Stanford's prestigious faculty, strong academic reputation and liberal environment provide the university's greatest attractions. Nearly all of the faculty (97 percent) have doctoral degrees, and they include Nobel laureates and Pulitzer prize winners. More impressive still is Stanford's enviable student-to-faculty ratio (10 to 1) and the fact that faculty teach and advise undergraduate students, and sometimes involve them in their research. Stanford's faculty, staff and student body are culturally diverse, with African-Americans represented at top levels of the administration, in such positions as Dean of Students and Vice President of Student Resources. Minority groups represent more than 40 percent of the student body, and international students make up another 4 percent of the population. This is attractive to many African-American students, and, though it's not perfect, they say the administration is supportive of the needs of all students. "Stanford is striving to create a pluralistic community," said one student. "From the very first day of frosh orientation, cross-cultural communication is encouraged." To demonstrate its seriousness about this issue, Stanford has established ethnic community centers for various student populations. The Ujamaa House, a cultural center and residence for select African-American students, is one of three ethnic theme houses on campus. The university supports a number of programs and cultural centers for African-American students, including the Black Student Volunteer Center (fondly referred to as the "Black House"). This center provides office and meeting space, program advising, and coordinating services for volunteer work in the predominantly African-American community of East Palo Alto. Stanford is also becoming a center for the study of the civil rights movement and houses the Martin Luther King, Jr., Papers Project, a fourteen-volume scholarly edition of speeches, sermons, correspondence and other writings. Coretta Scott King, Dr. King's widow, serves as the center's president.

Among the many programs available to students at Stanford is the Stanford/Howard University Exchange Program. Each year, two to five students exchange places for a semester or an academic year in an effort to enhance their academic and cultural experience. There are also numerous study abroad options, a library research program on African-Americans, and programs that encourage African-American students to consider earning a Ph.D.

Students will find campus life dynamic and varied, limited only by their imagination. As one student put it, "You name it and we've got it at Stanford, or you can start it!" Since most students (about 98 percent) live on campus, most of the social activities revolve around residential life. Everything from varsity athletics to student government, a campus newspaper and radio station, African-American fraternities and sororities, professional organizations like the Black Scientists and Engineers, and the Gospel Choir can be found at Stanford. Those interested in theater can get involved with the Committee on Black Performing Arts. For avid churchgoers, there's the Black Church at Stanford.

Besides offering the opportunity for a top-flight education, Stanford clearly has made a special effort to accommodate the academic, cultural and social needs of African-American students. The university's rate of graduating African-American students is very high, and the success of its students after graduation is well known.

Students who do well at Stanford are open to all types of people and want to be challenged academically and socially. One student said, "It would be very difficult to attend Stanford for four years and not have some of your beliefs and ideas challenged." If this kind of philosophy appeals to you, Stanford may be for you.

Colorado School of Mines
Twin Towers, 1811 Elm Street
Golden, Colorado 80401-9951
303-273-3220

Type: **4-year public science and engineering**
Overall campus environment: **Competitive**
Total enrollment: **2,750**
African-American students: **40**
Graduate students: **875**
African-American graduate students: **N/R**

Percentage of applications accepted: **80%**
Average SAT/ACT score: **1180/26**
Average SAT/ACT African-Americans: **N/A**
Special admissions programs: **N/R**
Percentage of African-American graduates: **60%**
Percentage receiving financial aid: **55%**
Average amount of award: **$7,700**
Percentage in ROTC programs: **N/R**
Number of faculty: **185**
Number of African-American faculty: **N/R**
Student/faculty ratio: **13 to 1**
Tuition: **$10,820**
Scholarship programs: **Black Student Achievement Scholarship**
Academic programs: **Chemistry; Chemical, Electrical, Mechanical, Geological, Mining, Metallurgy and Materials and Petroleum Engineering, general engineering programs, Geophysics, Mathematics, Physics**
Most popular majors: **Chemical, General, Petroleum Engineering**
Prominent African-American faculty: **N/R**
Prominent African-American graduates: **N/R**
African-American student organizations: **Society of Black Engineers**
Administrative services and programs: **Minority Engineering Program**

Colorado School of Mines is a state-run four-year college which specializes in science and engineering. Here you will find more types of engineering programs than you've ever imagined—chemical, geological, metallurgical and petroleum engineering and more. If there's an engineering specialty you want to study, you're bound to find it at Mines.

Mines is a fairly selective technical college. On average, students admitted here rank in the upper third of their high school class and score about 1200 on the SAT. Admissions requirements tend to hinge more on grades than at schools with a more liberal education policy. Students are expected to focus almost entirely on the technical aspects of the academic program, which is rigorous. Students who come to Mines need to be focused and serious about their work in order to do well. For many students who have excelled in high school, Mines can come as a shock. Doing well here is a challenge; students find that they have to work twice as hard to get "okay" grades.

Most of the students who attend Mines come from Colorado. Mines has been working to improve its low proportion of African-American students (about 1.4 percent) and has established a scholarship program as well as a Minority Engineering Program. This program provides intensive counseling, tutoring and support of African-American and other minority students, and helps them adjust to campus life. African-Americans, Hispanics and Asians combined make up 8 percent of the campus population. Foreign students, largely from the Middle East and Latin America, constitute about 15 percent of the student body.

Compared to other campuses, social life at Mines is almost nonexistent. There are a few fraternities and sororities but no African-American chapters. Most students tend to find their entertainment off-campus, either in nearby Denver (just twenty minutes away) or in the outdoors. Mines is near the Rocky Mountains, and skiing, mountain climbing and other sports are available a short ride from the campus.

Students do not come to Mines for the great social life or for a broad-based academic program. They come for superb technical training that translates into great job opportunities in engineering once they graduate. This is where the oil companies, energy firms and high-tech companies come to recruit. With a degree from the Mines you can expect to begin your career with an above-average salary.

If you're willing to work hard, give up on a "well-rounded" education and forgo a social life, you might look into Mines. Just be sure that it's the right choice for you.

University of Colorado—Boulder
Regents Administrative Center 125
Campus Box 30
Boulder, Colorado 80390-0030
303-492-4449/303-492-8384

Total enrollment: **25,008**
African-American students: **423**

Graduate students: **4,844**
African-American graduate students: **70**
Percentage of applications accepted: **75%**
Average SAT/ACT score: **1070/25.1**
Average SAT/ACT African-Americans: **810/21**
Special admissions programs: **N/A**
Percentage of African-American graduates: **38% (over 5 years)**
Percentage receiving financial aid: **50%**
Average amount of award: **$5,800**
Percentage in ROTC programs: **N/R**
Number of faculty: **1,094**
Number of African-American faculty: **23**
Student/faculty ratio: **18 to 1**
Tuition: **$2,080 (arts and sciences) in state/$10,870 out of state**
Scholarship programs: **Minority and Athletic Scholarships**
Academic programs: **Colleges of Arts and Sciences, Business and Administration, Engineering and Applied Science, Environmental Design, Music; Schools of Education, Journalism and Mass Communication, Pharmacy; Preprofessional Study**
Most popular majors: **Open Option, Sociology, Communication, Psychology, Pre-Journalism, Political Science, Kinesiology, Business**
Prominent African-American faculty: **N/R**
Prominent African-American graduates: **N/R**
African-American student organizations/activities: **Black Student Alliance**
Administrative services and programs: **CU Opportunity Program, Ethnic and Women's Advocacy Office**

The most outstanding feature of the University of Colorado—Boulder is the awesome beauty of the campus. Set in the foothills of the Rocky Mountains, UC—Boulder is dominated by the Flat-irons, dramatic rock formations which have become the university's most famous landmark.

Just walking around this scenic campus is bound to make any student feel good even on a bad day, and new students are likely to have a few of those before settling into this large university. Many first-year students report that classes are overcrowded and difficult to get into. Lecture classes may have up to 200 students.

Despite these drawbacks, UC—Boulder has a solid academic program, particularly in the sciences and engineering, as well as some of the best facilities in the nation. Students can choose majors from five colleges: arts and sciences, business administration, engineering and applied sciences, environmental design and music. Each college has its own entrance standards and requirements, and it's wise to examine them before applying. To qualify for admission into the College of Music, for example, you must audition.

UC—Boulder has plenty of state-of-the-art facilities, such as electron microscopes and a real space satellite—the only student-run satellite in the country. The university boasts that a number of its graduates have actually become astronauts and traveled in space.

UC—Boulder also offers programs in education, journalism and mass communications, and pharmacy, as well as preprofessional preparation in medicine, dentistry, law and other fields. However, like many large universities, UC—Boulder lacks a strong liberal arts program, and it has introduced an enrichment program to address this need. It has also established a study skills center and tutoring and counseling programs to help students adapt to campus and academic life. A residence hall academic program, however, has proved more successful by providing help to students in a small, more private setting.

The challenge of adapting to the large university setting is a great equalizer which brings together majority students and African-American and other minority students. Besides the general counseling and tutorial programs, the university has established the UC Opportunity Program, which provides guidance and academic assistance to prospective African-American and other minority students.

The university's liberal atmosphere is respectful of ethnic and cultural differences. It's perhaps because of this environment that the small number of African-American students here (about 2 percent) have been able to exert so much influence. The Black Student Alliance at UC—Boulder is strong, and along with other student groups has been pushing for the university to divest its financial interests in South Africa.

Nearly one-third of students admitted to UC—Boulder rank in

the top 10 percent of their high school graduating class, and 70 percent rank in the top quarter. While the administration gives a great deal of consideration to standardized test scores (the average SAT score is about 1000), the level of college-prep courses taken in high school and the demonstrated ability to succeed in college weigh more heavily. The university has a commitment to racial diversity and leans more toward admitting minorities given equal academic qualifications. Still, many students believe too few minorities are enrolled at UC—Boulder, and are always pressing the administration to admit more African-Americans.

Greater numbers of African-American students may be just what it takes to create a more comfortable environment for minorities, particularly those from economically disadvantaged backgrounds, since UC—Boulder attracts its share of wealthy and upper-middle-class students.

Students who enjoy the outdoors, especially skiing, hiking or mountain climbing, and want to be on a campus whose natural beauty is absolutely breathtaking, will enjoy UC—Boulder.

University of Northern Colorado
Greeley, Colorado 80639
303-351-2685

Type: **Public**
Overall campus environment: **Good**
Total enrollment: **10,259**
African-American students: **185**
Graduate students: **1,623**
African-American graduate students: **16**
Percentage of applications accepted: **71%**
Average SAT/ACT score: **890/22**
Average SAT/ACT African-Americans: **N/R**
Special admissions programs: **N/A**
Percentage of African-American graduates: **25% in 6 years**
Percentage receiving financial aid: **75%**
Average amount of award: **$4,400**
Number in ROTC programs: **N/R**
Number of faculty: **430**
Number of African-American faculty: **4**

Student/faculty ratio: **20 to 1**
Tuition: **$1,707 in state/$6,568 out of state**
Scholarship programs: **Cultural Diversity, Talent, Theater, Visual Arts, Athletic Awards**
Major fields of study: **Biological Sciences, Black Studies, Business Administration, Chemistry, Communication Disorders, Communications, Dietetics, Earth Sciences, Economics, English, French, Geography, German, Gerontology, Health, Hispanic Studies, History, Human Rehabilitative Services, Interdisciplinary Studies, Journalism, Kinesiology, Mathematics**
Most popular majors: **Business, Education, Health Sciences, Social Sciences, Visual and Performing Arts**
Prominent African-American faculty: **Dr. Hermon George, Jr.; Professor and Coordinator, Black Studies Program; Dr. Anthonia Kalu, Professor, Black Studies Program**
Prominent African-American graduates: **N/R**
African-American student organizations/Activities: **Marcus Garvey Cultural Center**
Administrative services and programs: **Interpersonal Growth Workshop, Black Studies Program.**

The University of Northern Colorado is a public university in Greeley, Colorado, about fifty miles north of Denver. Of interest to many is the fact that it's also the home of the Denver Broncos' summer training camp.

A university of about 10,000 students, UNC offers more than 100 undergraduate majors, including programs in education for which the university is well known. One of the largest teachers' job fairs in the United States is held here each year, attracting school district officials from across the country. UNC also offers twenty-four degrees in the liberal arts and sciences, as well as preprofessional programs in engineering, law and medicine.

The majority of students who attend UNC come from Colorado, attracted by reasonable tuition and career-oriented programs in business, education and the health sciences. Among the most popular majors is business and accounting, and for good reason: UNC has a highly computerized business curriculum which is said to be among the most advanced in the country. The university boasts that its graduates have achieved the state's highest scores on the national exam for certified public accountants. UNC's programs in music are also widely recognized, and the university's student vocal jazz group, the UNC Axidentals, received a Grammy nomination in 1987, making it one of only two university groups ever to be nominated.

A fairly culturally diverse institution, UNC has an African-American enrollment of about 9 percent—higher than most. It also offers a strong Black Studies program, administered by Dr. Anthonia Kalu, a renowned African-American professor. Students can make this field their major or a minor. UNC's philosophy of encouraging all students to take Black Studies to "enhance your multicultural education as well as your career opportunities" sets it apart. UNC has been offering this program to students since 1972, and it has become an integral part of the campus. Students are not only taught the historical aspects of African-American culture but are informed of the benefits of this study for their careers. "Black Studies will help you develop ethnic, racial, and cultural awareness and sensitivity," they are told, "and also develop insights and interpersonal skills that will permit you to work successfully in environments as varied as the American inner city and the international arena."

One of the most attractive features of the campus for African-American students is the Marcus Garvey Cultural Center, a meeting place for students and local residents. The center provides students with academic advising, counseling and overall educational and emotional support. It also extends services and support to the African-American community of Greeley.

Admission to UNC is moderately selective; however, students with a willingness to work hard and take advantage of the university's offerings will do well here.

Howard University
2400 6th Street, N.W.
Washington, D.C. 20059
202-806-2758

Type: **Private**
Overall campus environment: **Dynamic, Culturally Diverse**
Total enrollment: **12,299**

African-American Students: **8,111**
Graduate students: **3,023**
African-American graduate students: **2,048**
Percentage of applications accepted: **54%**
Average SAT/ACT score: **879/19**
Average SAT/ACT African-Americans: **879/19**
Special admissions programs: **N/A**
Percentage of African-American graduates: **45%**
Percentage receiving financial aid: **80%**
Average amount of award: **$6,000**
Percentage in ROTC programs: **N/R**
Number of faculty: **1,267**
Number of African-American faculty: **1,000**
Student/faculty ratio: **7 to 1**
Tuition: **$13,408**
Scholarship programs: **Trustee Scholarships, University Grants, Special Talent Grants-In-Aid, National Competitive Scholarships, SEOG, Pell Grants, State Student Incentive Grants, Laverne Noyes Scholarship**
Academic programs: **Allied Health, Architecture, Arts and Sciences, Business, Communications, Education, Engineering, Fine Arts, Nursing**
Most popular majors: **Allied Health, Arts and Sciences, Business Communications, Engineering**
Prominent African-American faculty: **Al Freeman, Drama Professor and Actor; Samuel Yette, Journalism Professor**
Prominent African-American graduates: **Debbie Allen, actress, dancer, producer; Ed Bradley, journalist; Kenneth B. Clark, psychologist; David N. Dinkins, Mayor, New York City; Michael Espy, U.S. Secretary of Agriculture; Roberta Flack, singer; Sharon Pratt Kelly, Mayor, Washington, D.C.; Thurgood Marshall, former Supreme Court Justice; Toni Morrison, novelist; Paulie Murray, priest; Richard Wesley, playwright; Douglas Wilder, Governor, Virginia**
African-American student organizations/activities: **Most organizations on campus, including Howard University March Band, Campus Pals, Cheerleaders, Howard Gospel Choir, Howard Players, Howard University Student Association,** *Hilltop* **newspaper and** *Bison* **yearbook, numerous fraternities and sororities, WHUR Radio, WHMM-TV.**

Administrative services and programs: **Educational Advisory Center, Center for Academic Reinforcement.**

Howard University! Just the name conjures up thoughts of great historical figures, prominent black doctors, lawyers, architects and engineers; and, of course, a great social life! Often referred to as the Black Harvard, Howard University is the preeminent African-American institution in the country, and its graduates are among the country's most prominent and well-respected professionals. A predominantly African-American university with a fair proportion of students of other races, Howard is a school with very high standards. Only 54 percent of the applications submitted each year are accepted. Once selected, students are put through the rigors they face at any major university—perhaps even more—in preparation for the real world. Getting a degree from Howard is no piece of cake. Howard's programs are intensive; in its pre-medical program, for example, students receive firsthand training at Howard University Hospital on the campus. Howard's communications, law, architectural, engineering and fine arts programs are among the most popular fields of study, and many graduates have become leaders in their fields. As at many predominantly African-American institutions, students will find a nurturing, supportive environment at Howard. The faculty and administration is predominantly African-American; the majority of the campus organizations and social and cultural activities are Afrocentric, and Howard sits in the heart of the country's predominantly African-American capital, Washington, D.C. The university is large; it's the largest African-American university in the country. Student housing is available, and freshmen are required to live on campus. It's believed that living on campus is an important part of a student's educational experience and personal development, but there's also a practical reason for the rule: it gives students an opportunity to adjust to life in Washington, D.C. Washington has a great many social and cultural offerings that African-American students can take advantage of, but there is a downside: like many urban centers, Washington is faced with the growing problems of crime, drugs and homicide among youths. However, the city's African-American administration, led by Mayor Sharon Pratt Kelly, is working hard to alleviate these problems and bring renewed investment and commitment to resolving them.

Howard University operates four campuses. The main campus houses most classrooms, dormitories and administrative offices; there is a separate Law Center, the Divinity School in northwest Washington, and the Beltsville campus in Prince George's County just outside Washington. Students at Howard are also exposed to a number of African-American-operated facilities associated with the university, including the Howard University Hospital, WHUR radio, and WHMM-TV. Qualified students have the opportunity to gain firsthand experience at these facilities, which on their own successfully serve Washington and the surrounding community. In addition, students can take advantage of a variety of internship programs in the city's news organizations, businesses, schools and government offices and can volunteer their services to community projects.

Traditionally, Howard has graduated a large majority of this country's African-American health care professionals, and it now has an accelerated medical and dental education program to allow students to pursue a joint degree: a B.S. and Doctor of Medicine, Doctor of Podiatric Medicine, or Doctor of Dental Surgery. Howard also has a student exchange program both within and outside the United States.

Students at Howard University become a part of an important institution and live and study among some of the nation's most successful and influencial professionals and leaders. They experience college life on a campus run by African-Americans, in a city of African-Americans. This combination of location, academic program, faculty and staff makes Howard University an attractive choice for many students.

Yale University
P. O. Box 1502A, Yale Station
New Haven, Connecticut 06520
203-432-1900

Type: **Private 4-year**
Overall campus environment: **Traditional, prestigious, competitive, supportive**
Total enrollment: **11,948**

African-American students: **935**
Graduate students: **6,516**
African-American graduate students: **N/R**
Percentage of applications accepted: **22%**
Average SAT score: **1270–1460**
Average SAT African-Americans: **N/A**
Special admissions programs: **Preorientation summer program**
Percentage receiving financial aid: **64%**
Average amount of award: **$15,900**
Percentage in ROTC programs: **N/R**
Number of faculty: **1,921**
Number of African-American faculty: **N/R**
Student/faculty ratio: **6 to 1**
Tuition: **$16,300**
Scholarship programs: **University, state and private scholarships and grants; in 1991–92, Yale had $25 million for undergraduate financial aid packages. No academic or athletic scholarships. Awards are based on demonstrated need.**
Academic programs: **Courses divided into 4 groups: Languages and Literature (includes English), Humanities, Social Science, Natural Sciences (includes engineering and mathematics). Majors of interest include African and African-American Studies and Women's Studies.**
Prominent African-American graduates: **Supreme Court Justice Clarence Thomas; Anita Hill, Professor of Law, University of Oklahoma; Ola Rotimi, playwright, director; Dr. Benjamin Carson, neurosurgeon, Johns Hopkins Hospital, Baltimore, MD; Erroll McDonald, Executive Editor, Pantheon Books; Barbara Chase-Riboud, sculptor, writer, poet.**
African-American student organizations/activities: **African-American Cultural Center, Heritage Theatre Ensemble, Yale Gospel Choir, Black Church at Yale, Black Student Alliance at Yale, Pre-Med Advisory Committee for Minorities, Black Pre-Law Society, Minority Business Association**
Administrative services and programs: **African-American Cultural Center, Pre-Med Advisory Committee for Minorities, Black Pre-Law Society, Minority Business Association**

Yale is one of the oldest and finest institutions in the country, and a Yale degree virtually guarantees career success. Yale has graduated U.S. presidents (including former President Bush, brilliant doctors like neurosurgeon Ben Carson, Nobel prize winners, Rhodes scholars, business and government leaders and diplomats.

What does this institution have to offer African-Americans? Plenty. Besides a top-quality education, Yale provides exposure to the real world through those in the front lines of politics, government and business. Distinguished educators and others in all fields come to teach and guest-lecture. Yale has the fourth-largest library in the country: more than 9 million volumes, including the James Weldon Johnson Collection, one of the country's most significant bodies of African-American artistic work. The university also offers excellent majors in African and Afro-American studies and women's studies.

Although African-Americans make up only about 7 percent of the students, their presence is felt through a number of campus organizations and activities which bring students together. Yale actively recruits minority students at college fairs and through a network of loyal African-American alumni. But it is no piece of cake to get into Yale; the average student scores between 1270 and 1460 on the SAT and the school admits only 22% of its applicants. Yale is also expensive: more than $20,000 a year in tuition and fees. Only 40 percent of students receive financial aid, which is allocated on the basis of need. Yale offers a preorientation program that brings entering African-American students to the campus each summer. Once admitted, each freshman is assigned a minority counselor and, for those who need extra support, an African-American student mentor to help him or her learn the ropes. Lots of remedial attention is also given to students once they're on campus. Pre-med, pre-law and business advisory committees provide academic assistance and professional guidance, in addition to internships for qualified students. African-American faculty are accessible, maintaining regular office hours and participating in student activities.

Interaction between students of different races is fairly good. African-American students will find that there is a tendency to separate along lines of socioeconomic status, educational background and hometown. Even the best-intentioned students may find it difficult to connect with other African-American students because students are scattered across the campus in twelve "residential colleges." These colleges are self-contained, each with its own living facilities; dining hall; library; seminar and music rooms; computer, game and TV rooms, and fitness facilities. However, students will discover they can connect through a number of Afrocentric organizations and through activities sponsored by the Afro-American Cultural Center, including annual events during Black History Month and Kwanzaa.

Yale sits in the center of New Haven, a predominantly poor and working-class African-American community. Since most students live on campus, they remain insulated from the realities of this urban environment, but the campus radio station, athletic organizations, theater and church groups offer chances to get involved. Many students also volunteer their time and efforts to the community by tutoring city children and participating in political and religious activities.

Florida A&M University
Tallahassee, Florida 32307
904-599-3796

Type: **Public**
Overall campus environment: **Traditional, Culturally Exciting, Academically Challenging**
Total enrollment: **7,500**
African-American students: **7,350**
African-American graduate students: **400**
Percentage of applications accepted: **N/A**
Average SAT/ACT score: **860–1050/20–25**
Special admissions programs: **N/A**
Percentage receiving financial aid: **74%**
Average amount of award: **$2800**
Percentage in ROTC programs: **N/A**
Number of faculty: **491**
Number of African-American faculty: **400**
Student/faculty ratio: **16 to 1**
Tuition: **$1,509 in-state/$5,648 out-of-state**
Scholarship programs: **President's Scholars Awards, Florida Undergraduate Scholars' Fund, Florida Teacher**

Scholarship-Loan Program, Florida Teacher Tuition Reimbursement Program, Florida Student Loan Forgiveness Program, National Merit Achievement Scholarships, ROTC Scholarships, departmental scholarships, etc.

Academic programs: **Colleges of Arts and Sciences, Education, Engineering Sciences, Technology, Agriculture; FAMU/FSU College of Engineering; College of Pharmacy and Pharmaceutical Sciences; Schools of Allied Sciences; Architecture; Business and Industry; General Studies; Graduate Studies, Research and Continuing Education; Journalism, Media and Graphic Arts; Nursing**

Most popular majors: **Business, Journalism, Engineering, Pharmacy**

Prominent African-American faculty: **N/R**

Prominent African-American graduates: **N/R**

African-American student organizations/Activities: **More than 100 organizations and clubs.**

Administrative services and programs: **Office of Special Programs and Services serving international students, minority (non-Black) students and disabled students**

Begun in the late 1800s as the State Normal College for Colored Students, Florida A&M University (FAMU) now enjoys a reputation as one of Florida's finest institutions of higher education. The key to FAMU's success has been a leadership with vision and a willingness to take risks to ensure the institution's future. Each of its eight presidents led the institution to greater heights in increased enrollments, academic offerings and educational standing. During the early 1970s, when federal laws forced a desegregated unitary system in education, FAMU's leaders pressed for the institution's autonomy, and in 1971 FAMU became a full partner in Florida's nine-university public system. By the late 1980s FAMU had grown to encompass eleven schools and colleges, a division of graduate studies and a doctoral program in pharmacology. Its student body grew to more than 7,500, and FAMU was ranked fourth in the nation in enrolling National Merit Achievement finalists, following only Harvard, Yale and Stanford.

FAMU has distinguished itself in many ways but is probably best known for its soulful, stepping Marching 100 Band. In 1989 the band was invited to participate in the French government's Bastille Day Parade as the official representative of the United States for the bicentennial of the French Revolution. Many also associate the university with its outstanding School of Business and Industry, which has involved corporate America in the training of students as well as in financial support of the institution.

Perhaps not as well known is the fact that FAMU was the first historically African-American university to have an accredited journalism program. FAMU is historically known for its agricultural and mechanical trade programs, hence its name, Florida Agricultural and Mechanical College.

African-American students will find that all of the programs and services are designed specifically for their interests and needs. FAMU offers a number of counseling and tutorial services for its students, as well as career programs, particularly for its business students. One program, the Skills Assessment Seminar, brings representatives from forty corporations to campus to help students assess their strengths and weaknesses in problem-solving, decision-making, leadership and interpersonal skills. The administration offers career workshops on everything from creating a professional image and dressing for success to global marketing and government service.

Non-Black students at FAMU are considered minorities. Although there are no official organizations for minority students, they are encouraged to participate in majority student programs and activities. The university does, however, have an Office of Special Programs and Services to meet the needs of minorities, foreign students and the disabled.

FAMU's more than 100 social and professional organizations include all the national Black Greek organizations, military, religious, honorary and scholastic groups. In addition, FAMU has a number of preprofessional organizations, including prelaw, premed, prenursing and preveterinarian groups, which sponsor seminars and are active in the field.

Overall, social life at FAMU depends on what you're interested in: theater, concert performances, the Greek life, or partying. Sports is a strong tradition, particularly football; the university has won eleven national championships. FAMU has membership in several intercollegiate athletic associations, including the

NCAA, and offers athletic grants for its outstanding students. In addition, the university boasts a 25,500-seat stadium, an athletic center with a track, Olympic pool, and men's and women's weight training rooms. Students who just want to cool out can take advantage of the many facilities offered at the University Union, including bowling lanes, billiards, a lounge area and a game area. FAMU's campus radio station features music, news and sports.

Florida A&M University is one of the larger and better-established predominantly African-American institutions in the country. Students who are looking for the supportive and nurturing environment of a predominantly Black university and an excellent program in business will want to place FAMU high on their list of schools to consider.

Stetson University
Campus Box 8378
De Land, Florida 32720-3771
904-822-7100

Type: **Private liberal arts**
Overall campus environment: **Cordial**
Total enrollment: **2,055**
African-American students: **40**
Graduate students: **136**
African-American graduate students: **N/A**
Percentage of total applications accepted: **72%**
Average SAT score: **1080**
Average SAT African-Americans: **893**
Special admissions programs: **N/A**
Percentage of African-American graduates: **33% (within 5 years)**
Percentage receiving financial aid: **95%**
Average amount of award: **$10,500**
Percentage in ROTC programs: **N/A (cross-enrollment program with Emory-Riddle Aeronautical University)**
Number of faculty: **185**
Number of African-American faculty: **4**
Student/faculty ratio: **12 to 1**

Tuition: **$11,500**
Scholarship programs: **George William Scholarship for minorities**
Academic programs: **Colleges of Arts and Science, Law; Schools of Business, Music**
Most popular majors: **Political Science, Business, Music**
Prominent African-American graduates: **N/A**
Prominent African-American faculty: **Dr. Patrick Coggins, Professor, multicultural researcher**
African-American student organizations/activities: **African-American Student Association (AASA); Multicultural Student Council**
Administrative services and programs: **Multicultural Education Institute; Summer Enrichment Program for Minority Students**

African-American students at Stetson find themselves at a university that offers a top-notch education in the arts and sciences, particularly business, law and music. Stetson is rated one of the top regional universities in the country and number three in the Southeast. More than 90 percent of the faculty hold doctoral degrees, and many are published scholars, performing artists, or active consultants in their field. Only 2 percent of the faculty is African-American—among them a professor renowned and much published in multicultural research.

While the African-American presence on this campus is minimal, the administration has recently made efforts to improve its relationship with African-Americans and other minorities through a cultural diversity committee, which consists of the president, provost, vice president of student life, dean of admissions and some other administrators and faculty. It's worth noting the administration's response to recent articles in the student newspaper indicating that many white students on campus were opposed to improving the racial mix. In an editorial, the provost restated Stetson's commitment to cultural diversity and invited minority students to write a similar editorial, which they did.

As is often the case at predominantly white colleges, many believe that Stetson can do more to meet the needs of African-American students. The university has already begun to institute programs such as the George William Minority Scholarship, the annual Multicultural Educational Institute and the Summer En-

92 / Stetson University

richment program, which brings African-American high school students to the university for a stay on campus. The administration also supports the African-American Student Association, which sponsors a number of cultural events every year. University officials have placed the handling of grievances high in the administration, with the vice president for student life. However, the administration recognizes that more needs to be done to bridge the gap between racial groups on campus. When pressed about the overall racial climate for African-American students, the administration admits that although interaction between all racial groups takes place, there continues to be a lack of understanding between white and African-American students. Much of this racial intolerance exists, administrators believe, because white students are ignorant of the history and culture of African-Americans, and because students mirror the attitudes of the general society about race and culture.

Still, Stetson has much to offer African-American students. The university has a highly regarded business school and music program, and offers opportunities to study abroad in Spain, Germany, France, England and the former Soviet Union. Qualified students can take advantage of a political science internship in Washington, D.C., or the business school's investment program, in which students actually manage an investment portfolio worth more than $1 million. One student confirmed that Stetson is both academically and socially challenging for African-American students. He pointed out that the limited cultural activities and social life for African-Americans contribute to a feeling of isolation from the rest of the student body, but, he added that the absence of these activities has had an unexpected benefit. "I can concentrate on academics better than I would be able to if most of my cultural interests were met," he said. "And when I want to satisfy these (cultural) interests, I can visit Bethune-Cookman College (a predominantly African-American college), which is only about fifteen minutes away." In an effort to connect with the local African-American community, many students attend a local African-American church, and the African-American Student Association often plans community activities. Students can also become mentors to children in the community through the Youth Motivator Program, visiting a local school regularly for one semester.

A private institution, Stetson is as affordable as many public colleges and universities. African-American students will find that they can get a good education at Stetson, and generous financial aid is available through a variety of school programs. One student summed up the advantages and disadvantages of the school this way: "Even though I sometimes long for the experience of attending a predominantly African-American college, I am proud to be at Stetson. I am receiving the best education in the state, have an excellent financial aid and scholarship package; and I have already made very important connections that will enhance my chances of a successful future. Overall, I am satisfied with my decision and if I had to do it again would probably make the exact same decision."

University of Florida
328 Tigert Hall
Gainesville, Florida 32611
904-392-0456

Type: **Public land-grant**
Overall campus environment: **Cordial**
Total enrollment: **36,227**
African-American students: **2,004**
Graduate students: **8,905**
African-American graduate students: **356**
Percentage of applications accepted: **71%**
Average SAT score: **1114**
Special admissions programs: **Individual Learning Plan**
Percentage of African-American graduates: **38% (after 7 years)**
Percentage receiving financial aid: **64%**
Average amount of award: **$3,859**
Percentage in ROTC programs: **N/R**
Number of faculty: **3,261**
Number of African-American faculty: **83**
Student/faculty ratio: **17 to 1**
Tuition: **$11,480**
Scholarship programs: **State of Florida programs, major field of study scholarships**
Academic programs: **More than 120 majors in 13 Colleges; Accounting, Architecture, Building Construction, Business**

Administration, Engineering, Fine Arts, Forest Resources and Conservation, Health and Human Performance, Health Related Professions, Journalism and Communications, Liberal Arts and Sciences, Nursing, Pharmacy
Most popular majors: **Business and management, engineering, social sciences**
Prominent African-American faculty: **N/R**
Prominent African-American graduates: **Too numerous to list**
African-American student organizations/activities: **Association of Black Communicators, Alpha Phi Alpha, Alpha Sweets, Beta Eta Sigma (Black honor society), Black Graduate Student Organization, Black Law Students Association, Black Student Union, Delta Sigma Theta, Kappa Alpha Psi, Minority Business Society, Minorities in IFAS, Minority Preprofessional Services Association, NAACP, National Association of Minority Contractors, Omega Psi Phi, Open Arms, Phi Beta Sigma, Presidential Scholars, Sigma Gamma Rho, Society for Black Engineers, University of Florida Gospel Choir, Zeta Phi Beta**

One of the most attractive features of the University of Florida is the wide variety of degree programs, major fields of study and social activities that the institution offers. With more than 35,000 students, 13 colleges and more than 121 majors (only two other universities in the country offer more degree programs), UF is one of the top twenty-five universities in the United States. As a research institution UF has incredibly fine facilities on campus, including the second-largest academic computer center in the South; one of the nation's few self-contained intensive-care hyperbaric chambers for the treatment of near-drowning victims; a powerful nuclear training and research reactor, and the second-largest astronomical research facility in the Southeast. The campus boasts a huge complex of excellent facilities, including a student union complete with bowling alley, billiards, table tennis, restaurants, specialty shops, hobby and arts centers and a photographic darkroom. Sports facilities are equally impressive, with a weight room, a 220-yard indoor track, a 50-meter Olympic-sized swimming pool and a seating capacity of 12,000 for basketball games and special events.

UF's academic programs are strong, and students will find

them challenging and exciting. Programs in the physical and biological sciences and in engineering, agriculture, architecture, and business are among the university's best and most popular. The communications and journalism college also enjoys a good reputation and affords students the opportunity to work at the university radio and television stations. UF was among the first to establish a state-of-the-art electronic newsroom on campus. In addition, the university has postgraduate programs in more than sixty major fields, through the doctoral level and including professional programs in medicine, dentistry, law and veterinary medicine.

A number of urban centers are accessible from UF, including Tampa/St. Petersburg, Jacksonville, Orlando, Miami, Atlanta and Tallahassee. All are within three hours of the campus except Miami and Atlanta, which are about six hours away. However, Gainesville (population about 85,000) is somewhat remote, and African-American students have little interaction with its residents.

African-Americans represent about 5 percent of the population at UF. The university has done a good job of recruiting, retaining and graduating African-American students and has established a number of programs and services to meet their needs. UF also has a respectable number of African-American faculty, a noteworthy African-American studies program, and an Institute of Black Culture. This facility serves as a meeting place for African-American students for formal and informal events. Finally, the university offers students a well-established Black Greek system, with chapters of the major national fraternities and sororities.

One truly special feature of UF is the real-life experience students are exposed to on campus. The university's Student Government Association, for example, is one of the most well-organized in the nation. The association holds elections, is responsive to its constituencies, makes political deals and generally operates like any local government in the United States. This provides African-Americans with a chance to practice negotiating in a governmental system that is a microcosm of the real world. Still, African-American representation in this process is weak—another way in which the university mimics the larger society. "I often feel like an outsider at UF," said one student, "so I channel my energies into helping other minority students in college, high school or grade school to achieve their goals."

Students reported few racial problems on this campus and said they socialize primarily with other African-American students. "UF has a reputable reputation, a fine faculty, a fair amount of African-American students and a good Afro-American studies program," said one student. "This university was a good choice and one that has provided me a quality education as well as life experiences that have helped me to grow."

Agnes Scott College
Decatur, Georgia 30030
404-371-6285/1-800-868-8602

Type: **Private women's liberal arts, affiliated with Presbyterian Church**
Overall campus environment: **Supportive/academically demanding**
Total enrollment: **600**
African-American students: **80**
Graduate students: **2**
Percentage of applications accepted: **81%**
Average SAT score: **1000**
Average SAT African-Americans: **N/R**
Special admissions programs: **N/A**
Percentage of African-American graduates: **60%**
Percentage receiving financial aid: **94%**
Average amount of award: **$9,200**
Percentage in ROTC programs: **N/R**
Number of faculty: **65**
Number of African-American faculty: **6**
Student/faculty ratio: **8 to 1**
Tuition: **$10,945**
Scholarship programs: **Agnes Scott College Scholarship Awards**
Academic programs: **Art, Art History/English Literature, Art History/History, Astrophysics, Bible and Religion, Biology, Biology/Psychology, Chemistry, Classical Languages and Literature, Classical Studies, Economics, English, English**

Literature/Creative Writing, French, German, Greek,
History, History/English Literature, International Relations,
Latin, Latin American Studies, Mathematics,
Mathematics/Economics/Physics, Music, Philosophy, Physics,
Political Science, Psychology, Sociology,
Sociology/Anthropology, Spanish, Theater
Most popular majors: **English, International Relations,
Psychology**
Prominent African-American faculty: **Bernita Berry, Sociology
Professor**
Prominent African-American graduates: **Angela Drake, Senior
Analyst, Lockheed Aeronautical Systems Company**
African-American student organizations/activities: **Witkaze,
Chimo Cultural Exchange Group**
Administrative services and programs: **Career Planning and
Placement**

Agnes Scott is one of the nation's leading women's liberal arts
colleges, with a reputation for turning out graduates who succeed
in many fields. Its alumnae have gone on to obtain postgraduate
degrees at Yale, Harvard, New York University, Johns Hopkins
and Stanford. Equally impressive are the numbers of alumnae
who have become television news anchors, successful attorneys,
Pulitzer prize-winning playwrights, and NASA engineers. Many of
these women say their liberal arts training at Agnes Scott was
invaluable in achieving their life goals. "My experiences at Agnes
Scott helped me realize there are two facets to success in any
discipline: a solid background in the discipline and good people
skills," said one graduate who now holds a management position
at a multinational corporation.

A small college of about 600 students in a suburb of Atlanta,
Agnes Scott is situated on a beautiful tree-lined campus, reminis-
cent of the "Old South" with its Gothic and Victorian buildings.
About 12 percent of the student body is African-American and
Hispanic, and the college prides itself on maintaining a good mix
of all types of women from all socioeconomic backgrounds, and
all ages including older returning students.

This college is not for the faint of heart. The academic program is rigorous, and students need to be serious to succeed.
Admission is fairly selective, most women have graduated in the

top quarter of their high school class. A proven ability to succeed, as well as qualities such as motivation, maturity and integrity, also rank high on the list of requirements that the administration looks for in a student.

Once admitted, students will find that their financial needs will be met. Agnes Scott is one of the best-endowed liberal arts colleges in the country, allowing it to provide the aid needed to fill the gap between tuition and what a student can afford to pay. The large endowment also means that the college can spend more per student to provide a good education.

Two of Agnes Scott's major attractions are a low student-to-faculty ratio and a supportive administration and faculty. However, students should know that this atmosphere of support does not mean a relaxation of high standards. "Our personal attention to students doesn't erode our ambition for their academic achievements," said one professor. Students will find that the most popular activity at Agnes Scott is hitting the books. In fact, students cite the highly academic atmosphere and lack of other activities as the college's downside. There are no sororities on campus, and most social interaction with men tends to take place off campus, either at one of the many predominantly Black colleges in Atlanta or at nearby Georgia Tech.

Overall, African-American students report that the college has an environment of racial respect and cooperation. Students also cite the college's Presbyterian affiliation and strict student honor code as having a positive impact on relationships. "Since most students live on campus, they get to know each other," said one student. "Your friends become your family away from home."

Most African-American students involve themselves in the student organization and activities on campus that interest them, with the administration's encouragement. An African-American student organization on campus called Witkaze coordinates many social and cultural activities, including a speaker series and panel discussions intended to further improve relations among all students.

Overall, Agnes Scott gets high marks for its excellent academics, supportive environment and liberal treatment of all its students. Here, women are pushed to fulfill all their ambitions.

Clark Atlanta University
James P. Brawley Drive at Fair Street, S.W.
Atlanta, Georgia 30314
404-880-8784/1-800-688-3228

Type: **Private historically African-American**
Overall campus environment: **Great**
Total enrollment: **2800**
African-American students: **2700**
Graduate students: **1060**
African-American graduate students: **1060**
Percentage of applications accepted: **75%**
Average SAT score: **781**
Special admissions programs: **N/R**
Percentage of African-American graduates: **97.4 (1988–89)**
Percentage receiving financial aid: **90%**
Average amount of award: **$7025**
Percentage in ROTC programs: **N/R**
Number of faculty: **246**
Number of African-American faculty: **200**
Student/faculty ratio: **12 to 1**
Tuition: **$5,800**
Scholarship programs: **University, Athletic and music scholarships.**
Academic programs: **Schools of Arts and Sciences, Business Administration, Education, Social Work; African and African-American Studies, Child Development, Hotel and Restaurant Management, ROTC; Preprofessional Programs in Engineering, Pharmacy, Medicine, Dentistry, Law, Seminary Studies**
Most popular majors: **Biology, Communications, Education, Health and Social Sciences.**
Prominent African-American faculty: **N/R**
Prominent African-American graduates: **Marva Collins, Founder Westside Preparatory School, Chicago, IL; Leslie B. McLemore, Professor Political Science, Jackson State University; Elsie L. Scott, Executive Director, National Organization of Law Enforcement Executives.**
African-American student organizations/activities: **Alpha Phi Alpha, Kappa Alpha Psi, Omega Psi Phi, Phi Beta Sigma**

fraternities, Alpha Kappa Alpha, Delta Sigma Theta, Sigma Gamma Rho, Zeta Phi Beta Sororities, Student Government Association, Clark Atlanta Magazine, Philharmonic Society, Clark Atlanta Players.
Administrative services and programs: **Office of Student Affairs**

Clark Atlanta University, recently consolidated from two historically African-American institutions, Atlanta University and Clark College, combines the offerings of a liberal arts college of high quality with those of a university on a shared campus. The consolidation promises to preserve the best of Clark and Atlanta U while eliminating duplication of programs and creating a more competitive institution.

The consolidated Clark Atlanta remains a part of the six-school Atlanta University Center, long known as a focus of African-American higher education and housing the country's largest assemblage of Black private colleges (besides Clark-Atlanta, the Interdenominational Theological Center, Morehouse College, Morehouse School of Medicine, Morris Brown College and Spelman College). Clark Atlanta distinguishes itself as the only totally private, urban, historically African-American university in the country offering comprehensive academic programs leading to the bachelor's, master's and doctoral degrees in a number of fields.

Such distinctions are not new for the Atlanta University Center. Its schools have educated Dr. Martin Luther King, Jr., and generations of his family, and more recently filmmaker Spike Lee, Olympic medalist Edwin Moses, Pulitzer prize–winning author Alice Walker and Marian Wright Edelman of the Children's Defense Fund.

The Center will continue to provide cross-registration and sharing of facilities with Clark Atlanta, including a $15-million library, a campus radio station (WCLK-FM, Atlanta's only jazz station), a cable television station and a $45-million state-of-the-art Science and Technology Research Center.

Being in an atmosphere where African-American students predominate certainly has its advantages for many students, and Clark Atlanta is one of the best such institutions a student can select. The predominantly African-American faculty is very supportive, and students are treated as though they are part of a family. African-American student organizations, events and culture abound, and students learn and grow together and often make friendships that last a lifetime. This explains why so many alumni want to send their offspring here and continue the tradition.

There's much to do culturally and socially—so much partying that students can easily go astray. However, there is an equal pull on the part of administration and faculty to keep students in good academic shape, and many students may find the truly caring administration a breath of fresh air and a strong incentive to do well.

If you want a predominantly African-American college with a strong academic program, great facilities and endless opportunities for you to learn and grow, Clark Atlanta offers all of that.

Georgia Institute of Technology
225 North Avenue
Atlanta, Georgia 30332-0320
404-894-4154

Type: **4-year state**
Overall campus environment: **Good/highly competitive**
Total enrollment: **12,814**
African-American students: **1,001**
Graduate students: **3,327**
African-American graduate students: **202**
Percentage of applications accepted: **53%**
Average SAT score: **1226**
Average SAT African-Americans: **1153**
Special admissions programs: **N/A**
Percentage of African-American graduates: **50%**
Percentage receiving financial aid: **55%**
Average amount of award: **$4,600**
Percentage in ROTC programs: **N/R**
Number of faculty: **607**
Number of African-American faculty: **17**
Student/faculty ratio: **21 to 1**
Tuition: **$4,300**
Scholarship programs: **Professional association and corporate**

scholarships for African-Americans from Mobil, Amoco, Kodak, AT&T, Bell Labs, Merck, Hewlett Packard, Texas Instruments, Phillips 66, Georgia Pacific, Delco, Eli Lilly, Intel, Southern Corporation, United Technologies
Academic program: **Colleges of Architecture, Computing, Engineering, Sciences and the Ivan Allen College of Management, Policy and International Affairs. 31 undergraduate majors, 32 master's programs, 23 doctoral programs; Pre-Medicine, Pre-Law**
Prominent African-American faculty: **N/R**
Prominent African-American graduates: **N/R**
African-American student organizations/activities: **Georgia Tech African-American Association, Fellowship of Christian Believers, Society of Black Engineers, Alpha Kappa Alpha, Alpha Phi Alpha, Delta Sigma Theta, Kappa Alpha Psi, Omega Psi Phi, Techwood Tutorial Program, Student Assistant Volunteers, Black Graduate Student Association**
Administrative services and programs: **Office of Minority Education Development, Challenge**

There's no question about it: students come to Georgia Tech for the strong academic program and the excellent chances of employment after graduation. Georgia Tech's reputation is well deserved. The institute has among the finest engineering, architecture and computer sciences programs in the country. Its faculty are extremely accomplished and well known for their research and consulting work for government and large corporations. Many large corporations and government agencies rely on Georgia Tech graduates to fill high-tech positions. "The best thing about Georgia Tech is the degree," one student said. "It is highly marketable and the opportunities for employment after graduation are outstanding."

Georgia Tech is highly successful in graduating capable engineering and science students, but some believe the program leaves much to be desired when it comes to providing a more well-rounded educational experience. The academic program is very demanding and tightly focused on the major field of study; it needs to be, as the subject matter is often difficult and mastering it is time-consuming. It is for this reason that Georgia Tech requires students to demonstrate their ability to succeed with good grades and high scores on standardized tests. Admission is based primarily on academics; the average student scores about 1200 on the SAT.

The requirements for African-American students are the same as those for other students, but African-Americans receive more personalized attention through recruitment and retention efforts. The majority of these efforts are administered through the Office of Minority Education Development, which provides individual counseling and academic advising services, as well as career planning and instruction in time management. Students also offer support through the African-American Association, the Society of Black Engineers and informal peer counseling.

It's not unusual for students to spend a large majority of their free time, including weekends, studying. But there is more to the school than just academics. Greek life, for one, is big on this campus, and African-American Greek organizations represent a large part of the social scene. There are also a number of professional and volunteer organizations for African-American students, and many say they rely on these organizations. "To have a social life on campus, you must get involved with special-interest organizations and Black Greek organizations," said one student. "It takes, in all honesty, a while to gain a sense of belonging at an institution which is 8 percent African-American, even though relationships with students of other races are good and strongly promoted by the administration."

Besides campus organizations, students take advantage of the rich cultural and social life of Atlanta. Georgia Tech is a convenient ride away on public transportation from clubs, theaters and the attractions of the city's Underground. Students can also join in more altruistic causes like the Big Brothers/Big Sisters, Saturday School program in which Georgia Tech students provide academic and tutorial assistance to local students. The city is also home to the Martin Luther King Center, which houses an enormous collection of materials on the civil rights movement.

One of the biggest attractions on campus is sports; Georgia Tech boasts a highly successful NCAA basketball team. The institute also has a very active intramural sports program, with nearly 5,000 student participants. Sports fans may also want to take in an Atlanta Braves baseball game or see the Atlanta Hawks basketball team.

Women who are contemplating Georgia Tech need to understand that they represent only about 20 percent of the student body and that the school is still very much a male bastion. But this is slowly changing as more women enter careers in engineering and the sciences.

Academics and opportunities abound at Georgia Tech, and if you have what it takes to complete a rigorous undergraduate program, you'll be rewarded handsomely once you graduate.

Georgia State University
P. O. Box 4009
Atlanta, Georgia 30302-4009
404-651-3010

Type: **Public nonresidential**
Overall campus environment: **Urban, Commuter campus**
Total enrollment: **24,024**
African-American students: **4,133**
Graduate students: **6,704**
African-American graduate students: **662**
Percentage of applications accepted: **72%**
Average SAT score: **880–970**
Average SAT African-Americans: **N/R**
Special admissions programs: **N/A**
Percentage of African-American graduates: **33%**
Percentage receiving financial aid: **33%**
Average amount of award: **$2,400**
Percentage in ROTC Programs: **N/R**
Number of faculty: **803**
Number of African-American faculty: **45**
Student/faculty ratio: **21 to 1**
Tuition: **$1778 in-state/$6080 out-of-state**
Scholarship programs: **University scholarships**
Academic programs: **250 majors in Colleges of Arts and Sciences, Business Administration, Education, Health Sciences, Law, Public and Urban Affairs**
Most popular majors: **Business, Computer Information Systems, Education, Psychology**
Prominent African-American Faculty: **N/R**

Prominent African-American graduates: **Lt. Gen. Henry Doctor, former Inspector General, U.S. Army; H. Jerome Russell, President, City Beverage Company; Mable Thomas, State Representative, Georgia House of Representatives; Dr. Barbara Whitaker, Assistant Superintendent, Atlanta Public Schools**

African-American student organizations/activities: **Black Student Alliance, Alpha Kappa Alpha, Delta Sigma Theta, Zeta Phi Beta, Alpha Phi Alpha, Kappa Alpha Psi, Phi Beta Sigma, Omega Psi Phi, Black Freshman Network, Baptist Student Union, NAACP, Black Students On White Campuses Conference, Black Life and Culture Committee, Minority Psychology Student Association, National Association of Black Accountants, National Black Business League, Organization for the Advancement of Students in Science (OASIS)**

Administrative services/programs: **Office of African-American Student Services, Office of Minority Affairs, Incept Orientation program, BRIDGE, Learning Resources Center, Division of Developmental Studies, Career Development Center, Office of Cooperative Education, INROADS, Governor's Intern program**

Georgia State University is a comprehensive public university in the heart of downtown Atlanta. Considered an "urban campus" for more reasons than just its location, GSU is nonresidential (no on-campus housing), and more than 92 percent of its students come from Georgia. Students here tend to be older; the average age of undergraduates is twenty-six. Many students have full-time jobs. Some have decided to obtain a degree after entering the work force; an equal number come to obtain advanced degrees.

With nearly 25,000 students, GSU is the second-largest institution in the University of Georgia system. The university awards degrees from the undergraduate through the doctoral level and offers 250 majors in its six colleges: Arts and Sciences, Business Administration, Education, Health Sciences, Law, and Public and Urban Affairs. Students say they come here because of the academic programs, convenience, and the support of the faculty, staff and administrators—and because of the low cost. Tuition for Georgia residents in 1991 was $1778—a real bargain considering the savings in cost of room and board. GSU's downtown location and varied class schedule are attractive to students as well. Whether a student is returning to school after beginning a family or is juggling work, family and school, GSU is very accommodating. This is perhaps the main reason that nearly 60 percent of the student body are women.

African-American students will find that GSU accommodates their needs as well. Besides a solid academic program, GSU provides a number of support services. The Office of Minority Affairs offers academic advising, help with developing good study skills, and assistance in selection of a degree program. The office also encourages students to get involved with campus life and sponsors many athletic, social and cultural events. Special events such as the annual Black Students on White Campuses conference bring together students from Georgia State University, Georgia Tech and Emory University to discuss ways for students to cope with being minorities at their schools. The university also has an African-American Student Services program which provides, among other things, university-wide assistance with issues of cultural and racial awareness. It coordinates mentoring, tutoring and supplemental advising programs through the minority affairs office and conducts a summer orientation program for potential students called BRIDGE.

Students who need additional academic support or tutoring can get help at the Learning Resources Center or in the Division of Developmental Studies. Each quarter the university holds a two-day workshop on improving study habits called the Study Skills Circus.

While GSU is nonresidential, it has traditional social offerings. There are a number of student organizations, including the Black Student Alliance and a number of black fraternities and sororities.

Students can participate in the Black Life and Culture Committee or become involved with the student government. Despite the small numbers of African-Americans on campus, four of the past ten student government presidents at GSU have been African-American. Of course, students can also take advantage of all of the cultural and social life that Atlanta has to offer. GSU is within a short drive of the Martin Luther King Center, the APEX Museum and the historic Auburn Avenue area. Atlanta is also the home of several of the nation's top African-American institutions, including the Atlanta University Center, which encompasses

Morehouse and Morris Brown and Spelman colleges, Morehouse School of Medicine, Clark Atlanta University and the Inter-denominational Theological Center.

Generally, students report that they're pleased with GSU and their interaction with faculty and staff. "I have had good experiences with the majority of my professors, both Black and white," said one senior. "Parts of the administration have been less than helpful in the past. However, I've since learned about the services directed toward us like the Black Freshmen Network and the Office of African-American Student Services. These programs help to orientate Black students, and they offer great support."

GSU makes available a fine education and plenty of academic support for students who would not otherwise have an opportunity to go to college. It offers good value to boot. However, students looking for a traditional college experience may be disappointed.

Morehouse College
830 Westview Drive, S.W.
Atlanta, Georgia 30314
404-215-2680

Type: **Predominantly African-American men's liberal arts**
Overall campus environment: **Traditional, Cultural, Academically challenging**
Total enrollment: **2,992**
African-American students: **2,950**
Graduate students: **Zero**
Percentage of applications accepted: **30%**
Average SAT score: **1003**
Average SAT African-Americans: **1003**
Special admissions programs: **N/A**
Percentage of African-American graduates: **100%**
Percentage receiving financial aid: **77%**
Average amount of award: **$4500**
Percentage in ROTC programs: **N/R**
Number of faculty: **178**
Number of African-American faculty: **N/R**
Student/faculty ratio: **17 to 1**

Tuition: **$5,800**
Scholarship programs: **N/A**
Academic programs: **Divisions of Social Sciences, Humanities, Mathematics and Natural Sciences, Education**
Most popular majors: **Biology, Engineering, Political Science, Management, Banking and Finance**
Prominent African-American faculty: **Dr. Robert Brisbane, Professor, political science; Dr. Anna Grant, Professor, sociology; Dr. A. Hornsby, Professor, history; Dr. Tobe Johnson, Professor, political science; Dr. Fred Mapp, Professor, biology; Dr. Willis Sheftall, Professor, economics and business**
Prominent African-American graduates: **Maynard Jackson, Mayor, Atlanta; Dr. Leroy Keith, President, Morehouse College; Rev. Dr. Martin Luther King, Jr., Nobel laureate; Spike Lee, filmmaker; Dr. Walter Massey, Executive Director, National Science Foundation; Edwin Moses, Olympic gold medalist**
African-American student organizations: **Morehouse College Glee Club, Marching Band, Maroon Tiger Newspaper, King Players, Pre-Alumni Club, International Students Association, STRIPES.**
Administrative services and programs: **Counseling Center, Summer Pre-Freshmen Science Program, National Alumni Association.**

Morehouse College produces leaders. This predominantly African-American, all-male college has produced some of the nation's heroes, chief among them Dr. Martin Luther King, Jr., Olympic gold medalist Edwin Moses, Atlanta's first African-American mayor, Maynard Jackson, and independent filmmaker Spike Lee. Morehouse takes pride in its academic excellence and its ability to develop the total student. One of only four colleges in Georgia honored with a Phi Beta Kappa chapter, Morehouse holds its own against any institution of higher education. "When I entered Morehouse, I didn't know Plato from Hemingway," said one student. "By my junior year, I was caught up in literature, world and African history and philosophy. If the liberal arts have taught me one thing, it's where to look for the answers. I know the rest is up to me."

One outstanding feature of Morehouse is its faculty, whose members are highly respected in their fields and come from the nation's top universities. No matter their background, all are committed to teaching and developing students' potential. Faculty and administrators are supportive and caring; it's not unusual for students and faculty to interact socially. Students believe that because a number of the professors are Morehouse alumni, they are especially sensitive to students' needs.

Morehouse men consider themselves heirs to a legacy unmatched by any college or university. There is a feeling of camaraderie; many students say life on this campus is "like being in one big fraternity." "When I first came to Morehouse, I thought all of the talk about 'brothers' was just that—talk," said a journalism student from New York. "But the men at Morehouse care about each other. When they ask, 'How are you doing?' they don't want to hear just 'fine,' they want to talk about your problems. I know that many of the friendships I've made here will last a lifetime."

Students concerned about life at an all-male college need not worry. Morehouse is part of the Atlanta University Center, which also consists of Clark Atlanta University, the Interdenominational Theological Center, Morehouse School of Medicine, Morris Brown College and Spelman College—where the women are. There's much socializing among the single-sex colleges, and there are always parties, sports events, Greek shows, and plenty of other activities in which to get involved. "I've got to tell you, Atlanta's what brought me to Morehouse, but Morehouse is what kept me here," one student said. "It's the whole package, actually. There's Spelman, of course, and all the other students we run across in the library and on campus. It's a family, really."

Morehouse is fairly selective—only 30 percent of applicants are accepted each year and SAT scores average 1000. Academics are not the only criterion for acceptance. The administration looks for students with ethics and principles who are concerned about making a contribution to society. The academic program is rigorous, and students feel they are getting a sound education. "I am comfortable with the academic programs offered at Morehouse," said a finance major. "In speaking with some of my counterparts who attend Ivy League schools, we all agree that Morehouse has one of the top curriculums in the country."

At the core of the academic program is a general studies concentration designed to introduce students to the liberal arts and develop their ability to think critically, reason and interpret knowledge as well as express their ideas through effective speaking and writing. Students may choose a major field of study from four divisions: the social sciences, humanities, mathematics and the natural sciences, and education. There is also an interdisciplinary major and dual degree program in engineering with Georgia Institute of Technology, and a similar program in architecture with the University of Michigan.

All students who are considering Morehouse are encouraged to visit the campus and take advantage of its formal open house, called the Prospective Student Seminar, which offers an extended visit each spring. Chances are if Morehouse appeals to you before you visit, you will be completely sold once you see the campus and interact with students and staff. "Being an African-American student on the campus of Morehouse is wonderful," said one student. "This institution is the best place for African-American males to cultivate their intellect inside and outside the classroom. If I had to choose a college again I would make the same choice because Morehouse has taught me how to be a man."

Spelman College
350 Spelman Lane, S.W.
Atlanta, Georgia 30314
1-800-241-3421

Type: **Private women's, predominantly African-American**
Overall campus environment: **Traditional, Strong Sisterhood**
Total enrollment: **1,900**
African-American students: **1800**
Graduate students: **zero**
Percentage of applications accepted: **30–40%**
Average SAT/ACT Score: **960/22**
Special admissions programs: **N/A**
Percentage of African-American graduates: **70–80%**
Percentage receiving financial aid: **86%**
Average amount of award: **$4,578**
Percentage in ROTC programs: **N/R**
Number of faculty: **167**

Number of African-American faculty: **130**
Student/faculty ratio: **16 to 1**
Tuition: **$6,150**
Scholarship programs: **Various Need-Based Scholarships Available.**
Academic programs: **Art, Biology, Chemistry, Biochemistry, Child Development, Computer and Information Science, Economics, English, Dual Degree in Engineering, French, History, Math, Music, Natural Sciences, Philosophy, Physics, Political Science, Psychology, Religion, Sociology, Spanish, Theater, Drama**
Most popular majors: **Psychology, English, Biology (pre-Med), Economics, Chemistry, Math/Computer Science**
Prominent African-American faculty: **N/R**
Prominent African-American graduates: **Selena Sloan Butler, Black PTA founder; Hershelle Challenor, Director, United Nations Educational, Scientific and Cultural Organization (UNESCO); Marian Wright Edelman, Founder/Director, Children's Defense Fund; Dr. Effie O'Neal Ellis, pediatrician and first Black to hold executive office in the American Medical Association; Varnette Honeywood, artist (works have appeared on** *The Bill Cosby Show* **and** *A Different World***); Clara Stanton Jones, first Black and female to direct a public library system in a major U.S. city; Dr. Deborah Prothrow-Stith, Assistant Dean for Government and Community Programs, Harvard School of Medicine; Elynor Williams, Vice President, Sara Lee Corporation**
African-American student organizations/activities: **All, including Student Government Association, student publications, musical organizations, Freshman Week, Living/Learning Program**
Administrative services and programs: **Student Affairs Office, Student Financial Services, Alumnae Recruitment Network, Pre-Freshman Summer Science Program, Summer Science and Engineering Program**

Spelman College has enjoyed a distinguished past and is now setting a course for an exciting future. Under its dynamic new president, Dr. Johnnetta Cole, whose leadership will undoubtedly take Spelman successfully into the twenty-first century, Spelman should remain one of this nation's outstanding institutions of higher education. Founded by and named for Mrs. Harvey Spelman, mother-in-law of John D. Rockefeller, in 1881, Spelman was the first college established to educate African-American women. It began as a training center for African-American female teachers, nurses and women who wished to enter the limited other professions open to them. Over the years Spelman expanded its programs. Today the college stands as a symbol of sisterhood and achievement. A great many of the nation's African-American female educators; community, religious and political leaders; artisans; doctors; lawyers, and businesspeople have graduated from Spelman, and the college continues to attract some of the brightest and best students.

In recent years, Spelman has attracted more than just students. In 1987, entertainer Bill Cosby and his wife, Camille, donated a record $20 million to Spelman, pushing its endowment up to more than $50 million, a record for a predominantly African-American college. The administration has already slated a portion of the funds for a new humanities building and other projects to increase the institution's value and prestige. And, in May of 1992, Readers Digest/De Witt Wallace topped that gift with a donation of $37 million to the college.

A large majority of Spelman students come from out of state; many are the children of Spelman or Morehouse graduates. Morehouse is known fondly as Spelman's brother college. Both schools, along with Clark Atlanta University, Morris Brown College, and the Interdenominational Theological Center, are members of the Atlanta University Center, sharing a campus and enjoying a cooperative relationship which allows students to take classes and use facilities at member colleges. Traditionally, women came to Spelman in search of two things: a college education and a husband. Although many women today put education, career and independence first, many still hope to find future husbands.

To help women take advantage of new opportunities and changing priorities, Spelman offers educational programs that keep pace with new career demands. Spelman's women not only get an education, they are pushed, prodded and cajoled into preprofessional study in medicine, law and the sciences, as well as into management, administration and engineering. Spelman has established an engineering program in conjunction with Georgia Institute of Technology, one of the finest engineering schools in the country.

Students accepted into Spelman are more often than not at the top of their high school graduating class and are courted by some of the most prestigious predominantly white schools (particularly the Seven Sister schools). But prospective Spelmanites are loyal and rarely succumb to pressure to attend these schools. Moreover, they come here, they say, because they want an opportunity to learn and work in an environment devoid of racial overtones and sensitive to their background and perceptions. "At another school I may be just another student," said one Spelmanite. "Here I am part of a legacy of women like myself who through nurturing, support and guidance at Spelman have achieved beyond their wildest dreams."

Getting through Spelman is no stroll in the park. The academic program is both demanding and exciting, and the faculty are achievers in their own right. Nearly 80 percent hold doctoral degrees, and a fair number are African-American women. Though plenty of support is offered, students have to work diligently and are expected to succeed.

Besides great academics and a supportive environment, students who attend Spelman will find a social and cultural life which centers around their interests and needs. There is a great deal of interaction with other Atlanta University Center schools (especially Morehouse), and students say there's always a party or another fun event. Recently Spelman allowed sororities on campus; however, only a small number of students have joined.

Spelman offers African-American women a special kind of college experience. If you're lucky enough to get in, you'll need to be prepared to work hard. Being part of a legacy, after all, has its price.

Illinois State University
Normal, Illinois 61761
309-438-2510/800-366-2478

Type: **Public**
Overall campus environment: **Cordial**
Total enrollment: **21,768**

African-American students: **1,359**
Graduate students: **2,670**
African-American graduate students: **112**
Percentage of applications accepted: **75%**
Average ACT/SAT score: **21.0**
Average ACT/SAT score African-Americans: **N/A**
Special admissions programs: **N/A**
Percentage of African-American graduates: **28%**
Percentage receiving financial aid: **N/A**
Average amount of award: **$2,444**
Percentage in ROTC programs: **1%**
Number of faculty: **1,003**
Number of African-American faculty: **32**
Student/faculty ratio: **22 to 1**
Tuition: **$1,980–$2,244**
Scholarship programs: **N/R**
Academic programs: **More than 50 majors, master's and doctoral programs; Undergraduate Teaching Assistants, High Potential Students program, Minority Professionals Opportunities program; Student Support Program for Disadvantaged Students; International Studies program; Study Abroad**
Most popular majors: **Pre-Business, Elementary Education, Special Education, Psychology**
Prominent African-American graduates: **Russell DeBow, circuit court judge in Chicago; Suzzanne Douglas, actress, *Tap*; Donald McHenry, former U.S. Ambassador to the U.N.; Rosetta Wheadon, community college president**
Prominent African-American faculty: **N/A**
African-American student organizations/activities: Black Student Union, NAACP, Black Greek fraternities and sororities
Administrative services and programs: **Cultural Retreat, MECCPAC, Minority Retention Committee, Minority Recruitment Committee, Minority Student Phon-a-thon, Minority Government Day, Black Action and Awareness Committee, REACH, Student Support Services program, Multicultural Center**

You may want to consider Illinois State University if you live in Illinois and do not want to go to school out of state. This public university, with more than 20,000 students, has a fine reputation and offers training from bachelor's to doctoral degrees. ISU has one of the highest percentages of African-American graduates in the state. Although students may be overwhelmed at times by the large campus, class sizes and the fact that only 6 percent of the student body is African-American, there is a tendency for students to work toward their common interests and goals. More than 30 programs, organizations, and special initiatives exist at ISU specifically for minorities. They range from peer counseling groups to support groups for student and faculty, and programs that promote academic and cultural excellence. The university also devotes a great deal of time and effort to recruiting African-American students and helping them succeed. Besides its continuing efforts through local high schools, community groups and its office in Chicago, ISU recently launched an ISU Associates program designed to increase enrollment by 10 percent over a two-year period. The Associates program is a joint effort of three states and African-American community leaders, educators, professionals and parents, who work to enhance minority student awareness of the academic preparation required for admission to and graduation from ISU. The administration credits the program with attracting more than one-third of the new minority students who entered ISU in the fall of 1991 and 1992. Once these students are enrolled, ISU supports them through a variety of academic and other programs. It also helps graduates find employment and get into graduate school through its Minority Job Fair and Minority Professional Opportunities (MPO) program, which acquaint students with graduate and professional schools and professions in which minorities are traditionally underrepresented.

ISU stands in the rural community of Bloomington/Normal, a town of about 100,000. Most students live on campus; because a fair number of the social and cultural programs take place through the residence halls, it is recommended that students live on campus, and freshmen and sophomores are required to do so. Off-campus, African-American students have formed bonds with the community churches and community organizations including the NAACP. In addition, ISU students and staff interact with human relations committees of Bloomington/Normal and have jointly developed a Black History Project which serves both residents and students.

ISU has much to offer African-American students both academically and socially. But the mere existence of numerous cultural and social organizations and multicultural committees is often not enough to help students feel a part of the university. According to one student, the answer to this dilemma may lie within the student. "I believe, whether you are Black or white, a resident student or not, the only way to make a difference is to get involved in voicing your suggestions and concerns to the committees and various boards on campus." This student went on to say that while racism does exist on campus, it is no worse than what exists in society and does not diminish the breadth of opportunity available to African-American students. "What I like about this university is that it gives all ethnic groups—African-Americans, Native Americans, Hispanics, Asian-Americans, and whites—a sense of reality about the world and that it is composed of many races and cultures with different values, ideals and morals." Although students complain that there are not enough African-American faculty or Afrocentric courses (in fact, the university offers a minor in ethnic and cultural studies and a major in ethnic origins/minority populations/ethnicity/Women's Studies), they are generally pleased with life on the ISU campus.

Illinois Wesleyan University
Bloomington, Illinois
309-556-3031

Type: **Private liberal arts, affiliated with United Methodist Church**
Environment: **Academically Challenging, Cordial, Supportive**
Total enrollment: **1,750**
African-American students: **48**
Percentage of applicants accepted: **46%**
Average SAT/ACT score: **1170/27**
Average SAT/ACT African-Americans: **1050/24**
Special admissions programs: **N/A**
Percentage of African-American graduates: **70%**
Percentage receiving financial aid: **85%**
Average amount of award: **varies**
Percentage in ROTC programs: **N/R**

Number of faculty: **140**

Number of African-American faculty: **4**

Student/faculty ratio: **13 to 1**

Tuition: **$12,120**

Scholarship programs: **National Achievement Scholarships, scholarships for each major field**

Academic programs: **College of Liberal Arts; Schools of Drama, Art, Music, Nursing**

Most popular majors: **Biology, Business, Music, Political Science, Psychology, Nursing, Accounting, Physics, Drama, Mathematics, English**

Prominent African-American Faculty: **Dr. Jan Rynveld Carew, Visiting Adjunct Professor, African-American Studies.**

Prominent African-American graduates: **Barrington Coleman, Assistant Professor, Wesleyan School of Music, and tenor soloist; Frankie Faison, actor** (*Coming to America, Manhunter, Mississippi Burning, The Money Pit*)**; Michelle Jones, engineer; Beverly Mayes-Hawkins, teacher and recipient of the 1991–92 Golden Apple Award for teaching excellence; Winnona Whitfield, Fulbright Professor in Ghana and Law Professor, Southern Illinois University**

African-American student organizations/activities: **Black Student Union, Minority Advisory Committee, Multicultural Events Committee, Black Greek fraternities and sororities**

Administrative services and programs: **Office of Minority Services, Multicultural Job Fair, Summer Enrichment Program**

Illinois Wesleyan University is a small private liberal arts institution with an excellent reputation. IWU has been cited by numerous college guidebooks as one of the best universities in the country. Located in the fast-growing community of Bloomington, Illinois, IWU is a tightly knit community where students receive a great deal of academic support from faculty and administrators. The ratio of students to faculty here is 13 to 1, and the majority of professors hold doctoral degrees. Liberal arts is strong here, many students go on to graduate and professional schools, many at Stanford, Harvard, Vanderbilt, Yale, Northwestern, Dartmouth and Princeton.

Students who attend IWU have average SAT scores of 1050 or

ACT scores of 25 or higher and rank in the upper 25 percent of their high school graduating class. Standards are not lowered for African-Americans though other attributes are considered. For example, the administration strongly considers intangible qualities such as motivation, leadership ability and determination to succeed. Generally speaking, IWU looks for students who will benefit from the resources and opportunities the university has to offer. It's no wonder, then, that IWU graduates 82 percent of those entering as freshmen within four years. The strong liberal arts program and opportunities for independent study, internships, and travel abroad help to shape a well-rounded person who is prepared for the working world or for graduate school. Within six months after graduation, more than 90 percent of students have either gained admittance into a graduate or professional school or landed a job related to their major field of interest.

While African-Americans currently represent a small proportion (about 3 percent) of the student body, the administration has made efforts not only to increase their numbers but to help current students achieve success. Incoming freshmen may benefit from the university's Summer Enrichment Program, which provides academic advising, tutoring and other services. The Black Student Union sponsors social and cultural events and provides general support. In addition, the administration makes use of a strong network of graduates who assist in recruitment and serve as role models for African-American students at IWU. These alumni represent successful professionals in medicine, law, education, business and industry. Their success, they say, proves that IWU is a good choice for African-Americans. "When I received acceptance into the University of Illinois College of Medicine, I realized that Wesleyan had been the best choice for me: I was prepared academically, intellectually and socially for the many roles that are necessary for a physician," said Janine James Cromwell, M.D., 1975 graduate and now assistant professor of Maternal-Fetal Medicine at the University of Wisconsin. Dr. Cromwell is also a trustee of IWU.

Encouraging students to become active on campus and in the community is a priority for the administration, and there's plenty of opportunity for students to get involved. They can serve on the Multi-Cultural Events Committee or the Minority Advisory Committee, or get involved with the university radio station, residential programs, or drama, music and theater groups. According to the current president of the Black Student Union, that organization and the Department of Minority Services are responsible for most of the social and cultural activities for African-Americans, but some students get involved in the mainstream. "The Greek system here seems to monopolize the party scene," the president said. "A few African-Americans belong to these predominantly white organizations; and while their events are open, you may feel like an outsider." Besides the Greek scene, events like the annual Dr. Martin Luther King, Jr., celebration and the Gospel Festival draw a good crowd, and even members of the community get involved.

Overall, students seem pleased with IWU's programs, faculty, staff and student body. "I like the university's small size, the attention professors give you, and the academic reputation," said one student. "I have matured academically, personally and socially and have learned many valuable lessons here."

If you're looking for a challenging and enriching college experience, consider IWU. Just be sure that you have good grades and a positive attitude and envision yourself as a leader.

University of Illinois at Urbana-Champaign
10 Henry Administration Building
506 South Wright Street
Urbana, IL 61801
217-333-0302

Type: **Public**
Overall campus environment: **Academically Challenging, Cordial**
Total enrollment: **36,139**
African-American students: **2,114**
Graduate students: **9,773**
African-American graduate students: **274**
Percentage of applications accepted: **77.5%**
Average ACT score: **27.6**
Average ACT African-Americans: **23.2**
Special admissions programs: **N/A**
Percentage of African-American graduates: **58.7 (based on 4 years)**

Percentage receiving financial aid: **83%**
Average amount of award: **$1,812**
Percentage in ROTC programs: **22% (Army, Air Force, Navy)**
Number of faculty: **3,070**
Number of African-American faculty: **55**
Student/faculty ratio: **8 to 1**
Tuition: **$6,808**
Scholarship programs: **President's Award Program (PAP), National Achievement Scholarship Program for Outstanding Negro Students (NASP)**
Academic programs: **Colleges of Agriculture, Applied Life Studies, Commerce and Business Administration, Fine and Applied Arts, Education, Engineering, Liberal Arts and Sciences; Institute of Aviation; School of Social Work**
Most popular majors: **Liberal Arts and Sciences, Engineering, Commerce and Business Administration, Architecture**
Prominent African-American faculty: **N/A**
Prominent African-American graduates: **David Blackwell, Professor, Department of Statistics, University of California—Berkeley; Jacqueline V. Gates, Manager, Human Resources, Time, Inc.; Grover G. Hankins, Principal Deputy General Counsel, U.S. Department of Health and Human Services; Robert L. Johnson, founder and owner, Black Entertainment Television (BET) Network; Roger L. Plummer, President and CEO, Ameritech Information Systems; Cordell Reed, Vice President, Commonwealth Edison; Joyce E. Tucker, Commissioner, U.S. Equal Employment Opportunity Commission; Eddie N. Williams, Executive Director, Joint Center for Political and Economic Studies**
African-American student organizations/Activities: **Black Student Union, African-American Cultural Center, University Black Chorus, Omnivov Dance Troupe, Black Greek fraternities and sororities, National Society of Black Engineers, more than 700 other organizations**
Administrative services and programs: **Office of Minority Student Affairs, Afro-American Cultural Program, Multicultural Career Conference, Multicultural Student Advisory Committee, Graduate College's Summer Research Opportunities, Career Services' Minority Employment Conference**

Robert L. Johnson, founder and owner of Black Entertainment Television (BET), Roger L. Plummer, president and CEO of Ameritech Information Systems, and Joyce E. Tucker, Commissioner, U.S. Equal Employment Opportunity Commission, all have something in common. They're all highly successful and are all graduates of the University of Illinois at Urbana-Champaign (or Illini, as it is often called). These successful African-American graduates are just a few of the long list of college professors, government and business leaders, and prominent members of various professional fields who attended Illini, one of the nation's largest and finest institutions of higher education.

A major research institution with more than 36,000 students, Illini sits between Chicago and Indianapolis on a campus that is the size of a small town. Ilini's prestigious faculty are widely published and research-oriented; in fact, the faculty represent one of the reasons students choose to come here. However, students will find that they must make trade-offs to succeed at a school of this size. The student-to-faculty ratio at Illini is about 8 to 1, and more than 80 percent of classes have fewer than thirty students. Students may find it difficult to develop the cozy kind of relationship with professors that they could have at a small liberal arts school. Still, students say they find professors accessible, even though they're often more interested in knowing a student's social security number than his or her name. One student said, "The classes are broken down. You might have a big lecture, but your discussion sessions are small. The professors are approachable, and the reputation the university carries is impressive."

For those with initiative and drive, opportunities abound at Illini. There are 150 major programs of study at eight colleges, a School of Social Work and the Institute of Aviation, which offers a certificate program for those interested in becoming pilots. Illini has top-ranked graduate and professional schools as well, and boasts that it is the only campus in the country with two supercomputer systems. The famous Plato, a highly sophisticated computer-based educational system, is connected to the university's twenty-three residence halls and is accessible to students. The system is also used for research and development by campus faculty and students.

Additional facilities include a major performing arts center, a newly constructed student union, two major sports facilities and an FAA-approved airport (about six miles off campus) used for aviation instruction and research. Students can avail themselves of numerous activities, cultural events, workshops, seminars and speaker series. "I was on my way to the Undergrad Library to study," one student said, "when I ran into some friends who said, 'Come with us, we're going to see Maki Mandela, daughter of ANC leader Nelson Mandela—she's speaking at the Auditorium.' So I decided that hearing this speaker was more important than studying right then, and it was one of the most interesting experiences I've ever had on campus."

In recent years, the university's African-American enrollment has increased substantially, thanks in large part to targeted recruitment efforts. In addition, the administration has become more culturally diverse and supportive of the needs of African-American and other minority students. Nearly 20% of the faculty are African-American although only 4 are deans and administrators. African-American enrollment at Illini is about 7 percent. Most students come from Illinois, many from Chicago and outlying areas. "As a minority student, I have seen a lot of changes on this campus," said a biology/prelaw student. "A lot of programs have emerged from the African-American Cultural Program—I wouldn't be as involved in things if it wasn't for their support."

The university has several scholarship programs for African-American students, as well as myriad academic and counseling services to help students make the transition to campus life at Illini. In addition, there are support systems at each college, including a dean who acts as liaison with the Office of Minority Student Affairs. Special programs such as the Graduate College's Summer Research Opportunities and the Career Services' Minority Employment Conference help African-American students move on to postgraduate work or the job market.

Students who attend Illini get a first-class education and have access to programs, facilities and opportunities unmatched at most schools. However, this is not the place for a student who needs a great deal of direction and nurturing to succeed. An independent go-getter will find Illini both challenging and gratifying; an introvert may feel like a fish out of water. An engineering student put it this way: "The university is definitely challenging. It has helped make me more confident in knowing that I can suc-

ceed in a competitive world. I have a higher cumulative GPA at
Illinois than I had in high school . . . that says a lot!"

Butler University
4600 Sunset Avenue
Indianapolis, Indiana 46208
317-283-9255/1-800-927-2882

Type: **Private liberal arts**
Overall campus environment: **Cordial**
Total enrollment: **4,000**
African-American students: **340**
Graduate students: **1,500**
African-American graduate students: **250**
Percentage of applications accepted: **89%**
Average SAT/ACT score: **1050/25**
Average SAT/ACT African-Americans: **900/20**
Special admissions programs: **N/A**
Percentage of African-American graduates: **60%**
Percentage receiving financial aid: **Nearly all students receive
aid**
Average amount of award: **Up to 100%**
Percentage in ROTC programs: **N/R**
Number of faculty: **213**
Number of African-American faculty: **5%**
Student/faculty ratio: **12 to 1**
Tuition: **$11,300**
Scholarship programs: **University and merit scholarships for
African-Americans**
Academic programs: **Colleges of Pharmacy, Education, Liberal
Arts and Sciences, Business and Fine Arts**
Prominent African-American graduates: **N/R**
Prominent African-American faculty: **N/R**
African-American student organizations/activities: **Black
Student Union, Minority Athletes Academic Achievement
Program, Career Challenges Workshop, Big Bro'/Big Sis'
Program, Multicultural Performing Arts and Film Series and
Reflections, African-American Visiting Scholars Program**

Administrative services and programs: **Office of Minority Student Affairs, Minority Alumni Council, Butler Mentoring Program**

Like many colleges and universities today, Butler University is moving toward greater cultural diversity in its student body. This four-year liberal arts university boasts student representation from all fifty states and more than a dozen countries. It not only offers a good academic program but has a strong reputation as a leader in athletics, cultural arts, medicine, research, science and technology, not to mention its world-class sports facilities, ranked second only to UCLA. But African-American students seem to be most impressed by the school's small size, cooperative and supportive faculty and administration, and support of financial aid to minority students. Some students receive aid that covers 100 percent of college costs, depending on demonstrated need—a generous package by any standards.

Students seeking a solid liberal arts education will find more than sixty majors from which to choose in education, liberal arts and sciences, fine arts, pre-Medicine, business, pharmacy and communications. The majority of the faculty hold doctoral degrees, and many have international reputations in their fields and invite students to work with them on research. Students can complete part of their education overseas at Butler's Institute for Study Abroad, which places students at more than thirty universities and institutions in Africa, Asia, Europe, Australia and the former Soviet Union. "I wanted to go to the Ivory Coast because I am African-American, and I wanted to see where we came from," said one student. "I learned more in two weeks there than I would have in a semester here."

Butler has a great deal to offer African-American students academically and socially, and the administration appears to be committed to improving the representation of African-Americans among administrators (seven) and faculty (about 5 percent). Its establishment of an Office of Minority Student Affairs is a positive step, as is its support of African-American cultural and social organizations and events. The Office of Minority Student Affairs, whose director is an African-American woman, coordinates, among other things, the Black Student Union, Minority Athletes Academic Achievement Program, Career Challenges Workshop,

Big Bro'/Big Sis' Program, and Multicultural Performing Arts and Film Series and Reflections, a look at the African-American experience in the U.S. The office also supports the African-American Visiting Scholars program, African-American fraternities and sororities, and the Visiting Writers Series, which has included major writers from various ethnic backgrounds. The university has also involved its African-American alumni in mentoring students on career planning and job placement.

Generally, students find faculty helpful but often feel unduly challenged. "As an African-American student I sometimes feel professors expect things out of you that they do not expect from other students," said one Butlerite. "For example, as a member of a jazz singing group I was expected on the first day of school to be familiar with certain forms of jazz music that most of the white students did not understand. However, I was able to turn this into a positive situation for me and take a leadership role in the group."

If you're looking for a small liberal arts institution that is academically competitive, yet personal enough that you can get to know the faculty, and at which you can feel culturally and socially accepted, you might want to look into Butler University.

Earlham College
Box 192
Richmond, Indiana 47374
1-800-327-5426

Type: **Private liberal arts, affiliated with Friends Meeting (Quaker)**
Overall campus environment: **Conservative, Culturally Supportive**
Total enrollment: **1,200**
African-American students: **70**
Graduate students: **N/A**
African-American graduate students: **N/A**
Percentage of applications accepted: **75%**
Average SAT/ACT score: **690–1570/19–34**
Average SAT/ACT African-Americans: **980/22**
Special admissions programs: **N/A**

Percentage of African-American graduates: **69%**
Percentage receiving financial aid: **80%**
Average amount of award: **$12,000**
Percentage in ROTC programs: **N/R**
Number of faculty: **102**
Number of African-American faculty: **3**
Student/faculty ratio: **11 to 1**
Tuition: **$18,297**
Scholarship programs: **Cunningham Cultural Scholarship, Indiana Enhancement Award**
Academic programs: **Arts and Sciences, Business, Social Sciences**
Most popular majors: **Biology, Literature, Politics, Human Development and Social Relations, International Studies**
Prominent African-American Graduates: **Francine Wright, IBM staff engineer**
Prominent African-American faculty: **Phyllis Bolanes, Director, African and African American Studies Department; Steve Butler, Professor, Sociology and Anthropology**
African-American student organizations/activities: **Umoja, Reggae Sunsplash, Black Leadership Action Coalition, Cunningham Cultural Center, Gospel Choir, Revelations**
Administrative services and programs: **Minority Affairs Office, Earlham Volunteer Exchange**

Warm, caring attitudes abound at Earlham College, and you get the feeling that people genuinely care about you—how you're settling in to campus life, whether you got enrolled in the class you want, and how you're treated by faculty and staff. Earlham College, a small liberal arts college in Indiana, was founded by Friends (Quakers) and attempts to provide a truly liberal education and environment for all of its students. At Earlham, students have a voice in the education they receive and the way they're treated. At the same time, they are expected to behave responsibly and not abuse these freedoms. Although only about 10 percent of the college's population are Quakers, Earlham's strong values and beliefs permeate the academic and social environment of the school. Quaker beliefs as well as Indiana liquor laws, for example, prohibit alcohol on campus. While not strongly enforced, this restriction has had an impact on the tone of parties at Earlham, and social life is generally comparatively low-key. However, there is plenty happening, and the administration and student groups work together to bring events to campus like the annual Reggae Sunsplash. Other amenities include a student run coffeehouse that showcases student performers, film forums and an annual May Day celebration. Some students may find these activities enjoyable; others may think them devoid of an African-American point of view.

Despite any social shortcomings, Earlham offers an excellent liberal arts program which, in keeping with the Quaker philosophy of service, is heavily slanted toward "people issues." International studies and human development and social relations are among the most popular majors, and the faculty emphasizes teaching rather than publishing. Classes average about twenty-two students, and the discussion-oriented format reflects a school whose interest is primarily students' needs. Overall student/faculty interaction is very good, and it's not unusual for discussions to move from the classroom into other areas of the campus or a faculty member's home. By graduation many students and faculty have formed close bonds that endure.

Earlham has a great deal to offer beyond the classroom. Perhaps the most important lesson the school imparts to its students is that of tolerance and understanding among all cultural and racial groups. "The Quaker affiliation creates a sense of community that very few schools can match," said one student. "I know that as an African-American student I am just as important to the college as anyone." For the student interested in study abroad, Earlham offers the country's most highly rated cooperative study program with Japan. More than 80 percent of students take advantage of study opportunities in Kenya, Israel and Mexico.

Although African-Americans represent only about 6 percent of Earlham's students, their numbers are growing. This increase is due in part to the administration's increased recruitment efforts, which through African-American churches, community organizations, publications and high schools encourage young people to apply. The result has been a proliferation of African-American organizations and services, including the Cunningham Cultural Center, which provides student housing and activities. (There are also a Japanese and a Spanish house.) These organizations plan activities for Black History Month and other events throughout the year. One of the activities of the center is Earlham Volunteer Exchange, a student volunteer program which provides tutoring to high school students and teenage mothers in the Richmond community. Programs like these not only support the "service" philosophy of Earlham but provide the much-needed connection between African-American students and their community. This is particularly important to students who live on campus without a car, as the nearest urban areas, Dayton and Cincinnati, are between one and two hours away.

African-Americans who are interested in attending a school that cares about its students, what they learn and how they will serve the world may enjoy Earlham. "From your roommate to the president of the college, Earlham is a very people-oriented school," said one student. "I like the academic program which allows me to gear the workload to my own pace, and I feel that I am guaranteed to be able to go on to graduate school or the work world once I graduate."

Goshen College
Goshen, Indiana 46526-9922
219-535-7535/800-348-7422

Type: **Private liberal arts, owned by Mennonite Church**
Overall campus environment: **Cordial/spiritual**
Total enrollment: **1,039**
African-American students: **26**
Graduate students: **0**
African-American graduate students: **0**
Percentage of applications accepted: **90%**
Average SAT score: **995**
Average SAT African-Americans: **N/A**
Special admissions programs: **N/A**
Percentage of African-American graduates: **2%**
Percentage receiving financial aid: **90%**
Average amount of award: **$7,495**
Percentage in ROTC programs: **0**
Number of faculty: **85**
Number of African-American faculty: **1**
Student/faculty ratio: **14 to 1**

Tuition: **$8,310**
Scholarship programs: **Minority Scholarships for African-Americans**
Academic programs: **Accounting; Business and Economics; Art; Bible, Religion and Philosophy; Biology; Chemistry; Communications; Computer and Information Science; Education; English; Foods and Nutrition; Foreign Language; Hispanic Ministries; History and Political Science; Intercultural Studies; Interdisciplinary Studies; Mathematics; Music; Natural Science; Nursing; Peace Studies; Physics and Pre-Engineering; Psychology; Sociology and Anthropology; Theater; Tropical Agriculture**
Most popular majors: **Business, Education, Nursing**
Prominent African-American graduates: **N/R**
Prominent African-American faculty: **N/R**
African-American student organizations/activities: **Black Student Union, International Student Club**
Administrative services and programs: **Multicultural Center (in progress)**

Goshen College is a four-year liberal arts college operated by the Mennonite Church in rural Indiana. Noted for its strong programs in liberal arts and international education, Goshen has attracted many students who might not otherwise have considered a church-affiliated school. Although students are not required to belong to the Mennonite Church, the college has strong religious principles, including mandatory attendance at certain religious services and a strong policy against use of alcohol, drugs and tobacco on campus. The college administration looks with disfavor on unmarried students who engage in sexual activity. Goshen's religious principles also prohibit racial intolerance, which college literature says is "inconsistent with the life and teachings of Christ and which will be addressed as a serious violation of campus standards."

To many students, Goshen College may seem very restrictive. Most students are affiliated with the Mennonite Church and have a lifestyle based on its principles. Religious teachings are interwoven into much of the coursework, and there is strong emphasis on Christian values. In addition, most students come from rural and middle America, and their exposure to African-Americans is

often limited to what they see in the media. Although the administration does not condone racial intolerance, students' lack of
contact with African-Americans can create difficulties, especially
since there are only a handful of African-American students on
the campus. The administration has made some effort to incorpo-
rate more African-American social and cultural activities into
campus life, and the noticeable presence of foreign students
helps; but many students are still not able to adjust, and they drop
out. However, for students who can make the adjustment, Goshen
offers a solid liberal arts education. "Being an African-American
student at Goshen College is both interesting and challenging,"
said one student. "When you are one of only a handful of African-
Americans you sometimes feel the pressure of representing yourself and the entire race. Learning to deal with these pressures has
not only enabled me to grow and mature as an individual, it has
made me socially and politically conscious."

Goshen has facilities that include state-of-the-art science, marine biology, computer graphics and video production laboratories. It offers internships and cooperative programs with other
universities in a variety of fields. It was one of the first colleges in
the country to implement an international education requirement. Today, more than 80 percent of students fulfill the requirement by taking advantage of the Study Service Term (SST)
program in such countries as Germany, Costa Rica, Guadeloupe
and China. Accompanied by well-traveled faculty, students spend
seven weeks studying the capital of a country and another six
weeks working and living in a small town or rural area, often with
a family.

Because Goshen has such high moral and religious standards
and so few secular distractions, those of strong religious backgrounds may be particularly attracted to this college. Foreign
students who are not familiar with the traditional trappings of
college life and are comfortable with missionary-type education
may also find it less difficult to adjust. However, any student
considering this college needs to be concerned with spiritual
growth—and primarily concerned with getting an education. One
African-American student put it this way: "I've found the faculty
and administration to be both friendly and helpful but the coursework demanding. I was attracted to Goshen because it was small,
had a low student-to-teacher ratio, and was known as one of the

best liberal arts colleges in the country. I like that the cultural awareness is emphasized nationally and worldwide and that there are many international students on campus. My education here and study abroad experience in China has helped me to grow academically and culturally and because of this, I'd choose Goshen again."

**Hanover College
Hanover, Indiana 47243
812-866-7021**

Type: **4-year liberal arts, affiliated with United Presbyterian Church**
Overall campus environment: **Cordial**
Total enrollment: **1,050**
African-American students: **75**
Percentage of applications accepted: **75%**
Average SAT/ACT score: **1050/24**
Average SAT/ACT African-Americans: **850/19**
Special admissions programs: **N/A**
Percentage of African-American graduates: **N/R**
Percentage receiving financial aid: **100%**
Average amount of award: **$6,000**
Percentage in ROTC programs: **0**
Number of faculty: **85**
Number of African-American faculty: **2**
Student/faculty ratio: **14 to 1**
Tuition: **$6,950**
Scholarship programs: **Hanover Pointe Scholarship, student offered admission**
Academic programs: **Liberal Arts**
Most popular majors: **Biology, Psychology, History, Business Administration, Chemistry, English, Communications**
Prominent African-American graduates: **N/R**
Prominent African-American faculty: **N/R**
African-American student organizations/activities: **Positive Image, Multi-Cultural Center**
Administrative services and programs: **N/R**

Hanover College is a small liberal arts college in the rural town of Hanover, which sits on the Kentucky state line, about an hour northeast of Louisville. Founded in the early 1800s and affiliated with the United Presbyterian Church, Hanover is the oldest college of its kind in Indiana. Beyond the traditional liberal arts training Hanover offers, the college distinguishes itself by requiring that graduates attain some proficiency in a number of disciplines including fine arts, a foreign language, Judeo-Christian thought, history and international studies, natural sciences, philosophy, physical education, social sciences, oral communication, and writing. A program that the college offers all its students is an opportunity to qualify for a Richter Grant, which supports innovative student projects anywhere in the world. Projects that the grant has funded at Hanover have ranged from riding the Trans-Siberian Railroad from Moscow to Irkutsk in order to study Russian culture, to building a computer-driven robot that is used in the study of robotics in the physics department, to studying what it means to be "White in a Black-Dominated Society in Zimbabwe."

Admission to Hanover is fairly competitive; the average student has a combined score of 1000 on the SAT or 24 on the ACT. Traditionally, students have come from privileged backgrounds, with more than 50 percent from Indiana. This is a very close-knit campus, partly because of its rural location and small size. Unless they live within commuting distance, students are required to live on campus, and the school has enough housing that a student can have a room for the entire four years.

Social life pretty much revolves around Greek organizations, which can place African-American students on the outside. There are only a handful of African-American students at Hanover, and many have found it difficult to adjust to an environment which almost totally leaves them out. The establishment of a support group called Positive Image has given African-American students an opportunity to socialize and discuss their concerns and problems. A recently completed Multi-Cultural Center, which plans a variety of ethnic events, also provides a sanctuary for students and a place to hang out. Some students have found the support of hardworking, caring administrators and faculty helpful. Many have been encouraged to get involved with the majority organizations and have found satisfaction in doing so. "At first I hated

Hanover College," recalled a female African-American student. "I felt out of place and because of it my grades suffered. The admissions staff and others helped me see that I belong at Hanover and that I could succeed here." Still, students find they must make their own fun. "Campus life can be boring, I must admit," the same student said. "You have to make it exciting. I found getting involved with the Student Programming Board challenging, and now I'm a chairman of a committee which brings all kinds of activities to the campus. There's also the school newspaper, student senate, and other organizations that are open to African-American student involvement."

Clearly, the administration wants to increase the number of African-American students on campus and understands that by doing so, it may make these students more comfortable and help keep them on campus through graduation. One of the incentives that the college offers African-American students is a Hanover Pointe Scholarship, which provides $3,000 to $6,000 toward tuition and expenses. This scholarship is given to every African-American student admitted to Hanover College. Besides its traditional recruitment practices, the college has begun bringing high school students to Hanover to experience campus life firsthand. It also works closely with local high school guidance counselors to encourage students to consider Hanover.

Students who believe they can handle being among a group of pioneers on a predominantly white campus that is both financially and emotionally supportive may want to consider Hanover. "Hanover has helped me grow immensely," said one student. "It has given me the opportunity to be a leader and I know I will be one of the first African-American women to graduate from the institution in a long time. I have become a better person because of my experience here and when I graduate, I will truly miss being here."

**Saint Mary's College
Notre Dame, Indiana 46556
219-284-4587**

Type: **Catholic women's liberal arts**
Overall campus environment: **Supportive**

Total enrollment: **1,675**
African-American students: **10**
Graduate students: **zero**
Percentage of applications accepted: **84%**
Average SAT score: **1020**
Average SAT African-Americans: **1020**
Special admissions programs: **N/A**
Percentage of African-American graduates: **75%**
Percentage receiving financial aid: **60%**
Average amount of award: **$12,950**
Percentage in ROTC programs: **zero**
Number of faculty: **122**
Number of African-American faculty: **1**
Student/faculty ratio: **11 to 1**
Tuition: **$11,080**
Scholarship programs: **Academic scholarships**
Academic programs: **Liberal Arts, Sciences, Business Administration, Music, Fine Arts**
Most popular majors: **Business, English, Humanistic Studies, Art**
Prominent African-American faculty: **N/R**
Prominent African-American graduates: **N/R**
African-American student organizations/activities: **Sisters of Nefertiti**
Administrative services and programs: **Minority, International, and Non-Traditional Office (MINT)**

Saint Mary's College, a Catholic women's college a short walk from the University of Notre Dame, provides its students with a unique educational opportunity that combines the best of each institution. At Saint Mary's a young woman can obtain an excellent liberal education in the supportive environment of an all-woman college, and at the same time enjoy the benefits of taking classes and socializing with men from Notre Dame. A prestigious college in its own right, Saint Mary's boasts an excellent faculty and strong academic programs in the sciences, English, psychology, and the arts.

Founded in the 1800s by four Catholic nuns, Saint Mary's is a relatively small college with a student body of about 1,700, but because of its coeducational relationship with Notre Dame and its solid academic offerings, many students think that the campus is more like that of a university.

What students most often cite about Saint Mary's is the support and nurturing they receive from faculty, staff, and fellow students. Most report that this environment helped them grow and succeed; almost every student has a story to tell about a faculty member who personally encouraged them to reach new heights of achievement. "The faculty never lose sight of our individual needs," said one student, "and have genuine interest in our overall success."

Saint Mary's religious affiliation (almost all students are Catholic) and the fact that it is a woman's college create a sensitivity and a feeling of mutual respect that are not present on many campuses. One of the few African-American students here points to an openness and acceptance on both sides. "I like Saint Mary's because it has allowed me to grow as a young woman with my own independent ideas," this student said. "I am not white. I am not Catholic. I am Black and I am Baptist. I have learned from Saint Mary's, but Saint Mary's has also learned from me."

African-American students say that the fact that it is a women's college gives them something in common with white students. "I feel like part of the Saint Mary's community because I do not allow myself to be 'shut out,' and I get involved in a variety of campus activities," one student said. "However, there are times when African-American students want to be together because we have a natural affinity for one another." While the administration encourages all students to get involved in campus life, it supports African-American student groups such as the Sisters of Nefertiti, which promotes film festivals, social gatherings, and volunteer activities like community toy drives.

"Saint Mary's is an excellent choice for women to learn from and support one another," said another African-American student. "The decision of which college to attend is a personal one and I chose Saint Mary's. I must say that despite naysayers who questioned the wisdom of my decision, attending a predominantly white women's college strengthened me in ways I never anticipated."

If you're looking for an opportunity to obtain an excellent education at a women's school (but with some advantages of coeducation), in an environment that is supportive and nurturing, and you are open to being one of a handful of African-American students on campus, Saint Mary's offers great value.

Cornell College
600 First Street West
Mount Vernon, Iowa 52314
319-895-4215/1-800-747-1112

Type: **4-year liberal arts, affiliated with Methodist Church**
Overall campus environment: **Academically Demanding, Small, Culturally Supportive**
Total enrollment: **1,150**
African-American students: **23**
Graduate students: **N/A**
African-American graduate students: **N/A**
Percentage of applications accepted: **85%**
Average SAT score: **1090**
Average SAT African-Americans: **N/R**
Special admissions programs: **N/A**
Percentage of African-American graduates: **75% (within five years)**
Percentage receiving financial aid: **79%**
Average amount of award: **$11,000**
Percentage in ROTC programs: **N/A**
Number of faculty: **75**
Number of African-American faculty: **0**
Student/faculty ratio: **13 to 1**
Tuition: **$13,129**
Scholarship programs: **Need-based grants, scholarships**
Academic programs: **Liberal Arts, Arts and Sciences; Business and Economics; preparatory programs**
Most popular majors: **Business and Economics**
Prominent African-American faculty: **N/A**
Prominent African-American Graduates: **Edgar Thornton III, Special Assistant to the Assistant Secretary for Land and Minerals Management, U.S. Department of Interior**
African-American student organizations/activities: **BACO**

(Black Awareness Culture Organization), Multi-Cultural Task Force
Administrative services and programs: **Multi-Cultural Affairs Office, Administrative/Student Mentoring Program**

Cornell College, with its historic buildings and traditional setting, could easily be mistaken for a New England school, and is probably the only college in the country whose entire campus is designated as a historic landmark. Cornell is in Mount Vernon, Iowa, a rural town of about 3,500. The college and community are very closely connected, with Cornell taking an increasingly important role in the town's adjustment to its growing multicultural population. Students have held "consciousness-raising" workshops on race relations in local grade schools and have sponsored mentoring programs for minorities in the community. After the verdict in the Rodney King beating case in the spring of 1992, students on campus organized a well-attended open forum for students, faculty, and staff to discuss the issues surrounding the case. The school is interested in other minority issues as well. Asian-American students, for example, work with a number of adopted Asian-American children in the community to teach them about their history and culture. Although African-Americans and other minorities represent a very small percentage of students on this campus, these efforts speak to Cornell's willingness to become a more culturally diverse college.

Cornell is a college for the serious-minded student. In fact, many liken its OCAAT (One Course At A Time) system of coursework to a job. Under this system, students focus their studies on one course every three-and-a-half weeks. It is a system that works well for some. "The OCAAT system taught me how to manage my time and helped improve my grades," says one student.

Most socializing revolves around small groups. There are no fraternities or sororities, and socializing for African-American students is centered largely around BACO (Black Awareness Culture Organization), which has a facility on campus called the BACO House. Students hang out there or participate in other campus events. Sports are big on campus; the school competes in the NCAA Division III, with several NCAA scholarship winners on campus. Since Cornell is just fifteen minutes from the University of Iowa and within a half hour of five other colleges, many students go off campus to participate in social and cultural events.

Cornell actively recruits African-Americans and other minorities through the traditional methods of college fairs, school visits, and direct-mail campaigns. It also employs some less traditional methods, such as advertising in black publications and assembling a special Multicultural Student Phone Team, who recruit other minorities to Cornell by sharing their own experiences at the school.

Once on campus, students will find the family-like atmosphere of Cornell to be responsive to student needs. The low student-to-faculty ratio of 13 to 1 allows for a great deal of interaction; and the school's small size affords students more opportunities to take on leadership roles. Recently, the administration began involving students in campus decision-making; it now includes students on all committees, including search committees that hire new faculty and staff. Students also evaluate faculty after each course, and this information is used during tenure evaluations. Finally, the administration recently established a mentoring program that requires each staff member to work with one to three students, helping them adjust to campus life. Additionally, African-American students can become leaders in organizations like BACO and the Multi-Cultural Task Force. "I never feel lost in the shuffle at Cornell, and am able to assume a leadership role within the campus. I serve on many committees side by side with faculty," said one student, "and it has been a great learning experience. I feel that they really listen to what I have to say."

The administration's efforts have paid off. Cornell College graduates about 65 percent of all students it enrolls. About 30 percent immediately go on to graduate school and 75 percent have completed postgraduate training within five years. For African-American students, this high rate of postgraduate training has produced a fair number of candidates for doctoral degrees at top colleges and universities, including the University of Michigan and the University of Iowa. The college can also point to African-American alumni in high-level jobs in business and government.

Like many predominantly white colleges, Cornell does have its problems. Students may feel isolated and frustrated with the slow way in which change occurs for African-American students, but most are generally pleased with their experience here. "Even with the few problems," one said, "I would choose Cornell because I feel that I am making a difference here and I hope to carry what I've learned into my work to improve conditions in society."

Drake University
2507 University Avenue
Des Moines, Iowa 50311
515-271-3181

Type: **Private**
Overall campus environment: **Friendly/Supportive**
Total enrollment: **3,524**
African-American students: **168**
Graduate students: **631**
African-American graduate students: **45**
Percentage of applications accepted: **91%**
Percentage receiving financial aid: **75%**
Average amount of award: **$9,000**
Percentage in ROTC programs: **0**
Number of faculty: **271**
Number of African-American faculty: **4**
Student/faculty ratio: **17 to 1**
Tuition: **$11,780**
Scholarship programs: **Luther T. Glanton achievement awards**
Academic programs: **Colleges of Arts and Sciences, Business and Public Administration, Education, Fine Arts, Journalism and Mass Communications, Law, Pharmacy and Health Sciences**
Most popular majors: **Biology, Chemistry, Pre-Law, Pre-Medicine, Psychology, Graphic Design/Commercial Art, Music, Accounting, Actuarial Science, Management, Education, Journalism, Pharmacy**
Prominent African-American faculty: **N/R**
Prominent African American graduates: **Fussell Davis, Major General, Virginia National Guard; Wendell Hill, Dean, Howard University School of Pharmacy; Joseph Howard, federal judge, Baltimore, Maryland; Felix Wright, football player, Minnesota Vikings**
African-American student organizations/activities: **Through**

Iowa State University Cooperative Program students can pledge Delta Sigma Theta, Alpha Kappa Alpha, Sigma Gamma Rho, Zeta Phi Beta, Alpha Phi Alpha, Kappa Alpha Psi, Omega Psi Phi, Phi Beta Sigma; Multicultural Theater, Gospel Choir, Black Cultural Advisory Board, Black Student Organization, National Association of Black Journalists, Black Greek Council, Drake Vine publication, Step Show, Talent Show
Administrative services and programs: **Minority Mentor Program**

There is a particular charm, almost an innocence, about the Midwest, particularly the Corn Belt and Wheat Belt. Drake University epitomizes this homey feeling, and shows a genuine concern for attracting and retaining African-American students. The administration is by no means unsophisticated about its efforts to achieve this goal. To the contrary, the administration has done its homework and has really listened to the concerns of African-Americans and other minorities.

A fairly selective university, Drake stands in urban Des Moines, a city of about 400,000. The university draws from the urban areas of Chicago to the farms of Iowa and appears to have had success in bringing together students from these divergent backgrounds to create an atmosphere that is educationally, socially, and culturally appealing. A thriving African-American community exists in Des Moines, and students get involved through African-American churches, local chapters of organizations like the NAACP and Greek organizations, and the local radio station and newspaper. From these ties Drake has been able to establish a Minority Mentor program, which assigns a mentor from the Des Moines community to each African-American freshman. The program is designed to give students a support system away from home; mentors often become like extended family. Although students may opt not to participate after the first year, it has been the university's experience that students not only remain in the program but stay with the same mentor.

Drake and Iowa State University have also developed a cooperative relationship which provides students the opportunity to pledge a Black Greek sorority or fraternity. These organizations do not exist on Drake's campus.

The administration exerts a great deal of effort to help majority and African-American students interact in more than just academics and in the informal settings of the dining halls and libraries. Some ingenious proposals have had a great deal of success, such as the effort which teamed up each chapter of historically African-American and majority fraternities and sororities in an all-Greek dance contest. The competition drew a huge crowd, and students report that everyone had a good time. In addition, Drake's president invites all student leaders to his home for dinner once a month, along with top administrators. Student life administrators regularly eat in student dining halls to stay in touch with students and hear their concerns. All of this is combined with a great academic program which offers numerous majors in seven colleges, including preprofessional programs in medicine, law, social work, and theology.

Drake seems to do a good job of creating a supportive and challenging environment for all its students. Students who are considering Drake must decide, however, whether they can adjust to the Midwestern lifestyle and the distance from major metropolitan areas (Chicago is the closest).

Iowa State University
Ames, Iowa 50011
515-294-1084

Type: **Public 4-year**
Overall campus environment: **Conservative, Academically Challenging, Culturally Supportive**
Total enrollment: **25,250**
African-American students: **593**
Graduate students: **4,395**
African-American graduate students: **82**
Percentage of applications accepted: **89%**
Average SAT/ACT score: **820–1150/22–27**
Average SAT/ACT African-Americans: **N/R**
Special admissions programs: **George Washington Carver Scholarship, Summer Enrichment Program**
Percentage of African-American graduates: **44%**
Percentage receiving financial aid: **67%**

Average amount of award: **varies**
Percentage in ROTC program: **N/R**
Number of faculty: **1,907**
Number of African-American faculty: **27**
Student/faculty ratio: **18 to 1**
Tuition: **$6,856**
Scholarship programs: **George Washington Carver Scholarship, University Scholarships, National Merit and National Achievement Scholarships, Athletic Scholarships, ROTC Scholarships (university also maintains a database of nearly 200,000 scholarships from more than 20,000 sources)**
Academic programs: **Colleges of Agriculture, Business, Design, Education, Engineering, Family and Consumer Sciences, Liberal Arts and Sciences, Veterinary Medicine; preprofessional programs in a variety of medical and technical fields**
Most popular majors: **Business and Management, Engineering, Education, Agribusiness and Agricultural Production, Social Sciences**
Prominent African-American graduates: **George Washington Carver**
Prominent African-American faculty: **N/R**
African-American student organizations/activities: **National Society of Black Engineers, African Students Association, Minority Support Group, Multi-cultural Action Group, Organization for Concerns of African-Americans and People of Color, Black Greek Association, Black Student Organization, Delta Sigma Theta**
Administrative services and programs: **Office of Minority Student Affairs, Educational Recovery Program, Minority Career Fair, Minority Orientation Banquet, Minority Alumni and Recognition Weekend, Minority Student Leadership Retreat, Black Cultural Center, Jack Trice Memorial Library (named for the first African-American athlete)**

Iowa State University is a four-year public university in America's heartland. With an enrollment of more than 25,000 and more than 120 undergraduate majors at its eight colleges, Iowa State offers, among other attractions, nearly 500 student organizations, including numerous ethnic groups; more student-edited and student-managed publications than any school in the country; homestyle dishes on its dining hall menu; entertainment from the New York Philharmonic to Stevie Wonder and speakers like writer Maya Angelou, Jamaican prime minister Michael Manley, and poet Nikki Giovanni; a special office to help students over twenty-five years old adjust to campus life; and sports activities that range from skydiving to tae kwon do to golf to juggling.

While the university attracts most of its predominantly white student body from the state's small towns, many African-American students do well here. They tend to be students who have the ability to adapt and flourish in a big school, where there's no "hand-holding." One student wrote, "Iowa State is a very conservative predominantly white university in which most students have had little if any contact with an African-American. I have found that most Iowans are more confused by race issues than they are racist. They have never really talked with a Black person, much less roomed with one." The university does provide a variety of academic and support services to help African-American students adjust to campus life and succeed academically. The Educational Recovery program provides academic, social, and career development support from faculty. Entering African-American freshmen are also encouraged to participate in a seven-week Summer Enrichment program that introduces them to campus life at Iowa State. Finally, the university sponsors a scholarship program named for its most famous African-American alumnus, George Washington Carver. The program awards merit scholarships to outstanding minority students and requires that they maintain a 2.5 to 3.0 average, live on campus, go to the Minority Student Affairs office for counseling, and serve the minority student community on campus. This service can take the form of organizing student projects, assisting new minority students, or working with campus organizations. The idea is to get the student involved with campus life and help develop leadership skills.

Still, African-American students may feel very challenged in this environment. "Iowa State is a tough school," wrote a student, "especially for students who for the first time ever are confronted with being the only African-American in a class of 100 to 300 other white students." Entrance to this school is fairly competitive; students average between 800 and 1100 on the SAT (22 to 27 on the ACT). African-Americans comprise about 2 percent of the student body, and nearly half of them drop out in the first year. But those who complete undergraduate studies tend to fare well, 20 percent go on to graduate school, many to Harvard, Yale, Stanford, Rice, MIT, Princeton, Northwestern, Cornell, and Johns Hopkins.

Iowa State offers one of the oldest veterinary medicine programs in the country; a popular engineering school which attracts more than 250 companies who recruit its graduates each year; a College of Family and Consumer Sciences, whose graduates have found employment in consumer affairs, nutrition, hotel management, consumer product management, and child care administration; a College of Agriculture, which offers training in careers from arborist to zoologist, and training in many other fields. In short, Iowa State offers a student many choices not only in career training but in campus life. Students who can adjust to the occasional isolation of being the only African-American student in a classroom or in a social situation can do well at this institution.

Kansas State University
Manhattan, Kansas 66506
913-532-6318

Type: **Public 4-year**
Overall campus environment: **Friendly**
Total enrollment: **20,712**
African-American students: **699**
Graduate students: **3,247**
African-American graduate students: **89**
Percentage of applications accepted: **81%**
Average ACT score: **22.5**
Average ACT African-Americans: **18.9**
Special admissions programs: **N/A**
Percentage of African-American graduates: **20%**
Percentage receiving financial aid: **88%**
Average amount of award: **$4,500**
Percentage in ROTC programs: **6.5% Army/6% Air Force**
Number of faculty: **1,102**

Number of African-American faculty: **5**
Student/faculty ratio: **17 to 1**
Tuition: **$6,002**
Scholarship programs: **Academic Achievement and Leadership, department scholarships**
Academic programs: **Colleges of Arts and Sciences, Health Related Pre-Professional Studies, Business Administration, Engineering, Agriculture, Education, Human Ecology, Architecture and Design, Technology (associate degrees), Veterinary Medicine**
Most popular majors: **Veterinary Medicine, Engineering, Architecture and Design**
Prominent African-American graduates: **N/R**
Prominent African-American faculty: **N/R**
African-American student organizations/activities: **African Student Union, Black Student Union, Ebony Theatre Company, Multicultural Student Council, United Black Voices Gospel Choir, National Society of Black Engineers, Minority Assembly of Students in Health, Minority Business Students in Action, Panhellenic Council, all traditional Black Greek organizations**
Administrative services and programs: **Multicultural Student Center, Racial/Ethnic Harmony Week**

Located in a small, rural community, KSU has an enrollment of more than 20,000, 3 percent of whom are African-Americans, from Kansas and nearby Midwestern states. In addition, the school has a fair number of students from Africa, Latin America, the Middle East, Europe and Asia. Students are generally attracted to KSU because of its wide variety of major fields of study, particularly architecture and design, engineering, and veterinary medicine, for all three of which the school is nationally ranked. However, many students are drawn here because of KSU's rich ethnic diversity. Its outreach to African-Americans and other minorities has resulted in a campus environment that is friendly and tolerant of a variety of cultural and social differences. This factor is an important consideration for African-American students uneasy about life on a predominantly white college campus. "Overall, the interaction between minority and white students on campus is good," said one student. "Many of us are the only minority in a class and it is only natural to make friends and try to learn and share our cultures."

As is the case on many predominantly white campuses, the number of African-American faculty and administrators at KSU is minimal. However, there are a number of support organizations for African-American students, including the Multicultural Student Organization and the Black Student Union, of which all African-American students are members, even if they choose not to be active. In addition, there are all the traditional Black Greek organizations, the National Association of Black Accountants, the National Society of Black Engineers, Minority Business Students in Action, Minority Assembly of Students in Health, and a number of cultural arts groups. These organizations are largely responsible for African-American social and cultural events on campus. Additionally, each year the administration sponsors Racial/Ethnic Harmony Week in an effort to bring together students from all racial and ethnic backgrounds to discuss any problems or incidents that may have occurred on campus. During that week, forums and workshops are held to allow students an opportunity to air their views and give suggestions on ways to improve relationships on campus.

African-American students tend to rate KSU fairly good for minority students but acknowledge that, "as in the real world," some racism does exist. The administration's commitment to a culturally diverse institution has had a role in circumventing any overt racial problem, and its continuing dialogue with students has also shielded KSU from many of the problems experienced on other campuses. Still, there is a lot of work to be done to assist African-American students in feeling comfortable here. Only 20 percent of African-American students who enroll complete coursework for graduation—a dismal figure for an institution this size. A student who needs a more nurturing environment would be wise to consider this fact before embarking on a collegiate journey at KSU. After all, fitting in at such a large university is not easy for any student, regardless of race or ethnic background. For students who are prepared to deal with the often impersonal world of a large institution, KSU may be less intimidating. One student said, "Many of us secretly wish to attend a predominantly black institution, but we know that we are in the real world here at K-State and feel this atmosphere will better prepare us for life after college."

Berea College
P. O. Box 2344
101 Chestnut Street
Berea, Kentucky 40403-9986
606-986-0341

Type: **Private liberal arts, nonsectarian with Christian focus**
Overall campus environment: **Strong Religious and Work Ethics, Culturally Supportive**
Total enrollment: **1,589**
African-American students: **150**
Graduate students: **N/A**
African-American graduate students: **N/A**
Percentage of applications accepted: **35%**
Average SAT/ACT score: **949/21.7**
Average SAT/ACT African-Americans: **N/A**
Special admissions programs: **N/A**
Percentage of African-American graduates: **N/A**
Percentage receiving financial aid: **100%**
Average amount of award: **$12,240**
Percentage in ROTC programs: **0**
Number of faculty: **113**
Number of African-American faculty: **8**
Student/faculty ratio: **13 to 1**
Tuition: **N/A**
Scholarship programs: **N/A**
Academic programs: **Agriculture, Art, Biology, Business Administration, Chemistry, Child and Family Studies, Classical Languages, Economics, Education, English, French, German, History, Mathematics, Music, Nursing, Philosophy, Physical Education, Physics, Political Science, Psychology, Religion, Sociology, Spanish, Technology and Industrial Arts, Theater**
Most popular major: **Business Administration**
Prominent African-American graduates: **Dr. James Burton, Chief, National Water Exchange Data Program, U.S.**

Geological Survey; Ophelia Weaver Burton, retired director of Program Planning, Internal Revenue Service; John Fleming, director, National Afro-American Museum of Culture; Julia Britton Hooks, first Black to teach white students in Kentucky; Constance Willard Williams, Professor of Ethics, Harvard Divinity School; Dr. Carter G. Woodson, scholar, educator, founder of Black History Month

Prominent African-American faculty: N/A

African-American student organizations/activities: **African Student Organization, Black Student Union, Black Ensemble**

Administrative services and programs: **Black Peer Counseling Program, Black Cultural Center, Interracial Education Program**

Berea College combines a sober lifestyle, a strong work ethic, and belief in God to help students succeed. It describes itself as a liberal arts college with a nonsectarian Christian focus. Although students are not required to take classes in religion, Berea maintains the philosophy of Christian missionaries who traveled to unheard-of places around the world to educate children and improve the condition of life among the poorest. Founded in the mid-1800s during the controversy over slavery in Kentucky, Berea set forth its mission as providing an education to all people of good character, and Berea condemned slaveholding and many discriminatory practices. For African-American students today, Berea's enduring commitment to cultural awareness is an attractive feature of the school. "All students are encouraged to associate with races other than their own at Berea," wrote one student. "When a student enters as a freshman, every effort is made to assign a roommate of a difference race to encourage them to explore nationalities other than their own. In my opinion, this method improves race relations on campus a great deal. It is an excellent way to teach students that stereotypes are not always realistic."

Berea is an unusual college. Students are admitted on the basis of financial need, making it possible for many disadvantaged young people to obtain a college education. There is no tuition, and parents contribute what they can afford (based on an income table) toward their child's education. Perhaps one of the most extraordinary aspects of Berea is its student labor program, in which every student is required to work at least ten hours per week while carrying a normal class load. The administration believes that students learn best by doing and that their education is enhanced when coupled with the experience of working. First-year students are usually placed where there is the most need; after that students can choose their own assignment, and every effort is made to place them in jobs directly related to their major field of interest. Hotel management majors, for example, may work at the local hotel; an English major may be assigned to work on a campus publication. These job assignments not only provide valuable work experience, but give students an opportunity to earn money to help defray college costs. The student labor program also helps Berea hold down its operating costs. The students' portion of the pay from this program ranges from $1.30 to $3.20 per hour and can go as high as $4.25 per hour for those who work over the summer.

Not surprisingly, many African-American students at Berea cite the college's commitment to principles of fairness and its strong work ethic as two of its strongest attractions. "One of the best things about Berea is the helpfulness and support of the faculty and administrators. In the classroom it is evident that the instructor wants to see students succeed and is more than willing to help," said a senior. "At Berea, there are no easy majors. For every hour in class, you are expected to spend two hours' study time. In other words, academics come first, but it is still possible to be a good student and have a social life." This social life for many African-American students revolves around a number of cultural events sponsored by the Black Student Union and African Student Association. And every year the African-American faculty prepare a home-cooked meal for beginning students. Several of them even open their homes to students to help them adjust to life on campus.

Berea offers an excellent academic program and has repeatedly been rated among the nation's "best buys in college" by national publications. It has a long history of educating some of the finest African-American leaders in our country, including scholar and educator, Dr. Carter G. Woodson, founder of Black History Month. And Berea's commitment to service and work provides a valuable education that will help a graduate succeed in almost any field.

Students who are looking for a more active "party" environment will find that Bera is not the college for them. Those who are fairly serious and focused on obtaining an education as their primary reason for being in college will find few distractions.

University of Kentucky
100 W. D. Funkhouser Bldg.
Lexington, Kentucky 40506
606-257-2000

Type: **Public**
Overall campus environment: **Cordial, Relaxed**
Total enrollment: **24,300**
African-American students: **1,000**
Graduate students: **6,550**
African-American graduate students: **180**
Percentage of applications accepted: **80%**
Average SAT/ACT score: **1000/24.0**
Average SAT/ACT African-Americans: **N/R/20.5**
Special admissions programs: **N/A**
Percentage of African-American graduates: **N/A**
Percentage receiving financial aid: **85%**
Average amount of award: **$2500**
Percentage in ROTC programs: **N/R**
Number of faculty: **1,500**
Number of African-American faculty: **30**
Student/faculty ratio: **15 to 1**
Tuition: **$5040**
Scholarship programs: **University Scholarships**
Academic Programs: **Colleges of Agriculture, Allied Health, Architecture, Arts and Sciences, Business and Economics, Communication, Dentistry, Education, Engineering, Fine Arts, Human Environmental Sciences, Law, Library and Information Science, Medicine, Nursing, Pharmacy, Social Work**
Most popular majors: **Business, Engineering, health programs**
Prominent African-American faculty: **N/R**
Prominent African-American graduates: **N/R**

African-American student organizations/activities: **Martin Luther King, Jr., Cultural Center**
Administrative services and programs: **Office of Minority Student Affairs**

Located in Lexington, Kentucky, the horse capital of the world, the University of Kentucky is the state's noted institution. UK appeals to students for different reasons. The Southern, aristocratic aspect of the school, with its Kentucky Derby image, is particularly attractive to more traditional Southerners, but there is also a more progressive and diverse side of this institution.

UK offers a variety of disciplines from education to medicine. Among its most notable programs are journalism, business, education and engineering. At the core of UK's program is an emphasis on the liberal arts principles of educating the total student by developing skills in writing, research and critical thinking. However, though the academic program here is good, what UK is probably best known for is its almost fanatical love of basketball. Outside of the Kentucky Derby, basketball reigns supreme. (Football is a close second.) Tickets for home games go quickly as both students and the community turn out to see the Wildcats play.

UK is a moderate-sized university with about 18,000 undergraduate students and more than 6,500 graduate and professional school students. About 5 percent of the student body is African-American. A smaller percentage of students come from abroad, representing nearly 100 countries. However, the large majority of students here come from Kentucky. That's no surprise, since the commonly held belief is that in Kentucky, a degree from UK is almost as valuable as one from an Ivy League school. For Kentucky residents, UK is the place to make political and business contacts. Almost all of the state delegates went to UK, as did former governor John Brown. It's said that if you get involved with the right political group, you're guaranteed a job once you leave college.

African-American students at UK generally report they are pleased with life on the campus, though sometimes they may experience the feelings of isolation often associated with being on a predominantly white campus of this size. Some classes, for example, are taught in a lecture format with hundreds of other students, and often an African-American student may be the only nonwhite in the class. However, some students say that the concern for students expressed by faculty and staff and the general friendliness of the university can help overcome these problems. "I was amazed to find out that three-fourths of my classes were not much larger than my classes in high school," says a biology/pre-Med major. "Even more so, I was overwhelmed by the friendliness and the patience that the faculty exhibited."

To help students adjust to life at UK, an Office of Minority Student Affairs provides counseling, orientation, nonacademic advising, and help with housing and financial aid. This office is also responsible for the Martin Luther King, Jr., Cultural Center, which sponsors yearlong cultural and educational programs and events based on the African-American experience.

The Southern hospitality, relaxed environment, and solid academics of UK make it a university worth considering, especially if you live in Kentucky.

Centenary College
Box 41188
Shreveport, Louisiana 71134-1188
318-869-5131/1-800-234-4448

Type: **Private liberal arts, affiliated with United Methodist Church**
Overall campus environment: **Conservative, Limited Diversity**
Total enrollment: **1043**
African-American students: **67**
Graduate students: **226**
African-American graduate students: **zero**
Percentage of applications accepted: **86%**
Average SAT/ACT score: **1020/25**
Average SAT/ACT African-Americans: **N/R**
Special admissions programs: **N/A**
Percentage of African-American graduates: **55%**
Percentage receiving financial aid: **76%**
Average amount of award: **$6,870**
Percentage in ROTC programs: **N/R**
Number of faculty: **N/A**

African-American faculty: **zero**
Student/faculty ratio: **11 to 1**
Tuition: **$7,550**
Scholarship programs: **N/A**
Academic programs: **37 majors in Arts and Sciences, Music, Pre-professional Engineering, Forestry, Law, Medicine, Medical Technology, Nuclear Medicine, Pharmacy, Physical Therapy, Theology, Dentistry, Veterinary Medicine; Career Preparations in Accounting, Business, Church Careers, Communications, Computer Science, Dance, Early Childhood Education, Elementary Education, Journalism, General Business, Museum Management, Petroleum and Land Management, Public Administration, Secondary Education**
Most popular majors: **Biology, Business, Education, Psychology**
Prominent African-American faculty: **N/R**
Prominent African-American graduates: **N/R**
African-American student organizations/activities: **N/R**
Administrative services and programs: **N/R**

A liberal arts college affiliated with the United Methodist Church, Centenary College offers students a program that combines academics and exposure to a variety of disciplines as it strives to educate the total person. Centenary requires that all of its students take a core curriculum of courses that include cultural awareness, writing and speaking, and career exploration in addition to a student's selected major field of study.

The Centenary Plan has students taking a two-semester course in the freshman year that encourages them to broaden their perspective through attendance at art, drama, and music events. In the sophomore year, students are involved in an assessment program that helps guide them in career decisions. By the junior year, students are fulfilling a number of requirements, including a writing course that focuses on their major field of study, as well as a speech course in which the required oral presentation is critiqued on the basis of its content and delivery, and in which students are also evaluated on impromptu responses to questions about the presentation.

Besides the core curriculum, students can choose from more than thirty-seven major fields of study as well as pre-professional preparation in engineering, medicine, law, forestry, veterinary science, religion and education.

It is the administration's goal to help students acquire the skills they need to think, deduce, and reason to solve problems, and to write and communicate effectively. Understanding the past and learning how to work with people of all cultural and social backgrounds are of most importance in the philosophy of teaching at Centenary, a philosophy that is found at some of the top Ivy League and liberal arts institutions.

Centenary's small size and supportive faculty create an environment which lends itself to this kind of learning. Its faculty are highly qualified, coming from such prestigious institutions as Columbia, Darmouth, Emory, Oberlin and Yale. They bring with them a commitment to teaching. "Through the Centenary curriculum, students and faculty study and discuss the best thought and literature in various fields," said one professor. "And even more important, our students learn to exceed their time-space limitations through the informed life of the mind and interact intellectually with the people behind these readings representing thousands of years of human experience."

The vast majority of students who attend Centenary come from the South; more than half are from Louisiana. About 5 percent of students are African-American; many say they came because of Centenary's excellent academic program and faculty and the financial support the college provides. "I especially like the personal attention you get at Centenary," said one sophomore. "I've had occasions when a professor has literally spent hours helping me with a particular class assignment."

However, some students complain that there are no organizations specifically for African-American students. "Most of us have to go off campus to find entertainment that appeals to us." One student laments that attempts to start African-American student organizations have not been successful. "There are so few of us on campus that it's difficult to get a chapter of a fraternity or a sorority on campus; and many students are not supportive of standing up to the administration to get support of an African-American student organization." Yet most students say that racial relations on campus are good and that they feel comfortable getting involved in other student organizations.

When asked about the academics and faculty at Centenary,

students overwhelmingly rate them excellent. However, students who want an active social life and great academics, or who want to attend a school in the forefront of political and cultural change on campus, will find that Centenary leaves much to be desired.

Bowdoin College
Brunswick, Maine 04011
207-725-3100

Type: **Private liberal arts**
Overall campus environment: **Friendly/supportive**
Total enrollment: **1,400**
African-American students: **58**
Graduate students: **0**
Percentage of applications accepted: **32%**
Average SAT score: **Not required**
Special admissions programs: **Several**
Percentage of African-American graduates: **80%**
Percentage receiving financial aid: **43%**
Average amount of award: **$12,950**
Percentage in ROTC: **N/A**
Number of faculty: **137**
Number of African-American faculty: **5**
Student/faculty ratio: **11 to 1**
Tuition: **$17,035**
Scholarship programs: **John Brown Russwurm Scholarship for African-American Students**
Academic programs: **Liberal arts with 35 majors including Afro-American Studies, Art, Biological and Physical Sciences, Economics, English, History, Government, Music, Psychology, Religion, Romance Languages, Sociology**
Most popular majors: **Sciences, Government, Humanities, General Liberal Arts, Economics**
Prominent African-American Faculty: **N/A**
Prominent African-American graduates: **Kenneth I. Chenault, business leader; Oliver Otis Howard, founder, Howard University; John Brown Russwurm, second Black college graduate in America**

African-American student organizations/activities: **John Brown Russwurm African-American Society**
Administrative services and programs: **Multi-Cultural Affairs, Student of Color Counselors**

The familiar adage "one person can make a difference" rings true about the alumni of Bowdoin College, who have made a difference in the lives of many African-Americans. John Brown Russwurm, an 1826 graduate of Bowdoin and the second African-American male to graduate from an American college, left a legacy as a newspaper publisher, pan-Africanist, and Third World leader. He was followed by Oliver Otis Howard in 1850, whose great vision and strong belief in education as a way to real freedom for African-Americans gave rise to some seventy educational institutions, chief among them Howard University, Hampton, Atlanta, Fisk, and Lincoln Memorial. Russwurm and Howard are only the first in a long line of prominent African-American alumni of Bowdoin.

This legacy of achievement is at the heart of Bowdoin's educational mission. A small private liberal arts college, Bowdoin is proud of its outstanding academic program, renowned and committed faculty, nontraditional curriculum structure, and recently revised non-letter grading system. Bowdoin and its staff and faculty truly care about students. "I feel that Bowdoin is genuinely concerned with my needs as a student of color," said one student. "Although I find Bowdoin to be academically demanding, I enjoy the challenges and find the faculty tend to be very accessible for advice and encouragement."

Bowdoin approaches liberal arts education in a way that places primary responsibility on the student. During the first two years, students must complete at least two courses in each of the academic areas of the humanities, natural sciences, mathematics and social sciences. In an effort to expose students to other cultures, attitudes and history, each student is required to select two courses in "non-Eurocentric" studies. Once these requirements are completed, a student may select courses from more than thirty-five major fields of study, including the most popular, the sciences, economics, humanities, government and general liberal arts.

Bowdoin is in Brunswick, a small coastal town of about 20,000. Of the approximately 1,400 students on campus, only 4 percent are African-American, and less than 1 percent of the Brunswick population is African-American.

The college is near the mountains, and students take advantage of backpacking, skiing, and numerous other activities. The facilities on campus are good and the dormitories are especially comfortable. The town of Brunswick is the home of the famous sports and outdoor apparel mail order company, L. L. Bean, which has an outlet store here that stays open twenty-four hours. Not surprisingly, everyone here seems to have stepped out of the pages of an L. L. Bean catalog.

Bowdoin is very sensitive to the special needs of African-American students in such a culturally isolated environment, and the administration supports student organizations, cultural activities, and events to help students adjust. Recently, the John Brown Russwurm African-American Society, named for the famous alumnus, celebrated its twentieth anniversary. The college also has the African-American Center, which houses a 1,600-volume library of materials relating primarily to African-Americans in the diaspora. According to one student, the center is also a meeting place. "The African-American Center provides students of color a haven of support."

The very small number of African-American students has produced a very close group who report that they are generally pleased with life at Bowdoin. Students admitted here are generally bright and committed and do very well. In fact, Bowdoin reports an 80 percent graduation rate and notes that one class graduated 100 percent of its African-American students. Again, the college's philosophy of caring for students seems to make the difference. "The college is continuously seeking out ways in which to better fulfill the needs of its students," said one student. "Not only am I impressed with the outstanding faculty, but also with Bowdoin's appreciation for and sensitivity toward students of color."

While life at Bowdoin may not always be easy, the academic program, caring faculty and staff, and special efforts for students place it high on the list of colleges to consider seriously.

Goucher College
1021 Dulaney Valley Road
Baltimore, Maryland 20204
410-337-6100

Type: **Private 4-year liberal arts**
Overall campus environment: **Liberal, Culturally supportive**
Total enrollment: **950**
African-American students: **52**
Graduate students: **65**
African-American graduate students: **N/A**
Percentage of applications accepted: **70%**
Average SAT/ACT score: **1110/26**
Average SAT/ACT African-Americans: **N/R**
Special admissions programs: **N/A**
Percentage of African-American graduates: **46%**
Percentage receiving financial aid: **77%**
Average amount of award: **$11,300**
Percentage in ROTC programs: **N/A**
Number of faculty: **133**
Number of African-American faculty: **1**
Student/faculty ratio: **9 to 1**
Tuition: **$13,446**
Scholarship programs: **College Scholarships, need-based grants**
Academic programs: **Arts, Humanities, Natural Sciences, Mathematics, Social Sciences, Interdisciplinary Studies**
Most popular majors: **Natural Sciences, Politics, Public Policy, English**
Prominent African-American graduates: **Jewell Robinson, first Black Goucher graduate; Actress**
Prominent African-American faculty: **N/R**
African-American student organizations/activities: **Black Students Association, Ethnic Religious Minority Affairs Committee, African-American Student Alliance, African-American Speakers Bureau**
Administrative services and programs: **Minority Mentoring, Internships, Career Development and Placement for Minorities**

Once a small, private liberal arts college for women that catered to the offspring of Baltimore's wealthy families, Goucher today has shed its parochial image in favor of one that is coed and culturally diverse. While many of the young women who attend Goucher still come from prominent families, attendance is no longer restricted to the elite. Goucher has become a college that prepares women for careers in the sciences, medicine, law, and other demanding fields. "Goucher is in the midst of transition," one student pointed out. "Formerly a school for women, Goucher is now a college committed to the well-being of both male and female students from various ethnic and economic backgrounds. Although it is still a predominantly white institution, Goucher promotes cultural diversity."

Goucher has an excellent academic program that is particularly strong in the natural sciences, politics and public policy, and English. Its reputation in the sciences is outstanding, and graduates are nearly ensured admittance to medical, dental, veterinary and other graduate-level programs. At the core of Goucher's program is a highly accomplished and committed faculty. More than 85 percent of professors have a doctorate or the highest degree in their field, and they must publish. However, what many students find most satisfying about Goucher is the relationship they have with the faculty. Because of the small faculty-to-student ratio (9 to 1), students get a lot of one-on-one attention. The combination of small class size and sensitive faculty has led to student-faculty relationships that extend beyond the classroom and campus. "The amount of personal attention granted here is simply amazing," said one student. "When I was having a lot of problems adjusting to my French course, the professor invited me to her apartment for coffee several times a week just so we could converse in French together and increase my comprehension. This kindness gave me renewed confidence in the classroom." A number of students recount similar stories about the faculty, and many say the faculty is the primary reason they chose Goucher.

Located in an upper-class suburb of Baltimore, Goucher is surrounded by both residential and commercial areas and is easily accessible to malls, pizza parlors, restaurants and movies. It is also within four miles of several other well-known colleges and universities, including Towson State University, Loyola College, the College of Notre Dame of Maryland and Johns Hopkins University. Students often take courses at these colleges; Goucher sponsors a Goucher–Johns Hopkins shuttle which runs hourly seven days a week. In addition, Goucher is about eight miles from Baltimore's attractive Inner Harbor development and the new Oriole Park stadium.

African-American students will find an administration increasingly sensitive to and involved in issues surrounding cultural heritage and racism. Officials are currently developing a marketing strategy to interest more African-Americans in enrolling in Goucher, and have established a multicultural internship position in which a student conducts an evaluation of the college's existing effort. In this way Goucher hopes to develop realistic strategies for improvement in recruiting and retaining students. In addition, the administration supports a number of organizations on campus, including the Black Students Association (BSA) and the Ethnic Religious Minority Affairs Committee (ERMAC), which assist students in adjusting to life on campus.

Beyond Goucher's commitment to cultural diversity, students will find a spirit of activism that creates an awareness among students that they can make a difference in life. "Goucher students proclaim and protest, march and mingle, serve and sanction throughout the nation," said one student. "This collective spirit to make a difference in world events is born and fortified within our small community and escapes into soup kitchens, rallies, inner-city schools, demolished houses, courthouses, and impoverished neighborhoods of Baltimore." An example of this activism is Goucher's partnership with an inner-city middle school through the RAISE (Raising Ambition Instills Self-Esteem) program, in which students provide tutoring and mentoring to students at risk of academic failure. The college is also actively involved with the Habitat for Humanity housing organization, and students regularly participate in the restoration efforts of this group, as well as in efforts for the homeless and other social causes.

For students who want a solid education in a socially conscious environment, Goucher is a college to consider. "As an African-American student at Goucher, I have a valued voice in the face of transition," said one student. "Goucher is an excellent college and instills in students both a habit of expecting the best and an awareness of the ability of each individual to make a difference."

Hood College
Rosemont Avenue
Frederick, Maryland 21701-8575
301-696-3400

Type: **Private women's**
Overall campus environment: **Cordial/Improving**
Total enrollment: **2,000**
African-American students: **141**
Graduate students: **900**
African-American graduate students: **24**
Percentage of applications accepted: **82%**
Average ACT score: **1000/24**
Average ACT/SAT African-Americans: **894/22**
Special admissions programs: **N/R**
Percentage of African-American graduates: **60%**
Percentage receiving financial aid: **95%**
Average amount of award: **$13,300**
Percentage in ROTC programs: **N/A**
Number of faculty: **78**
Number of African-American faculty: **4**
Student/faculty ratio: **12 to 1**
Tuition: **$12,078**
Scholarship programs: **Hood Opportunity Awards**
Academic programs: **Bachelor of Arts in Art, Biochemistry, Biology, Chemistry, Communication Arts, Early Childhood Education, Economics, English, Environmental Studies, French, German, History, Information and Computer Science, Latin American Studies, Law and Society, Management, Mathematics, Philosophy, Political Science, Psychobiology, Psychology, Religion, Religion and Philosophy, Social Work, Sociology, Spanish, Special Education; Bachelor of Business Administration; Bachelor of Science in Computer Science, Home Economics, Medical Technology**
Prominent African-American faculty: **N/R**
Prominent African-American graduates: **Winifred King, M.D., medical reporter WMAR-TV, Baltimore; Sarah Brumbach Roache, high school vice principal, Frederick, MD; Carol Smith, financial analyst, GTE Spacenet, McLean, VA**
African-American student organizations/activities: **Black**

**Student Union, Office of Multicultural Affairs, Gospel
Ensemble, Annual Liberation of the Black Mind Weekend,
Teaching Our Little Ones Workshop, Kwanzaa Celebrations**
Administrative services and programs: **Office of Multicultural
Affairs, College EEO Officer, Minority Concerns Committee,
Grievance Board for Complaints of Racial and Sexual
Harassment**

A small private women's liberal arts school in beautiful western
Maryland, Hood College prides itself on being a teaching college
whose faculty are selected on the basis of their strengths as teachers; all but a handful have doctoral degrees. The college encourages self-reliance and the development of leadership skills, and it
is small enough to see to it that students get the attention they
need to succeed.

Opportunities abound at Hood College, where students can
work independently on research projects as freshmen; participate
in one of the numerous internship programs; learn a foreign
language and live in a dormitory where only that language is
spoken; participate in one of the cooperative programs between
Hood and George Washington University or the American University in Washington, D.C., or study abroad in Spain, the Domin-
ican Republic, Germany, Japan, and other countries where Hood
operates a program.

At Hood, the student is treated as an independent, thinking
person and is expected to live by the choices he or she makes.
Supported by a strict honor code, Hood assigns responsibility for
governing residence halls and managing student organizations
and campus activities to students. Hood is so confident of its
honor code system that it allows students to schedule and admin-
ister exams without faculty supervision. This confidence in student behavior underpins Hood College's philosophy of providing
a complete education to students by helping then develop the
skills to be responsible and assume leaders' roles.

African-American students at Hood represent about 7 percent
of the population and are given a great deal of attention in terms
of their cultural, educational, and remedial needs. Hood's Office
of Multicultural Affairs (OMA) monitors the progress of African-
American and other minority students and intervenes when they
have problems. Students who achieve excellence are recognized

with congratulatory letters, and each year a special program is held in their honor. OMA also serves as a bridge between the college establishment and African-American students. Faculty, for example, refer students to OMA for special help. The needs of the larger college community are also addressed by OMA through special programs and activities.

Hood College's commitment to cultural diversity is evidenced by its hiring of African-Americans, who now comprise 5 percent of the faculty and 20 percent of administrators, and by its support of African-American student organizations. The Black Student Union, which is student-governed and self-managed, is well funded by the Student Government Association, receiving the second-highest level of funding of student organizations. The BSU is a focal point for African-American students and sponsors a variety of events, including the annual Liberation of the Black Mind Weekend, a tutorial program for middle and high school students, and an annual workshop called Teaching Our Little Ones for elementary students. The college supports Kwanzaa events and regularly brings African-American leaders and organizations to campus.

For all of its commitment, Hood is not free of racial intolerance. "Personally, I get along very well with other-race students," said one student. "But other African-Americans feel that the racism on this campus is very strong, and I sometimes feel it, too." A recent incident on campus bears that out. An altercation between invited and uninvited African-American male guests at a dance resulted in three African-American female students being arrested by local police. The college president supported the young women, and eventually all charges were dropped. However, some white students felt bitter about the president's support of the students, and racial tension remained high on campus afterward. Hood's administration responded by bringing in professionals from the National Coalition Building Institute, which has since held open forums to give students an opportunity to address this incident and similar concerns. By the administration's own admission, interaction between racial groups on campus still leaves a lot to be desired, and the college holds regular workshops on prejudice for students, faculty and staff. A recent survey conducted by the college indicated that while students were concerned about racial tension, the majority expressing concern believed that the administration should help them manage it. Clearly, the will is strong on all sides to move toward a true embrace of one another.

Hood has a lot to offer African-American students. The school's small size allows for individual attention and access to professors—a feature that many students say draws them to attend predominantly African-American colleges. Hood's honor code and its overall philosophy of building leadership skills are particularly attractive to African-American students, who often feel left out of campus life. The school has had some success in grooming African-American leaders. One of the graduates Hood is most proud of is both a practicing medical doctor and the medical reporter for a television station in Baltimore. Two others have settled close to the school, including a financial analyst with GTE Spacenet in McLean, Virginia, and a vice principal at the largest high school in Frederick, Maryland. One student said about Hood, "I like that the school has a lot of clubs and organizations that represent the diverse interests of students on this campus. I like that the lecturers and speakers have been informative and that we are in between Washington, D.C., and Baltimore. I like that most students are great, wonderful and friendly, and basically that it is a student-run campus." When asked whether she would select Hood again, the student said, "I would most definitely make the same choice again because this school is one where I can strengthen my leadership skills and know that I have the support if I need it."

Morgan State University
Baltimore, Maryland
410-319-3130

Type: **Public, predominantly African-American**
Overall campus environment: **Supportive, Culturally Diverse, Traditional**
Total enrollment: **5,100**
African-American students: **4,900**
Graduate students: **1,000**
African-American graduate students: **900**
Percentage of applications accepted: **78%**
Average SAT score: **820**

Average SAT African-Americans: **820**
Special admissions programs: **N/A**
Percentage of African-American graduates: **70%**
Percentage receiving financial aid: **90%**
Average amount of award: **$2,000**
Percentage in ROTC programs: **1%**
Number of faculty: **217**
Number of African-American faculty: **187**
Student/faculty ratio: **20 to 1**
Tuition: **$2,470**
Scholarship programs: **N/A**
Academic programs: **Accounting; African-American Studies;
Art; Biology; Business Administration and Education;
Chemistry; Civil, Electrical, and Industrial Engineering;
Elementary Education, English; Fine Arts; Foreign Languages;
History; Music; Medical Technology; Mental Health;
Philosophy; Physical Education; Physics; Political Science;
Psychology; Religious Studies; Social Work; Sociology;
Speech; Telecommunications; Theater Arts; Urban Studies;
Pre-Dentistry; Pre-Pharmacy; Pre-Law; Information Systems;
International Studies; Geography; Human Ecology;
Marketing; Computer Science; Economics**
Most popular majors: **Business/Accounting,
Telecommunications, Engineering, Biology/Chemistry**
Prominent African-American faculty: **Dr. Milford Jeremiah,
English and Language Arts**
Prominent African-American graduates: **Brenda Alford, singer;
Joe Black, Vice President, Greyhound, Inc.; Earl Graves,
publisher/CEO** Black Enterprise **magazine; Zora Neale
Hurston, poet and writer; Kweisi Mfume, U.S. Congressman
(Maryland); Parren Mitchell, former U.S. Congressman;
Verda Welcome, first African-American state senator
(Maryland); Deniece Williams, singer; Samm Art Williams,
producer,** Fresh Prince of Bel Air
African-American student organizations/activities: **A variety of
social and professional clubs, Black Greek fraternities and
sororities, Umoja Student Affairs Council,** The Spokesman
newspaper, The Promethean **yearbook**
Administrative services and programs: **Student Affairs Office,
Career Counseling, Counseling Center, Pre-College Program**

Morgan State University is among the best-known historically African-American institutions in the country and has survived rising economic and political barriers to its existence. Before African-Americans were being wooed to predominantly white universities, Morgan State, like Howard University, was the college that everyone wanted to attend. During the 1960s and 1970s Morgan State was in the vanguard of the civil rights movement, with students staging sit-ins at local lunch counters and shopping malls. Today Morgan State is still at the forefront, but now its concerns lie increasingly with the community-related issues of an urban college. Although the university reports about 40 percent of its students come from outside Maryland, it is still mostly a state university, and a large majority of its students live within commuting distance. The university's focus has become more urban and centered on issues that affect African-Americans disproportionately. It works closely with the community on issues of education, health care, nutrition, aging, and human resource development. It is especially concerned with the problems of African-American men and houses the Center for Educating African American Males. The university academic offerings reflect this concern, as well as the need to prepare students for future job demands in engineering, communications and the sciences. Indeed, Morgan State's engineering program is rated among the best in the United States.

The majority of faculty here are African-American. They have earned many distinctions, including Guggenheim and American Council on Education fellowships. Morgan State has six Fulbright scholars and one MacArthur scholar and a host of published faculty. While the ratio of students to faculty is 20 to 1, students report that faculty are very helpful, supportive and understanding of the special needs of African-Americans.

Morgan State is becoming more selective in its admissions process as the number of applicants increases. For the first time in several years, the administration reports it has had to turn away students because of the upgraded requirements for admission. Scores on standard admissions tests are considered, but the administration seems more concerned with admitting students who are determined, industrious and committed to achieving excellence.

Graduates of the university have achieved excellence in business, politics, entertainment and the arts. Its list of prominent alumni reads like a *Who's Who* and many alumni like Earl Graves, publisher and CEO of *Black Enterprise* magazine; Congressman Kweisi Mfume and former congressman Parren Mitchell, remain supportive and involved with the university administration.

Besides a solid academic program, Morgan State offers students an exciting social life, with myriad student social and professional organizations and cultural activities including music, the performing arts, theater and fine arts exhibits. Morgan State's Fine Arts Center houses a fine collection of American, African and European art. The Greek life has always been big at Morgan State, and all the national Black fraternities and sororities are represented. One real success at Morgan is its independent and powerful radio station WEAA, well known in the community for its consciousness-raising talk shows and culturally diverse music. Morgan State students can work on the air or behind the scenes.

Sports have traditionally been an important aspect of life at Morgan State, especially at homecoming, when hundreds of alumni return to the campus to reminisce about their college days with old friends and pass on the tradition to their children. While football is the sport many have associated with Morgan State, it is the men's wrestling team that has won several championships and produced several all-American athletes, including a 1984 Olympic alternate. Women's track is also prominent here; the Lady Bears have garnered a great deal of attention at the NCAA finals over the past few years.

As is the case on many predominantly African-American campuses, students feel nurtured here and energized by the cultural awareness. "I am proud to be a part of a historically Black university," said one female student. "My experiences at Morgan have been enriching and enjoyable. The administrators and faculty have encouraged me beyond measure; and being here has given me a rich education and helped me to define who I am as an African-American."

St. John's College
P.O. Box 2800
Annapolis, Maryland 21404-2800
Camino De Cruz Blanca
Santa Fe, New Mexico 87501
1-800-727-9238

Type: **Private 4-year**
Overall campus environment: **Congenial, Intellectual, Creative**
Total enrollment: **417**
African-American students: **9**
Total graduate students: **64**
African-American graduate students: **2**
Percentage of applications accepted: **75%**
Average SAT/ACT score: **Not Required**
Percentage of African-American graduates: **50% (in 4 years)**
Percentage receiving financial aid: **N/A**
Average amount of award: **$12,167**
Percentage in ROTC programs: **N/A**
Number of faculty: **61**
Number of African-American faculty: **N/R**
Student/faculty ratio: **8 to 1**
Tuition: **$15,400**
Scholarship programs: **St. John's Grants**
Academic programs: **No major areas of study; curriculum is divided into several areas: Seminar, Preceptorial, Tutorials, Laboratory, Formal Lecture. The core curriculum is the Great Books Program.**
Most popular major: **N/A**
Prominent African-American graduates: **Charlotte King, Chairman of the Board, Catholic Archdiocese of Washington, D.C.; Theophus Smith, Professor of Theology, Emory University**
Prominent African-American faculty: **N/R**
Student organizations/activities: **N/R**
Administrative services and programs: **N/R**

St. John's college is not for everyone. The third-oldest college in the country, St. John's offers students a liberal arts education through a unique program that is both traditional and radical in its approach to teaching. The primary focus of education is reading and discussion in which students ponder highly intellectual and philosophical theories. Applicants to this school are selected primarily on the basis of a series of essays. According to the college, "Academic records, recommendations and college testing scores (SAT and ACT) are supplemental and may be made irrelevant by what a candidate writes." Students come from varied backgrounds and geographic locations.

African-American students liken St. John's program to the kind of education once afforded only the upper classes of society. While the school now aggressively seeks minority applicants, the presence of African-American students on the campus is nearly negligible, and the administration makes no apologies for it. Still, the school has graduated African-Americans of prominence, including a professor at Emory University and the chairman of the board of the Catholic Archdiocese in Washington, D.C.

St. John's is a small, cozy campus of just over 400 students. Applicants need to be aware that this is a college for a very independent and self-motivated student. What St. John's has to offer African-American and other students is a liberal arts education that provides an understanding and appreciation of language, mathematics, natural science and music as well as the development of the skills needed to effectively speak and write, measure, deduce and demonstrate. An opportunity also exists for students to attend one or both of the college's campuses in Annapolis and Santa Fe. Students with an interest in the fine arts, museums, archaeology and historical research will find the Santa Fe campus attractive. Overall, the curriculum on both campuses is designed to encourage students to think for themselves. It is believed that students should be able to envision and properly analyze real-life situations and arrive at a proper choice in a given situation.

The curriculum centers around the reading and discussion of what's called the Great Books Program. It is a seminar in which a group of students and two faculty members meet twice weekly to discuss readings from a set list, beginning in the freshman year with Homer and ending in the senior year with Freud. In the course of four years students read, among many others, Plato and Aristotle, Frederick Douglass, Sophocles and Aeschylus, the Bible and St. Augustine, Shakespeare and Cervantes, Kant and Hume, Rousseau and Lincoln, Hegel and Marx. It is the goal of St. John's to help students build a life philosophy and value system based on knowledge learned from Western civilization's greatest thinkers.

Traditionally, this kind of thought-provoking education has eluded African-Americans as they struggle with issues of basic survival and the distractions of family life and community responsibilities. Ironically, it is perhaps this kind of education that can most benefit African-American students as they are challenged to deal with an increasingly tense society.

St. John's has a poor record of attracting African-American students (about 2 percent of its student body), but it has made some attempts to create an environment in which these students can learn and grow. Some attention is paid to the classic works of African-Americans, including Frederick Douglass, Langston Hughes, Gwendolyn Brooks and Ralph Ellison, in required and elective courses. The very nature of the college facilitates a close relationship between students and faculty (called tutors), and the concerns and needs of African-American students are aired in that environment. There is also an effort to recruit African-Americans through a variety of means, including college fairs, direct mail, advertisements in African-American publications, and outreach programs with middle schools in Fairfax, Virginia, and Baltimore.

However, as one female African-American student pointed out, "St. John's is first and foremost a white college, perhaps not altogether on purpose, but in fact." She went on to say that students and tutors are fairly open-minded and that while there is discussion of African-American issues, they are usually singular in nature and not a part of the general educational program. "Do not imagine you will learn your history here. Know it before you come," she advised. Having said this, she praised St. John's as "quite exceptional" and suggested that "if learning excites you this is a school that has a lot to offer. It is very possible to come here as an African-American, gain much academically and be reasonably content socially."

St. Mary's College of Maryland
St. Mary's City, Maryland 20686
301-862-0380

Type: **Public/honors/liberal arts**
Overall campus environment: **Rural, Friendly, Innovative**

Total enrollment: **1511**
African-American students: **125**
Graduate students: **zero**
Percentage of applications accepted: **45%**
Average SAT score: **1174**
Average SAT African-Americans: **N/R**
Special admissions programs: **N/R**
Percentage of African-American graduates: **65%**
Percentage receiving financial aid: **74%**
Average amount of award: **$2500**
Percentage in ROTC programs: **N/A**
Number of faculty: **147**
Number of African-American faculty: **7**
Student/faculty ratio: **13 to 1**
Tuition: **$3,000 in state/$5,100 out of state**
Scholarship programs: **Matthias D'Sousa Fellowships, Maryland State Scholarships, St. Mary's College Scholarships**
Academic programs: **Divisions of Arts and Letters, History and Social Science, Human Development, Natural Science and Mathematics**
Most popular majors: **Biology, Economics, English, Human Development, History, Political Science, Psychology**
Prominent African-American faculty: **Lucille Clifton, poet and author, Professor of Literature**
Prominent African-American graduates: **N/R**
African-American student organizations/activities: **N/R**
Administrative services and programs: **Office of Minority Affairs**

St. Mary's in Maryland, a small "honors" liberal arts college on the southern shore of Maryland, is a college on the move. St. Mary's steadily rising SAT scores and its accomplished student body and faculty have made it a college to take notice of—and many have. A close look at the campus, its programs and its administration reveals why St. Mary's has become nationally recognized as one of the best small liberal arts colleges in the country.

Founded as a seminary for women, St. Mary's College has always been committed to providing a sound and affordable education. By the late 1960s the school had evolved into a four-year college, and in 1991 the state legislature named it an honors college—one of only two public honors colleges in the nation.

Until recently, St. Mary's was mostly unknown, but an ambitious capital program aimed at transforming the campus, physically and otherwise, has breathed new life into the school. Already in place is a modern complex of townhouse-style student residences and a new campus community center. The existing dormitories have all been refurbished and a major addition to the library has been completed which includes a new computer and media center. Plans are under way for a new science center, expansion of the gymnasium and a campus redesign which includes new courtyards, walkways and gardens.

In an effort to maintain adequate funding in these volatile economic times, St. Mary's president has proposed to the governor and state legislature an innovative plan that would in effect drop the state's share of the cost of running the college by about 8 percent while gradually doubling tuition over a five-year period. The plan would supply St. Mary's with a steady funding stream in the form of a block grant that would remain about the same each year, leaving the administration free to plan without fear of budget cuts. It would also, according to the administration, allow the college to continue providing financial assistance to students and families with limited incomes, ensuring the college's commitment to the diversity of its student body. Though some are concerned about the high tuition cost projected, others hail the college's president for such forward thinking.

It is this willingness to be unconventional that is attractive to many students, including many African-Americans, who say that this college offers a solid education in an atmosphere that is friendly, supportive and cooperative. There is plenty of evidence to support this opinion. A copy of the college's newspaper reveals that African-Americans have a significant role in college life at St. Mary's, from serving as college deans to receiving national achievement awards. In 1992, St. Mary's announced the college's first African-American valedictorian, an honors economics graduate who won more than 100 trophies in two years as a national forensic champion.

While the numbers of African-American students on campus remain very small, there is support for students, largely through the minority affairs office and the few African-American and other minority professors on campus. One of the college's most distinguished faculty members is poet and author Lucille Clifton. Students say the college's small size and reputation for supportiveness are major reasons they selected St. Mary's. "It takes a lot to keep up with the academics here and the support you receive from the faculty does help," said one student. "I don't think I would have gotten that kind of support from a larger school."

Besides an excellent faculty, students enjoy a curriculum that mirrors those of the most prestigious private liberal arts colleges, including impressive internships and study abroad opportunities that take students from Oxford to Paris and Costa Rica. The college also offers an exchange program with Johns Hopkins University and an independent study program.

Then there is the beauty of the campus, which sits on the tip of a peninsula where the Chesapeake Bay and Potomac River meet. Students who like the outdoors and living on the water will appreciate this still largely rural setting. St. Mary's is not totally isolated, however. The entire area is undergoing a transition into a more suburban area, marked by the recent construction of a hotel and an eclectic shopping mall including a movie theater and restaurant.

If you want to attend a good liberal arts college but cost is a factor, put St. Mary's at the top of your list.

Towson State University
Office of Admissions
8000 York Road
Towson, Maryland 21204-9940
410-830-2112/1-800-CALL-TSU

Type: **Public**
Overall campus environment: **Friendly, Supportive**
Total enrollment: **9,193**
African-American students: **827**
Graduate students: **1,568**
African-American graduate students: **110**
Percentage of applicants accepted: **64%**

Average SAT score: **800–1000**
Average SAT African-Americans: **N/R**
Special admissions programs: **N/A**
Percentage of African-American graduates: **40% in five years**
Percentage receiving financial aid: **35%**
Average amount of award: **$2500**
Percentage in ROTC programs: **N/R**
Number of faculty: **460**
Number of African-American faculty: **N/A**
Student/faculty ratio: **17 to 1**
Tuition: **$2,258 in state/$4,380 out of state**
Scholarship programs: **BUILD, Minority Award for Academic Excellence, CEEP, State Scholarships**
Academic programs: **Colleges of Allied Health Sciences and Physical Education, Education, Fine Arts and Communication, Liberal Arts, Natural and Mathematical Sciences; School of Business and Economics**
Most popular majors: **Mass Communication, Education, Business, health-related fields**
Prominent African-American faculty: **N/A**
Prominent African-American graduates: **N/R**
African-American student organizations/activities: **Black Student Union, The Brotherhood/The Sisterhood, NAACP College Chapter, Alpha Kappa Alpha, Delta Sigma Theta, Sigma Gamma Rho, Zeta Phi Beta, Alpha Phi Alpha, Iota Phi Beta, Kappa Alpha Psi, Omega Psi Phi, Phi Beta Sigma fraternities,** *Mahogany Magazine* **(radio show), Distinguished Black Marylanders Awards, Minority Students Reception, SAGE (Students Achieve Goals Through Education), African-American Cultural Center**
Administrative services and Programs: **Office of Minority Affairs, Minority Student Open House, Homecoming Sleeping Bag Weekend**

Towson State University is a public institution in a suburb of Baltimore. Begun more than 100 years ago as a teaching college, TSU has grown into one of Maryland's finest institutions of higher education, offering strong programs in communications, arts and sciences, business, fine arts and allied health sciences, as well as teacher education.

TSU's success is a direct reflection of the institution's ability to keep up with the times and the changing needs of students, employers and the community at large. Still largely a commuter college, TSU has kept its enrollment growing by responding to the needs of nontraditional adult and part-time students, transfer students and senior citizens, as well as business and industry, with special training programs.

However, TSU does attract a fair number of traditional students as well and boasts a residential population of 40 percent. The university currently has thirteen residence facilities, ranging from modern high-rises to more traditional two-story buildings. There are also apartment-style residences for upperclassmen.

Over the years, TSU has become increasingly popular with African-American students, who now represent almost 10 percent of the student population, reflecting the administration's recent effort to step up recruitment of this population. Through the Office of Minority Affairs, the administration developed a comprehensive strategy not only to attract African-American students to TSU but to ensure admission and enrollment of these students. Among other things, the administration visits more high schools with large enrollments of African-American students in and outside the state, has established a special weekend event (Homecoming Sleeping Bag Weekend) that gives students an opportunity to stay on campus, and holds an annual open house for prospective minority students. The university uses currently enrolled African-American students in its radio and television commercials, and in a very successful Phon-A-Thon, which gives potential students the opportunity to ask questions of current students. TSU has also increased its contact with African-American alumni.

Once on campus, African-American students are supported by a number of academic and cultural programs sponsored by the Office of Minority Affairs, including a mentoring program, an African-American Cultural Center and a number of student organizations, including a Black Student Union and chapters of national fraternities and sororities. University academic advising and counseling services serve all students on campus. One of the major attractions of the university is its increasing financial support of African-American students through various scholarship programs, including the Minority Award for Academic Excellence and the BUILD Scholarship, which cover full tuition and fees, and the CEEP (Community Enrichment Enhancement Partnership) awards, which offer up to $2,000 to students in good academic standing.

Although there are other minorities on campus, African-Americans are the largest group, and their increased involvement in campus life has not only changed the complexion of the university but created an environment that is comfortable for majority and minority students alike. "I attended TSU over a decade ago and while African-American students attended the school at that time, the level of involvement was not nearly as great," one graduate said. "Today, the campus is larger but in many ways it is a more friendly and tolerant environment."

TSU offers students a solid academic program, and unlike many universities, its professors focus on teaching rather than research and publishing. The program here is challenging but not so competitive that you will not be able to keep up with the work or have to focus all of your energies on academics rather than the total college experience. However, if you want more demanding courses, you can take advantage of the university's cooperative arrangements with nearby institutions like Johns Hopkins University, Goucher and Loyola colleges and the University of Maryland.

If you live in or near Maryland and are particularly interested in a good communications, business or health-related program but don't have a lot of money to spend, Towson State University is a good school with excellent academics and a reputation for its support of all its students.

University of Maryland–College Park
College Park, Maryland 20742
301-405-5595

Type: **4-Year public**
Overall campus environment: **Cordial, Supportive**
Total enrollment: **34,623**
African-American students: **3,438**
Graduate students: **9,262**
African-American graduate students: **617**
Percentage of applications accepted: **69%**

Percentage receiving financial aid: **19%**
Average amount of award: **$3,218**
Percentage in ROTC programs: **14% (Air Force)**
Number of faculty: **2,504**
Number of African-American faculty: **99**
Student/faculty ratio: **14 to 1**
. Tuition: **$2,214**
Scholarship programs: **Benjamin Banneker Scholarship, Frederick Douglass Scholarship, Presidential Minority, National Achievement scholarships, departmental scholarships**
Academic programs: **More than 300 majors including Business, Engineering, Education, Social Studies, Arts and Humanities, Agriculture**
Most popular majors: **Government and Politics, Psychology, English, Electrical Engineering, Computer Science, Business Administration**
Prominent African-American faculty: **Carmen Balthrop, Metropolitan Opera singer, Associate Professor of Voice.**
Prominent African-American graduates: **Carmen Balthrop, Metropolitan Opera singer; Richard Douglas, Vice President, Sun Diamond Growers, former Undersecretary of Agriculture; Len Elmore, Washington, D.C., attorney, CBS Sports commentator, former NBA player; Edith House, Vice President, Trahan, Burden & Charles Advertising; Jefferi Lee, Vice President, Operations, Black Entertainment Television; Parren Mitchell, former U.S. congressman, first Black undergraduate at UM–College Park; DeWayne Wickham, syndicated columnist, Gannett News Service**
African-American student organizations/activities: **Black Student Union,** *The Black Explosion* **Newspaper**
Administrative services and programs: **Minority Student Education Office, Intensive Education Development program, Remedial Math, Maryland English Institute, Office of Human Relations**

With nearly 35,000 students, the University of Maryland–College Park is one of the largest universities in the country; according to recent statistics it is a leading predominantly white institution in the number of African-American students it graduates each year.

That the University of Maryland should garner this distinction, given the bad publicity it has received over the past five years, is surprising. Its image has been tarnished by a number of incidents including the death of basketball star Len Bias and the departures of basketball coach Bob Wade, and its first African-American chancellor, John Slaughter. Most recently UM was challenged by a court ruling involving the university's popular Banneker minority scholarship program and a lawsuit filed by African-American employees at the university alleging discrimination.

These events may lead one to think that UM is an uncomfortable place for an African-American student. To the contrary, the university has worked to improve conditions for African-American students for a number of years and is commited to increasing enrollment. While admission to UM is fairly competitive, with average students scoring between 900 and 1000 on the SAT, the administration recognizes the importance of providing academic and cultural support to help African-American students graduate. Among other things, it has established a Minority Student Education office, which provides tutorial and mentoring services. There are also efforts through individual departments, such as the science and engineering department's BRIDGE program, which helps students make the transition from high school to college. A number of university and departmental scholarships provide needy minority students with financial support. While there is no data to support it, administrators believe that African-American students are succeeding at UM because of these kinds of interventions and want to continue to provide them.

UM is a huge campus which sits in the small town of College Park. There are plenty of fast-food restaurants, movie theaters and shops. But students need not go off campus for entertainment. The university's huge student union has restaurants, stores, lounges, bowling alleys, game rooms and even a movie theater. Students with transportation may want to also take advantage of the vast cultural and social life available in Washington, D.C. The nation's capital is within a half hour by car, and Baltimore is about an hour and a half away. Dormitory rooms are generally available (freshmen are encouraged to live on campus) and there is ample off-campus housing. For those who live on campus, a number of student organizations including the Black Student Union and Black Faculty and Staff Association organize social and cultural events. There is also a newspaper that deals with African-American student issues, called *The Black Explosion*. In addition, African-American students are strongly encouraged to participate in general campus activities, particularly the school newspaper, *The Diamondback*, which has received national recognition.

The university offers more than 300 major fields of study and has strong programs in agriculture, journalism, government and politics, engineering, and computer science. UM also has a prestigious faculty, including nearly 100 African-American professors, many of whom support students in one-on-one relationships and attend African-American student events.

Students considering UM need to know that they follow a long list of successful African-American graduates, including a former U.S. congressman, who was the first African-American to obtain an undergraduate degree at UM; a Metropolitan Opera singer; an advertising agency executive; a former NBA star and CBS sports commentator, and numerous business executives, political leaders, journalists and others. Students will also find a university environment supportive of African-American success.

Boston University
881 Commonwealth Avenue
Boston, Massachusetts 02215
617-353-9818

Type: **Private**
Overall campus environment: **Urban, Cosmopolitan, Liberal, Strong Academics**
Total enrollment: **28,660**
African-American students: **849**
Graduate students: **10,428**
African-American graduate students: **225**
Percentage of applications accepted: **73.1%**
Average SAT score: **1132**
Average SAT African-Americans: **1124**
Special admissions programs: **N/R**
Percentage of African-American graduates: **53%**
Percentage receiving financial aid: **70%**
Average amount of award: **$14,673**

Percentage in ROTC programs: **N/R**
Number of faculty: **1,908**
Number of African-American faculty: **N/R**
Student/faculty ratio: **15 to 1**
Tuition: **$16,590**
Scholarship programs: **University scholarships, need-based grants.**
Academic programs: **More than 130 majors including dentistry, medicine, law, theology**
Most popular majors: **Economics, English, Biology, Psychology, Engineering**
Prominent African-American faculty: **N/R**
Prominent African-American graduates: **Edward Brooke, first African-American U.S. Senator (Massachusetts); Barbara Jordan, professor LBJ School of Public Service, U of Texas–Austin, and member of Watergate Committee**
African-American student organizations/activities: **Black American Law Students, Minority Pre-Law, Minority Engineering, Pre-Health associations; NAACP; Caribbean Club; Black Drama Collective; Black Greek fraternities and sororities**
Administrative services and programs: **Office of Minority Affairs, Martin Luther King, Jr., Center for Career Education and Counseling Services, Learning Assistance Program, Black Mentoring Program, A Better Chance, Upward Bound**

Boston University, the largest private university in the country, is traditionally known as the "other university," after Harvard and MIT. Students will find the pace here typical of most big Northeast cities, with the full complement of busy streets and traffic jams. BU's campus, however, is not typical. The campus is spread around the city in a conglomeration of Gothic buildings, highrises, and brownstones. You'll be hard-pressed to spot a grassy area here, and it is not unusual to see a Burger King or car dealership next to a campus building. It may take a while to learn where the campus ends and the city begins.

Because of its cosmopolitan urban setting, BU has typically attracted upper-middle-class students from Long Island, New York City, and New Jersey, although many also hail from the

Midwest as well as from outside the United States. Minorities represent only about 6 percent of the student body, with about half of those African-American. To improve that number, the administration has an active recruitment program. Its membership in the Upward Bound summer program and ABC (A Better Chance), which identifies disadvantaged students and prepares them for college life, is one way the administration attracts more students. Once on campus, students generally fare well, and the university boasts a 53 percent graduation rate for African-Americans who make it past freshman year. A minority affairs office provides students with a menu of services, counseling and tutoring, and educational programs. The Martin Luther King, Jr., Center for Career Education and Counseling provides many of these services and holds workshops and seminars on test-taking, stress, and time management. A free service helps students develop better writing skills. The center also maintains a tape library of many of Dr. King's speeches and other materials. Additionally, the university's Mugar Library houses many African-American historical and literary collections in its Alcove and African Studies Library. Works by poet Nikki Giovanni and cartoonist E. Simms Campbell, and by Dr. King, are among this collection.

While African-American students are a small minority at BU, they report that the support services as well as the academic offerings have had a positive impact and contributed to their success at BU. African-American student organizations abound, too, and include a number of professional student groups like the Black American Law Students Association, Minority Engineering Society, and Minority Finance Society. There are a number of national Black Greek organizations on campus, although Greek life among the majority population is almost nonexistent.

Students report that faculty are fairly responsive to students' needs and that racial relations between white and African-American students are fairly good. Academics are demanding, and many students who have demonstrated potential but do not have the grades to match enroll in the College of Basic Skills, which provides a vigorous college-prep program. While there is some stigma attached to being in this program, it has enjoyed great success, the majority of its graduates enter other colleges of BU, and many go on to graduate programs at the university.

BU's urban location provides plenty of entertainment and cultural outlets for all students. There is an active Black drama group on campus, and students interact with the community through a number of organizations, including the NAACP and sororities and fraternities.

BU has a history of graduating successful African-Americans, many of them pioneers, like Edward Brooke, the first African-American U.S. senator, and Barbara Jordan, who sat on the Watergate Committee and is now a professor of Public Affairs at the LBJ School of Public Service, University of Texas–Austin.

Students who want a contemporary university setting with good academics and a solid reputation in a cordial atmosphere will want to consider Boston University.

Emerson College
100 Beacon Street
Boston, Massachusetts 02116
617-578-8610

Type: **4-year school of communications**
Overall campus environment: **Relaxed/Creative/Liberal**
Total number of students: **2,500**
African-American students: **100**
Graduate students: **500**
African-American graduate students: **15**
Percent of applications accepted: **72%**
Average SAT score: **968**
Average SAT African-Americans: **N/R**
Special admissions programs: **N/A**
Percent of African-American graduates: **N/R**
Percent receiving financial aid: **88%**
Average amount of award: **$5000**
Percent ROTC programs: **N/A**
Number of faculty: **100**
Number of African-American faculty: **N/R**
Student/faculty ratio: **18 to 1**
Tuition: **$12,695**
Scholarship Programs: **College scholarships, need-based grants**
Academic programs: **Divisions of Communication Disorders,**

Communication Studies, Mass Communications, Performing Arts, and Writing, Literature, and Publishing
Most popular majors: **Mass Communication, Film, Theater Arts**
Prominent African-American faculty: **N/R**
Prominent African-American graduates: **N/R**
African-American student organizations/activities: **AHANA, EBONI Cultural Center**
Administrative services and programs: **Office of Multicultural Affairs**

Emerson College offers a very specialized undergraduate and graduate program in the communication and performing arts. Students who attend this college are interested in pursuing careers in the media, the arts, business or education. Emerson has a longstanding reputation for offering excellent preparation in these fields.

Originally known as the Monroe Conservatory of Oratory, the college was renamed for its founder, Charles Wesley Emerson, in the late 1800s, when the school began offering a full college program. Emerson pioneered the communication arts specialty; in 1919 it became the first institution to establish a children's theater program; and it was one of the first to grant degrees in dramatic arts, speech pathology and public communication, including broadcast journalism. The college also opened New England's first educational FM radio station and first closed-circuit television studio with broadcast capabilities.

Today, Emerson offers programs in five divisions: Communications Disorders, Communications Studies, Mass Communication, Performing Arts, and Writing, Literature, and Publishing. The college offers a variety of internship opportunities as an integral part of its program. Students have the opportunity to work at local television and radio stations, advertising agencies, and production facilities. Emerson also maintains a close relationship with its alumni and other associates in the communications field. These people are regularly called on to provide career advice and job opportunities to students and graduates.

At Emerson you will not find a sprawling green campus, big athletic teams, or concentrations of study in fields outside communication arts. A small college in the historic Back Bay area of

Boston, Emerson is housed in a series of brownstone buildings. The atmosphere of the college is relaxed, creative and informal and there is a great deal of interaction between faculty and students. There is some housing on campus, but some students say it is often cramped, and they prefer living off campus.

African-Americans represent about 5 percent of the student population, but the number is slowly growing as the administration increases its efforts to attract students of color. One of its strategies is to have current African-American students recruit others over the telephone. In this way, potential students can get a firsthand account of campus life from students of color.

While small in number, African-American students at Emerson do have clout. Their student-run organization, EBONI (Emerson's Black Organization with Natural Interest), sponsors most of the social and cultural activities for African-American students and also acts as a support group for students who are having trouble adjusting to campus life. Students have also been influential in how they are perceived and even referred to: preferring the term AHANA (African-American, Hispanic, Asian, Native American), students are no longer called minorities. "AHANA is the term used when referring to students of color," said a graduate student. "We prefer AHANA to the word 'minority,' which is often interpreted as inferior or with deficiency."

Emerson is not without its problems. A recent incident in which a student appeared in a performance in blackface raised a flurry of questions and concerns from students and parents alike. "It was discovered that the young woman involved was the president of a campus organization and her resignation was called for by members of her organization and many other students on campus," said a student. "There are bound to be more incidents like this as students adjust to the culture shock of having more students of color on campus. However, I have to admire a school that takes this step and others to make people of color feel at home."

Students looking for training in the communications field in an environment that is creative, in a metropolitan area that promises the opportunity for real-life experience, would do well to consider Emerson College.

University of Massachusetts—Boston
Boston, Massachusetts
617-287-5420

Type: **Public**
Overall campus environment: **Supportive/friendly**
Total enrollment: **11,606**
African-American students: **1,119**
Graduate students: **2,155**
African-American graduate students: **90**
Percentage of applications accepted: **77%**
Average SAT score: **921**
Average SAT African-Americans: **832**
Special admissions programs: **Developmental Studies Program**
Percentage of African-American graduates: **20.4%**
Percentage receiving financial aid: **14.8%**
Average amount of award: **$5,543**
Percentage in ROTC programs: **N/A**
Number of faculty: **445**
Number of African-American faculty: **31**
Student/faculty ratio: **16 to 1**
Tuition: **$10,197 out of state/$4,094 in state**
Scholarship programs: **Dr. Benjamin Carson Scholarship for Minorities**
Academic programs: **54 majors—Colleges of Arts and Sciences, Management, Public and Community Service; African-American studies**
Most popular majors: **Management, English, Psychology, Nursing**
Prominent African-American faculty: **N/R**
Prominent African-American graduates: **N/R**
African-American student organizations/activities: **Black Student Center**
Administrative services and programs: **Developmental Studies Program, Affirmative Action Office, Office of Student Affairs**

The University of Massachusetts—Boston is an urban commuter campus about five miles outside Boston's downtown. Founded in 1965, the university recently absorbed Boston State College, expanding program offerings. U Mass—Boston offers fifty-four majors in a variety of fields, including an African-American studies program, through its Colleges of Arts and Sciences, Management, and Public and Community Service. A fair number of the university's programs are community- and human resource-based and provide students with skills needed to enter the work force after graduation.

One of the major attractions of this university for African-American students is its extensive academic support services and counseling. Its Developmental Studies Program provides disadvantaged inner-city students with an intensive eight-week summer program of remedial math and English to help them qualify for admission. Once students qualify, their progress is followed closely under a federally funded program called ACCESS that attempts to link high schools and colleges to improve the chances that urban students will succeed in college. This program and similar ones work closely with the Boston-area public schools.

About 95 percent of U Mass—Boston students come from Massachusetts, and more than 20 percent of the student body is minority. About 10 percent of the minority population is African-American. The urban setting of this public institution has attracted many students who are older or have family responsibilities; the university has responded to their needs by providing on-campus day care facilities on a sliding fee basis. Bilingual counseling is available for Hispanic students.

Students report that interaction with faculty and administrators on campus is good, particularly with African-American staff, who are supportive and encouraging. The university demonstrates its commitment to being a culturally diverse institution through its hiring of African-American faculty and staff. More than thirty faculty and fourteen administrators, including three deans and one vice chancellor, are African-American. There also seems to be good interaction between white and minority students on campus. The university's affirmative action office handles any complaints of harassment or discrimination and has established a formal grievance procedure through the Vice Chancellor of Student Affairs.

The Black Student Center is the focal point for most of the entertainment, conferences, and other activities on campus. One of the major events of the year is the Black Graduates' Ball, which takes place just before commencement. In addition, all students are encouraged to participate in all campus activities, including intramural sports, student government, publications and the campus radio station.

If you are from the Boston area or nearby, you may want to consider U Mass—Boston, particularly if you are interested in a less competitive school. This university provides an excellent education with programs similar to that of its more prestigious counterpart, the University of Massachusetts—Amherst, but in an environment that is more responsive to the special needs of African-American and other minority students.

Michigan State University
East Lansing, Michigan
517-355-0333

Type: **Public—Big Ten institution**
Overall campus environment: **Friendly**
Total enrollment: **42,088**
African-American students: **2,950**
Graduate students: **8,404**
African-American graduate students: **408**
Percentage of applications accepted: **79%**
Average SAT/ACT score: **1100/23**
Average SAT/ACT African-Americans: **N/A/19**
Special admissions programs: **CAAP (College Achievement Admissions Program)**
Percentage of African-American graduates: **66%**
Percentage receiving financial aid: **50%**
Average amount of award: **$6,120**
Percentage in ROTC programs: **15% Air Force, 7% Army**
Number of faculty: **2,668**
Number of African-American faculty: **N/R**
Student/faculty ratio: **9 to 1**
Tuition: **$8,700**
Scholarship programs: **Distinguished Minority Freshman Scholarship, National Achievement Scholarships, Minority Academic Excellence Awards**
Academic programs: **Colleges of Agriculture and Natural Resources, Arts and Letters, Business, Communication Arts**

and Sciences, Education, Engineering, Human Ecology,
Natural Science, Nursing, Social Science, Veterinary Medicine
Most popular majors: **Business, Education, Engineering**
Prominent African-American faculty: **N/R**
Prominent African-American graduates: **Ernest Green, Member
of "Little Rock 9," which integrated Arkansas schools; Magic
Johnson, former NBA star; Craig Polite, psychologist and
author; Ron Quincy, Director, Martin Luther King Center for
Nonviolent Change; Bubba Smith, former sports star and
actor**
African-American student organizations/activities: **More than
50 student clubs, Greek and social organizations; Workshop
for Excellence; Black Male Conference**
Administrative services and programs: **Office of Minority
Student Affairs, Minority Aide Program, Multi-Ethnic Center
Alliance, Minority Student Career Fair, Cultural Heritage
Rooms, Office of Supportive Services, Tutorial Program**

Michigan State University holds a number of distinctions for African-Americans. It is the university where Clifton Wharton, Jr.,
became the first African-American president of a major predominantly white university. MSU is also the university that produced
NBA and all-American star Magic Johnson, as well as a number of
other well-known and successful African-Americans such as
Mitchell Titus, partner in the largest African-American owned
CPA firm, and psychologist and writer Craig Polite.

MSU is a Big Ten school, one of the largest universities in the
country, with more than 42,000 students on a sprawling 5,000-
acre campus near Detroit. Students come from all over the state
and country and from more than 100 countries outside the
United States. They do so in search of a high-quality, diverse
education and access to the programs and services that a university of this size can provide. MSU offers more than 150 majors in
everything from agriculture and veterinary medicine to interior
design, textiles and clothing, and Latin American and Caribbean
studies. The university also boasts a plethora of facilities and
services, including a modern dormitory system that is the largest
in the country, with a capacity of 17,000 students. Many of the
dorms have health care facilities, weight rooms, game rooms,
libraries and study lounges. The university boasts the largest intra-

mural program in the nation and facilities that include three indoor pools and racquetball and tennis courts. Those who appreciate the arts will enjoy Kresge Art Museum and Wharton Center for the Performing Arts.

The mere size of this institution can create a feeling of isolation for any student, and the administration seems to understand that the challenge for minority students is even greater. African-American students comprise about 7 percent of the student body, and the university provides a number of programs and services to ease them into campus life. The minority student orientation program offers African-American, Hispanic, American Indian and Asian-Pacific Islanders academic counseling and tutoring. Many academic departments also provide their own programs for minority students—for example, Minority Students in Engineering, Vetward Bound and the Charles Drew Science Enrichment Program. The Office of Minority Student Affairs has also established a number of programs for students, such as the Minority Aide Program, which provides "resource agents" who offer peer counseling in each residence hall. The minority students' office also oversees minority student organizations, including the Office of Black Affairs, hosts workshops and conferences that benefit minorities, fields complaints of racial harassment and acts as a liaison between students and administrators.

African-American students are encouraged to get involved in campus life, and there are more than fifty minority student organizations, including chapters of the national Black Greek organizations and Black Caucus organizations in many of the residence halls—in addition to the more than 350 other student organizations, in which all students are encouraged to take an active part. One thing that brings students together here is sports. MSU has a number of African-American athletes and has won several national football and basketball championships over the years. There is tremendous school spirit and plenty of rivalry between MSU and the other Big Ten schools.

Students who want a diverse education in a setting that provides access to up-to-date facilities will find that MSU fits the bill, and is student-friendly. "One of the first things you notice about MSU is the diversity in the student population," said a freshman. "People are friendly here and you never need to feel alone."

Surprisingly, for an institution of this size, a fair number of the courses are taught by professors, not teaching assistants. Students say they are comfortable with the relationships they have with the faculty. "I make it a point of visiting my professors at least once a term," said a junior from Detroit. "For the most part I have found that professors are accessible. I have developed a good working relationship with one of my professors and we sometimes meet to talk and have a cup of coffee."

Students agree that MSU is what you make it and that if you feel shy and uncomfortable in a big place where you can easily get lost, MSU may not be for you. One student said, "My advice to new students is to take advantage of all the things MSU has to offer. Take everything and go further with it."

Hamline University
1536 Hewitt Avenue
St. Paul, Minnesota 55104-1284
612-641-2207/800-753-9753

Type: **4-year liberal arts, affiliated with Methodist Church**
Overall campus environment: **Supportive, Liberal, Academically Challenging**
Total enrollment: **1,448**
African-American students: **37**
Graduate students: **237**
African-American graduate students: **7**
Percentage of applications accepted: **84%**
Average SAT/ACT score: **1100/25**
Average SAT/ACT African-Americans: **1100/25**
Special admission programs: **N/A**
Percentage of African-American graduates: **65%**
Percentage receiving financial aid: **85%**
Average amount of award: **$11,200**
Percentage in ROTC programs: **N/A**
Number of faculty: **128**
Number of African-American faculty: **3**
Student/faculty ratio: **14 to 1**
Tuition: **$12,190**
Scholarship programs: **Scholarships for Students of Color at Hamline Law School**

Academic programs: **Liberal Arts and Sciences, Business, Physical Sciences, Communications, Masters Programs in Public Administration, Liberal Studies, Education, Professional Program in Law**
Most popular majors: **Psychology, English, Business Administration and Management, Pre-Law**
Prominent African-American graduates: **Jennifer Flack, J.D., first African-American Hamline Law School graduate to clerk for a Minnesota State Supreme Court Justice; Damon Ward, J.D., Editor-in-Chief,** *Hamline Law Review*
African-American student organizations/activities: **PRIDE (Promote Racial Identity, Diversity and Equality) House Program, Hamline Open Organization for Diversity**
Administrative services and programs: **Multicultural Affairs Office**

This four-year liberal arts college in St. Paul, Minnesota, has as its overriding goal for students to "examine critically your own values and recognize the existence of other value systems." This statement underlies a Hamline University tradition which holds that to be well educated, a student needs to develop a clear understanding of the values he or she uses daily; and further, that to be well prepared in life, one must also be able to recognize, understand and appreciate the values of others. Hamline challenges its students to achieve this overriding goal in every class.

The University takes a straightforward approach to the education it provides and has established 10 basic educational goals for all of its students. Graduates of Hamline should have developed an understanding of the liberal arts; be able to communicate effectively in writing and speech; use computers; reason logically; have gained work experience; be able to work independently; understand various disciplines; become familiar with American culture and how it interacts with others; develop an awareness of the experiences and contributions of women, minorities and other ethnic groups; and know in great depth at least one major field of study. These goals may seem ambitious, but are certainly attainable for students who put their minds to succeeding. Hamline faculty and administrators give all students and, in particular African-American students, a great deal of academic and emotional support. Hamline offers new minority students a two-day orientation program before they enroll. Once a student has been accepted, peer tutors in all majors can help them with their studies. There is also a Professional Mentoring Program, through which students can get firsthand advice from professionals on what it's like to work in a variety of fields. The university's Multicultural Affairs Director is specifically designated to work with students of color, give them support and help them succeed at Hamline. There are several cultural organizations on campus, such as PRIDE (Promote Racial Identity, Diversity and Equality) and the Hamline Open Organization for Diversity, which offer additional support to African-American students, plan cultural activities and generally promote cultural diversity among all students. "A supportive social environment is of utmost importance to me as an African-American student," said a 1991 graduate and current law student at the University of Minnesota. "A university that is utopian in structure, without racism, sexism, classism, is probably nonexistent. But I can certainly appreciate an atmosphere that is constantly pushing for and wanting change. Hamline's quest for cultural equality and diversity has been clear and insistent for the past four years."

While the number of African-American students at Hamline is small (about 2 percent), the university has begun a more aggressive recruitment effort to attract students from the community through churches, high schools and community agencies as well as through the traditional college fairs, direct mail and advertising. To demonstrate just how serious the administration is about attracting African-American students, Hamline has begun offering "travel grants" to admitted students to visit the campus before making a decision to enroll. It also awards preferential need-based financial aid to students of color. Additionally, students may apply for residence in a special dormitory called PRIDE House, which provides housing and social and cultural activities for African-American students.

Most of the inroads for African-American students at Hamline thus far seem to have been made in the law school. The university's recent efforts to increase the numbers of African-Americans at the undergraduate level have not yet borne fruit, but judging from the current crop of students it is just a matter of time. "I have talked with hundreds of students from colleges and universities across the country and I am convinced that Hamline is ahead of most when it comes to multiculturalism and diversity," said the Student Congress president who is African-American. "Students, faculty and staff realize that talent comes in all shapes, sizes and colors. Not every school is comfortable with the notion of electing an African-American to lead the student body."

University of Mississippi
University, Mississippi 38677
601-232-7378

Type: **Public**
Overall campus environment: **Cordial**
Total enrollment: **11,033**
African-American students: **1,000**
Graduate students: **1,741**
African-American graduate students: **295**
Percentage of applications accepted: **88%**
Average SAT/ACT score: **710/18**
Average SAT/ACT African-Americans: **N/A**
Special admissions programs: **N/A**
Number of faculty: **438**
Number African-American faculty: **16**
Student/faculty ratio: **19 to 1**
Tuition: **$3,683**
Scholarship programs: **African-American Student Scholarships; departmental, merit, and other scholarships**
Academic programs: **Art, Biology, English, History, Home Economics, Biomedical Science, Journalism, Music, Political Science, Psychology, Social Work, Criminal Justice, Business, Accounting, Education, Exercise Science and Leisure Management, Engineering, Computer Science, Pharmacy, Law, Southern Studies**
Most popular majors: **Business and Management, Education, Engineering, Health and Life Sciences**
Prominent African-American faculty: **N/R**
Prominent African-American graduates: **N/R**
African-American student organizations/activities: **Black Student Union, Black Campus Ministry, Black Greek sororities and fraternities**

Administrative services and programs: **Office of Minority Affairs, Learning Development Center**

A public university with an excellent academic reputation, the University of Mississippi, or Ole Miss, is a "traditionally Southern" university. Students have come here in the past not only for the academics but as a rite of passage into political and business careers, and sometimes to find a husband. This is a cohesive campus, and African-American and white students have each created an insular environment as a means of coping with campus life. Ole Miss is a school of contradictions. Nationally reputed to offer one of the best values in education, Ole Miss is also known as a "party campus" with too much emphasis on the Greek life. Located in the small town of Oxford, population about 10,000, Ole Miss is very much a part of the community. Many here show a desire to go back to a time when African-Americans "knew their place." For others, the experience at Ole Miss has been cordial and accommodating. "Being an African-American student at Ole Miss has been a surprisingly pleasurable experience," said one student. "Not at any point have I felt like an outsider."

In many ways Ole Miss is a big school masquerading as a small one. Besides an extensive undergraduate program, the university has a graduate school, a law school and a medical center in nearby Jackson, Mississippi. Yet there is a caring and nurturing side to the school, and an overall belief that students come first. One attractive feature of Ole Miss is its variety of admissions programs, which consider a wide range of academic levels from honor student to average student, transfer student to athlete. Admission is not very competitive, and requirements are made flexible depending on the student's needs and proven potential. However, although the university attempts to accommodate special needs, it does not compromise its standards of student achievement.

Ole Miss provides academic advisers, student development counselors and access to an on-campus learning center to help African-American students adjust to campus life and graduate. There is tutorial assistance in English, math and reading through the Center, Learning Development and one-on-one tutoring by residence hall advisers in each dormitory.

The Office of Minority Affairs works closely with minority students to help plan social and cultural events and to act as a liaison between students and administration should any problems arise. This office is also responsible for assisting in the recruitment of minorities and has established a program in which outstanding African-American students from state high schools stay on campus for several days, visiting with professors, students and staff.

A focal point of activity for African-American students at Ole Miss is the Black Student Union, which sponsors many cultural and social events, including an annual beauty pageant, homecoming dance, speaker series and activities for Black History Month. But when it comes to parties, the Greek organizations still prevail. Black Greek organizations on campus include Delta Sigma Theta and Zeta Phi Beta sororities and Kappa Alpha Psi and Phi Beta Sigma fraternities. Attempts are made to include all students in majority campus activities, but students complain that most are not culturally diverse, and they stick to socializing within their own groups. One area where there is a fair amount of interaction is sports, both intramural and varsity; the university has a strong reputation in intercollegiate football and basketball.

When all is said and done, Ole Miss has much to offer students who can put the past behind them and deal with the present. One student who has had a favorable experience advises others to consider the school's good points. "Ole Miss has great people, outstanding academics, caring faculty and an irrefutable reputation that makes it one of the top schools for anyone to attend."

Mississippi State University
Drawer EY
Mississippi State, Mississippi 39762
601-325-3920

Type: **Public**
Overall campus environment: **Conservative**
Total enrollment: **13,740**
African-American students: **1,698**
Graduate students: **2,134**
African-American graduate students: **159**
Percentage of applications accepted: **73%**
Average ACT score: **23.1**
Average ACT score African-Americans: **19.7**

Special admissions programs: **N/A**
Percentage of African-American graduates: **31.3%**
Percentage receiving financial aid: **N/R**
Average amount of award: **$1,000**
Percentage in ROTC programs: **11% Air Force/20% Army**
Number of faculty: **840**
Number of African-American faculty: **26**
Student/faculty ratio: **14 to 1**
Tuition: **$1,996 in state/$3,956 out of state**
Scholarship programs: **Weyerhauser Black Scholars, Dow Black Scholars, Thurgood Marshall Scholarship, Black Student Scholarships**
Academic programs: **Colleges of Agriculture and Home Economics, Arts and Sciences, Business and Industry, Education, Engineering, Veterinary Medicine; Schools of Accountancy, Architecture, Forest Resources; Graduate School**
Most popular majors: **Business Administration; Elementary Education; Chemical, Electrical, Mechanical Engineering; Marketing; Pre-Accounting; Communications; Psychology**
Prominent African-American faculty: **N/R**
Prominent African-American graduates: **Steven Cooper, Assistant to Jackson, Mississippi, Mayor Kane Ditto; Dr. Richard Holmes, emergency room physician; Dr. Sebetha Jenkins, President, Jarvis Christian College**
African-American Student organizations/activities: **Black Student Council, National Society for Black Engineers (NSBE), STAR Drama Society, Black Voices Choir, Black Business and Professional Association, Greek Association, Alpha Kappa Alpha, Delta Sigma Theta, Sigma Gamma Rho, Zeta Phi Beta, Alpha Phi Alpha, Kappa Alpha Psi, Omega Psi Phi, Phi Beta Sigma, NAACP, Black Outreach for Leadership and Development (BOLD) conference, Black History Trivia Bowl, Center for Cultural Diversity**
Administrative services and programs: **Holmes Cultural Diversity Center, Peer Counseling, Summer Program for Entry, Enrichment and Development (SPEED), IMAGE**

Mississippi State University is an example of an institution working to overcome a stereotypical image of schools in the South.

Mississippi State University / 197

With a 12 percent African-American student population, MSU is above average in its enrollment of students of color and has established myriad support programs to keep these students through graduation. The university has been able to minimize its dropout rate. "When I first came to Mississippi from Illinois, I expected to find deep racial hatred because of all the movies and stories I had seen and heard," one student said. "All of those things I found were very untrue."

The state's principal research university, MSU offers a first-rate education, particularly in the sciences and engineering. To attract more students to the school and to these fields in particular, the university has several full-tuition scholarship programs for students who have demonstrated academic ability. Among these programs are the Weyerhauser Black Scholars and Dow Black Scholars programs, the Thurgood Marshall Scholarship and the university Black Students program.

MSU offers academic programs in ten colleges and schools and has the state's only accredited programs in architecture, forestry, landscape architecture and veterinary medicine. Admission requirements are minimal, and though the majority of students are from Mississippi, a fair number come from other states in the South.

Besides traditional recruitment methods, the university employs student recruiters. Part of the attraction of MSU for African-American students is the financial support and the increased emphasis on cultural diversity. Many are also impressed by the number of African-American student organizations, and the cultural, social and academic advising programs. The Summer Program for Entry, Enrichment, and Development (SPEED) is one such program, designed to assist students whose ACT Score is below the required level for regular admission. Students are brought onto campus for a summer live-in program that combines group study sessions and personal development seminars. Housing and meal costs are split between the university's Department of Housing and Office of Academic Affairs, and students receive six credit hours for participating. When they return for the academic year students must enroll in a learning skills course and a freshman seminar course in addition to their regular studies.

The IMAGE program, sponsored by the College of Engineering, provides a similar program for engineering and science majors and offers tutoring, study groups and laboratory assistance. Additional help is provided to students through peer counseling and a number of other programs. The Holmes Cultural Diversity Center, for example, hires twelve peer counselors each year to work closely with freshmen and transfer students, acting as big brothers and big sisters to help them learn the ropes at MSU.

Students say taking advantage of the many African-American and other student organizations is the key to adjusting to campus life. "In my four years at MSU I have participated in a number of events and held positions in various organizations including the University Choir, the Phi Beta Sigma Convention and the Black Student Council as a member, tutor and president," wrote one student. "I am also a member of the student chapter of the NAACP. Being involved in this way has helped me feel a part of the school community."

Students can get involved in professional organizations such as the National Society of Black Engineers (NSBE), the STAR Drama Society, Black Voices (one of the school choirs), the Black Student Council or one of eight Black Greek organizations. Activities like the Black Outreach for Leadership and Development (BOLD) conference, the Black History Trivia Bowl and others also bring African-American students together.

Although MSU puts on its best cultural diversity face and has established a new attitude and programs to bring the university into the twenty-first century, the campus remains conservative and students still segregate themselves along racial lines. Students say they deal with this reality by remembering the sacrifices that so many people made so that they could attend schools like MSU and work hard to get the most out of the educational opportunities the school affords them. "I am taking a stand to gain the competitive edge that is needed to survive in this world today by getting a good education," said one student. "I feel that it is a responsibility, indeed, an obligation to take advantage of these opportunities given the struggles that so many of our forefathers encountered in our behalf."

Students say that their experience at MSU is generally good and that their peers, faculty and administrators are helpful. "I have learned a lot academically and personally at MSU," said one student, "and have developed many friendships that I know will last a lifetime."

St. Louis University
St. Louis, Missouri 63103
1-800-325-6666

Type: **4-year liberal arts jesuit (Catholic)**
Overall campus environment: **Good/culturally diverse**
Total enrollment: **6,423**
African-American students: **578**
Graduate students: **1,867**
African-American graduate students: **N/R**
Percentage of applications accepted: **49.6%**
Average ACT score: **21–29**
Average ACT African-Americans: **15–20**
Special admissions programs: **N/A**
Percentage of African-American graduates: **43%**
Percentage receiving financial aid: **80%**
Average amount of award: **$8,740**
Percentage in ROTC programs: **N/A**
Number of faculty: **788**
Number of African-American faculty: **36**
Student/faculty ratio: **14 to 1**
Tuition: **$9,880**
Scholarship programs: **Ernest A. Calloway Scholarship, Roy Wilkins Scholarship (St. Louis residents)**
Academic programs: **More than 80 major fields of study including Aeronautical Engineering, Business Administration, Nursing, Social Services, Allied Health Professions, Education, Mathematics**
Most popular majors: **Business, Allied Health (Physical and Occupational Therapy), Social Work, Pre-professional Medical Program, Aeronautical Studies, Nursing**
Prominent African-American graduates: **N/R**
Prominent African-American faculty: **N/R**
African-American student organizations/activities: **Black Student Alliance, Black Pre-Med Club, Black Business Student Association, Black Law Students Association, Black Alumni Association, Afro-American Studies Club, Afro-American fraternities and sororities**
Administrative services and programs: **START (Students**

Together Against Racial Tension), Student Educational Services Center

St. Louis University is a four-year liberal arts institution affiliated with the Jesuit order of the Roman Catholic Church. SLU (Slew), as it is called, is a midsized institution in the metropolitan area of St. Louis, Missouri. More than 25 percent of the 6,500 students enrolled here are minorities, with African-Americans comprising just under 10 percent of that number. SLU's philosophy of producing academically and morally prepared graduates seems to have a positive impact on African-American and other minority students. Students report that race relations are generally good, and they seem to interact well.

A historic institution, SLU is said to have been the first college established west of the Mississippi. Today it is primarily a commuter college that is enjoying a revival of interest and attendance due in part to recent renovation and a rebuilding of St. Louis's urban center. The campus is now a combination of Gothic buildings and futuristic structures. Its new look and solid programs attract students mostly from within the state and nearby areas in the Midwest.

SLU has much to offer, with more than eighty courses of study, including its most popular programs in pre-med and pre-law as well as business, allied health (physical and occupational therapy), social work, aeronautical studies and other technical majors. Academic requirements for admission are less competitive than at many other universities; the programs and faculty have a good reputation in the community. In keeping with the Jesuit philosophy of educating the whole person, SLU has a core curriculum of humanities, math and natural and social sciences which all students are required to complete. This base of courses is designed to develop a student's ability to think analytically and sharpen his or her communication skills. It is the administration's belief that this kind of training will help students grow and become people who can think, reason and deduce, and in that way find solutions to the many societal problems they will face as adults.

SLU sets an admirable standard of decency and fair play. The administration has professed a commitment to cultural diversity, and it seems that a great deal of effort has gone into fostering good relations among students of all cultural, social and racial backgrounds. Perhaps the university's most successful effort is its START (Students Together Against Racial Tension) program, which promotes greater understanding of all cultural and ethnic groups. The administration has been supportive of events like the silent vigil for peace held after the verdict in the Rodney King beating trial in spring 1992, which attracted more than 400 participants from all over the St. Louis area. It is also concerned about poverty, illiteracy, poor health care and other ills of society, and strongly supports student involvement in alleviating these problems through volunteerism. Indeed, student involvement in the community is well known and encouraged, with volunteers working as tutors, counselors and mentors in such programs as Big Brothers/Big Sisters.

African-American students will find a number of academic and counseling support services at SLU, including the university's Student Educational Services Center and a very helpful and concerned faculty. There are also myriad African-American student organizations, such as the Black Student Alliance, Black Business Student Association, Black Pre-Med Club, Black Law Students Association, Black Alumni Association, and a number of African-American national fraternities and sororities. Students who choose SLU will find an institution of high moral standards and respect for the individual. "Never did I lose my dignity or understanding of what and who I am: an African-American male," remarked one student. "In fact, as I graduated I realized that I was a winner with my degree and my heritage."

Creighton University
2500 California Plaza
Omaha, Nebraska 68178
402-280-2703

Type: **Private Jesuit (Catholic)**
Overall campus environment: **Conservative**
Total enrollment: **6,100**
African-American students: **186**
Graduate students: **2,000**
African-American graduate students: **70**
Percentage of applications accepted: **85%**

Average ACT score: **20**
Average ACT African-Americans: **N/A**
Special admissions programs: **N/A**
Percentage of African-American graduates: **68%**
Percentage receiving financial aid: **100%**
Average amount of award: **$10,181**
Percentage in ROTC programs: **5%**
Number of faculty: **609**
Number of African-American faculty: **11**
Student/faculty ratio: **14 to 1**
Tuition: **$9,370**
Scholarship programs: **Presidential Black Scholars, Mildred D. Brown Journalism Scholarship, SEEDs Program**
Academic programs: **50 undergraduate majors and professional schools in medicine, law, dentistry, pharmacy, and allied health**
Most popular majors: **Chemistry, Biology, Psychology, Political Science, Accounting, Finance, Nursing**
Prominent African-American faculty: **N/A**
Prominent African-American graduates: **Susan McNiel, J.D., Colonel, U.S. Army; Clarence Shields, team physician for L.A. Rams; J. Clay Smith, J.D., law professor, member Creighton Board of Directors**
African-American student organizations/activities: **African-American Student Association, Black Greek clubs**
Administrative services and programs: **Peer Advising, Minority Retreat, Mentoring Program, Minority Student Orientation, Minority Student Advising**

One thing that African-American and white students agree on about Creighton University is that it is a no-nonsense university that provides excellent training for students interested in medicine, law and the sciences. A Jesuit (Catholic) university, Creighton is a rather conservative institution and is the type of college that many parents will feel comfortable about because of rules such as those that prohibit unescorted men on women's dorm floors after midnight and mete out strict punishment to student couples caught "cohabitating" in dorm rooms. There are also restrictions on alcohol use on campus. Generally, the university subscribes to a "values-based" education seeking to develop stu-

dents well rounded in academics, social behavior and competition
(through sports) whose morals are based on religious principles.
Students who have attended Catholic secondary schools would
do well here because the philosophy and expectations are very
similar.

African-Americans comprise only about 3 percent of the student population, and the administration has stepped up its recruitment efforts. Students who are accepted receive generous
financial assistance based on need, and the university has several
academic, counseling and tutoring services to assist students in
making the transition to the sometimes demanding curriculum.
Although the administration reports a fairly low student-to-
faculty ratio, 14 to 1, it seems that African-American students are
not comfortable reaching out to faculty for academic assistance
and counseling. Rather, they rely on administration academic
advising and tutoring programs such as the Peer Advising program, Mentoring Program, Minority Student Advising and Student Support Services, which is open to all students but is much
used by minority students. However, many students develop close
relationships with professors.

Interaction between African-American and white students on
this campus is fairly good, and the administration reports no
racial incidents. Still, the administration has established awareness programs and similar forums to discuss cultural and racial
issues. African-American students tend to socialize among themselves through student organizations like the African-American
Association, professional organizations which sponsor cultural
events, mixers, movies and other entertainment. The Greek life is
big on campus here, and African-American fraternities and
sororities are popular and are responsible for a lot of the parties.

Creighton offers students a great deal of support to achieve
academically and socially, but for African-American students who
are not from the area or at least the Midwest, life here may cause
culture shock. Students must be fairly independent and not require the nurturing of a small liberal arts or predominantly African-American institution. For those who can handle this and who
want a strong academic base in medicine, law or science, Creighton may be a candidate.

Trenton State College
Hillwood Lakes
CN 4700
Trenton, New Jersey 08650
(609) 771-2131
1-800-345-7354 (NY, PA, DE, CT)

Type: **Public**
Overall campus environment: **Cordial/competitive/supportive**
Total enrollment: **7,143**
African-American students: **471**
Graduate students: **973**
African-American graduate students: **14**
Percentage applications accepted: **39%**
Average SAT score: **1120**
Average SAT African-Americans: **N/R**
Special admissions programs: **Educational Opportunity Fund**
Percentage African-American graduates: **N/R**
Percentage receiving financial aid: **55%**
Average amount of award: **$3,250**
Percentage in ROTC programs: **N/R**
Number of faculty: **315**
Number African-American faculty: **13**
Student/faculty ratio: **15 to 1**
Tuition: **in-state $3,687/out-of-state $5,289**
Scholarship programs: **TSC Minority Scholarships,**
Presidential Scholarships
Academic programs: **Schools of Arts and Sciences, Business,**
Education, Technology, Nursing and Teacher Preparation.
Most popular majors: **Biology, Business Administration,**
Elementary/Early Childhood Education, English, Law and
Justice
Prominent African-American faculty: **Dr. Gloria Dickinson,**
Professor, African-American Studies; Don Evans, Associate
Professor, African-American Studies
Prominent African-American graduates: **N/R**
African-American student organizations/activities: **Over twenty**
minority organizations including the Gospel Choir, *Utimme*
Umana/La Voz Oculta **Magazine**

Administrative services and programs: **Minority Mentoring Program, Educational Opportunity Fund, Expectations.**

Founded in 1855 as New Jersey's first public college, Trenton State College is highly regarded for its strong emphasis on teaching, small class size, and the wide range of academic programs offered in its five schools of arts and sciences, business, nursing, technology and education. TSC has been rated as one of the best educational values in the nation by several national publications that rank colleges each year.

Public institutions often are viewed as having lower standards than private ones, but this is not true of TSC. The average SAT score of students accepted to TSC is 1000 or better. SAT scores and good high school grades are not the only criteria used in the selection process, however. Those seeking admission to TSC should demonstrate that they have participated in sports, community or volunteer work, hobbies, part-time and/or summer jobs, or other pursuits. In short, like many top schools, TSC is looking for well-rounded students with a strong desire to succeed.

Students come to TSC for a number of reasons, including its excellent academic reputation, variety of programs, beautiful campus (bordered by two natural lakes), and proximity to New York and Philadelphia. However, one of its most appealing features is its distinguished and dedicated faculty. "My most important goal as an educator is to create an environment in the classroom that enables students to become proficient in creative thinking," says an economics professor.

At TSC, the emphasis is on teaching rather than research and publishing—although many of its faculty are active researchers, authors, artists, performers, and regular contributors in their fields—and it is not unusual for faculty members to give students an opportunity to assist them in their work. The average class size at TSC is small (usually less than 20 students) and all classes are taught by professors, not graduate assistants. More important, students say that professors are accessible, willing to help, and generally supportive. "I love watching creative people—students—develop," says an African-American Studies professor. "I don't care if their work is brilliant or not. It's their evolution that

I find fulfilling. I always begin with the assumption that everyone in the class is an artist."

The belief that all students can achieve excellence is pervasive at TSC as is the administration and faculty commitment to help students do so. TSC has an impressive record of retaining a large majority of its students, and its four-part freshman orientation program, "Expectations," is nationally renowned for achieving this result. Expectations (a program for all students), includes June Advisement Week, a summer reading program, a Welcome Week of seminars and other activities, and a 10-week college seminar. Over the past five years, the rate of students returning for their sophomore year has increased from 89 to 92 percent.

Additionally, a Minority Mentoring program pairs African-American and Hispanic students with members of the faculty and staff to advise, guide, and encourage them through graduation from TSC. There also is the Educational Opportunity Fund for students with demonstrated potential who were academically underprepared in high school. Students admitted to TSC through this program must complete a six-week summer remedial program, during which they are given academic advisement, study skill–building, tutoring, career counseling, and motivational seminars.

Students interested in pursuing professional degrees in medicine and law will find that TSC provides excellent preparation and that its graduates are accepted at the finest schools, including Columbia University College of Physicians and Surgeons, University of Pennsylvania School of Medicine, Howard University College of Medicine, Harvard University, Cornell and Stanford, to name a few. In addition students can take advantage of a combined BS-MD degree program offered in conjunction with the New Jersey Medical School in Newark. Students admitted to this six-year program must, among other things, maintain a 3.0 average for three years at TSC and undergo interviews at both schools. TSC offers a similar seven-year combined BS-OD (optometric doctor) degree program with SUNY College of Optometry in New York City.

The supportive atmosphere of TSC is particularly beneficial to African-American students, who say that the faculty at TSC sincerely care. "Professor Karras teaches the Roman Empire and the Roman Republic," says a history student. "He is so tough—you really have to rise to the occasion to meet his standards. I know I have become a better writer because of him and plan to take as many of his courses as I can."

In addition to fine academics, TSC offers more than 140 student organizations and 20 minority organizations including *Utimme Umana/La Voz Oculta,* the minority magazine, Gospel Choir, and cultural activities like visits to the famous Apollo Theater in New York City. African-American students will find that there is plenty of room for their involvement in campus activities and they are encouraged by the administration to become so engaged.

TSC offers all students an excellent education in a caring and supportive environment in which any student interested in succeeding can learn, and African-American students will find that even their small numbers on this campus will not adversely affect that fact.

University of New Mexico
Albuquerque, New Mexico
505-277-2446

Type: **Public**
Overall campus environment: **Cordial**
Total enrollment: **25,009**
African-American students: **496**
Graduate students: **4,940**
African-American graduate students: **58**
Percentage of applications accepted: **85%**
Average ACT score: **22**
Average ACT African-Americans: **20**
Special admissions programs: **N/A**
Percentage of African-American graduates: **12% (over 6 years)**
Percentage receiving financial aid: **63%**
Average amount of award: **$4,392**
Percentage in ROTC programs: **4.9%**
Number of faculty: **1,420**
Number of African-American faculty: **10**
Student/faculty ratio: **15 to 1**
Tuition: **$5,000**

Scholarship programs: **ZIA Scholarships, Abraham Lincoln Mitchel Scholarship**
Academic programs: **Numerous majors in Arts and Sciences, Engineering, Law, Medicine, Education, Business, Fine Arts**
Most popular majors: **Psychology, Business, Education, University Studies**
Prominent African-American graduates: **Robin Cole, Pittsburgh Steelers; Michael Cooper, Assistant Coach, Los Angeles Lakers; Ed Lewis, Publisher, *Essence* magazine; John Lewis, musician/composer, Modern Jazz Quartet; Don Perkins, Dallas Cowboys**
African-American student organizations: **Black Student Union, National Society of Black Engineers, NAACP, Black Greek fraternities**
Administrative services and programs: **African-American Student Services, African-American Student Center, African-American Studies, Student Diversity Council**

Besides the excellent academic programs it offers, the multicultural environment and the great climate in which you can play tennis in the morning and ski in the afternoon, there are no special reasons to attend the University of New Mexico. Seriously speaking, this large university in Albuquerque, on the banks of the historic Rio Grande and bordered by the majestic Sandia Mountains, offers students more than great weather and a great view. African-American students will find a strong academic program with an entire interdisciplinary unit on Ethnic and African-American studies that includes courses like Emancipation and Equality, the Black Experience in the United States, as well as courses in Swahili and Arabic, Black theology and philosophy, and a menu of related subjects. Additional Afrocentric courses are interwoven in major fields of study like history, art and economics. However, African-American students considering the University of New Mexico need to be aware they are a minority within a minority. The dominant minority is Native Americans and Hispanics, who are indigenous to the area. The university places a great deal of emphasis on these groups and the study of their history, art and culture, and African-Americans may think that little attention is given to their needs. Indeed, the administration admits that a recent racial incident led to the establishment of a

Student Diversity Council which discusses issues of all cultural groups in an effort to foster greater understanding and tolerance.

Perhaps one question that African-Americans here must answer is whether they can function at a large institution which by its nature is impersonal and sometimes insensitive to individual needs. More than 25,000 students are enrolled at UNM, and African-Americans represent less than 2 percent of the total. Because of their small numbers, even the administration's best intentions may fail to prevent the isolation a student can feel on a campus of this size. Admittedly, increasing the numbers of African-American students on campus will improve life for all students, but if a student is mismatched to the school, it will do little to improve his or her chance of success.

For students who can thrive in a large university setting, UNM offers plenty of opportunity and services. In the past twenty years, UNM has moved into the twenty-first century of high technology and computers. For a small fee students can tap into the university's system and gain access to the undergraduate catalog, campus phone directories, current class schedules, library catalogs, a selected schedule of courses, and modems and electronic mail systems. The administration provides a computer consultant to troubleshoot and gives students discounts on purchases of computer equipment and software. UNM has seven libraries on campus, six museums and four centers of performing arts, as well as vast media and communication services including videotaped courses, computer graphics and extensive state-of-the-art audiovisual equipment.

Social life for African-Americans centers around events sponsored by student organizations such as the Black Student Union and Black Greek fraternities. Students are also involved with the African-American community of Albuquerque. Sports are big on the UNM campus, and the university has produced a huge share of professional African-American athletes in football, basketball and track.

UNM is moderately competitive, and students will find a number of support services to help them adjust to campus life. The African-American Student Services Program provides academic advising, tutorial and financial aid services. However, many students find this is not enough to help them through the maze of academic and social life. One student said, "The African-

American faculty and administrators are very helpful but at times I feel like an outsider at UNM." In general, the university does a good job of providing academic and cultural support to African-Americans, but students will need to decide whether they can handle being on a campus where they are a double minority.

Columbia University
212 Hamilton Hall
Columbia Undergraduate Admissions
New York, NY 10027
212-854-2522

Type: **Private Ivy League**
Overall campus environment: **Urban, Intellectual, Academically Demanding**
Total enrollment: **4,200 (Columbia College)**
African-American students: **420**
Graduate students: **12,000**
African-American graduate students: **600**
Percentage of applications accepted: **30%**
Average SAT score: **1230–1400**
Average SAT African-Americans: **N/R**
Special admissions programs: **Yes**
Percentage of African-American graduates: **90%**
Percentage receiving financial aid: **75%**
Average amount of award: **N/A**
Percentage in ROTC programs: **N/A**
Number of faculty: **400**
Number of African-American faculty: **12**
Student/faculty ratio: **10 to 1**
Tuition: **$23,551**
Scholarship programs: **Higher Education Opportunity, National Opportunity Programs**
Academic programs: **African-American Studies, Ancient Studies, Anthropology, Applied Chemistry/Geophysics/Mathematics/Physics, Archaeology, Art History, Astronomy, Astrophysics, Biochemistry, Bioengineering, Biology, Biology-Psychology, Chemical Engineering/Physics,**

Chemistry, Civil Engineering, Classics, Comparative
Literature, Computer Science, East Asian Studies,
Economics, Economics-Mathematics/Philosophy/
Statistics, Electrical Engineering, English, Environmental
Sciences, Film Studies, French, Geochemistry, Geology,
German, History, History-Sociology, Human Rights,
Industrial Engineering, Italian, Mathematics, Mechanical
Engineering, Medieval and Renaissance Studies, Metallurgy
and Materials Science, Middle East Studies, Mining and
Mineral Resources Engineering, Music, Operations Research,
Philosophy, Physics, Political Science, Pre-Law, Pre-Medicine,
Psychology, Regional Studies (African, Central European,
Latin American, Russia and the Republics), Religion, Russian
and Slavic Languages-Literature, Sociology, Spanish,
Statistics, Theater Arts, Urban Studies, Visual Arts, Women's
Studies
Most popular majors: English, Political Science, Economics,
Electrical Engineering, Computer Science, Mechanical
Engineering
Prominent African-American graduates: Langston Hughes,
poet; Paul Robeson, actor, singer, civil rights activist; George
Starke, former captain, Washington Redskins; Franklin
Thomas, President, Ford Foundation; Mario Van Peebles,
actor and filmmaker
Prominent African-American faculty: Barbara J. Fields,
Professor of History and author, *Slavery and Freedom on the
Middle Ground: Maryland During the 19th Century*; Charles V.
Hamilton, Professor of Political Science
African-American student organizations/activities: Black
Students Organization, Charles Hamilton Houston Pre-Law
Society, Charles Drew Pre-Medical Society, National Society of
Black Engineers, Roundtable, Gospel Choir, *Black Heights*
magazine, Kwanzaa Celebration, Black Heritage Month, Third
World Weekend
Administrative services and programs: United Minorities Board

Columbia is the smallest of the nation's Ivy League colleges and
one of the best. Its reputation as a leading educational institution
is worldwide and its graduates are leaders in politics, government,

business, science and the arts. They include Nobel prize winners, fourteen New York City mayors, ten New York State governors and a graduate in every session of the U.S. Congress.

Columbia's faculty are also renowned, having made major contributions in a number of fields. The first experiments with X rays were developed here, as well as the technology that led to long-distance telephone. FM broadcasting, the laser and the discovery of the cause of hepatitis are all products of research by Columbia faculty. It's no wonder that many key advisers and presidential cabinet members have been recruited from the ranks of the Columbia faculty.

Columbia offers students a highly intellectual and academically rigorous program. With emphasis on a strong liberal arts education, the sciences and engineering, Columbia prepares its students to meet the challenges of the real world by teaching them the skills to reason and think independently. The core curriculum of Contemporary Civilization, Literature and Humanities, and Fine Arts and Music provides the foundation for study in any major field of interest from journalism to chemical engineering.

Many African-American students agree that adjusting to Columbia can be challenging. "Generally, Columbia is like any other predominantly white college, and a student's adjustment has more to do with how hard a student is willing to work," said one student. "There are problems, like on any campus. However, there are support systems in place to help you adjust." Among Columbia's most popular programs for African-Americans and other minority students is its Higher Education Opportunity Program (HEOP) and the National Opportunity Program (NOP), which provides admissions assistance and financial aid to students who otherwise would not have an opportunity to attend Columbia. Under these programs, both in-state and out-of-state students are provided assistance, including a summer on-campus program before the freshman year and tutoring and academic and career advising after admission.

In addition, Columbia's African-American student organizations provide academic and social support to students; there are preprofessional groups like the Charles Hamilton Houston Pre-Law Society, the Charles Drew Pre-Medical Society, the National Society of Black Engineers and the Roundtable business society. Students may also take advantage of the social and cultural activities offered through the Black Student Organization, such as the Kwanzaa Celebration and Black Heritage Month, as well as appearances by speakers such as Angela Davis and Kwame Toure and shows such as *The Wiz*.

One of the very special features of Columbia is its location in New York City—the arts, culture and entertainment center of the world. Students at Columbia are exposed to enormous cultural and social opportunities through the city's museums, jazz clubs, theaters and music and dance centers. Just being on the streets of New York, hearing the many languages spoken and being exposed to people of all cultures and countries, is an education in itself.

And because of Columbia's location in Harlem, African-American students will find an opportunity to experience their culture in a way they cannot anywhere else in the country. The home of many great African-American leaders, artists and institutions, Harlem remains today a symbol of African-American culture and pride, and even with its problems is a center of hope for the future. The Columbia community at large often does not like to deal with the fact that it is located in Harlem, and indeed strives to set itself apart from the community; but African-American students can use this opportunity to connect with Harlem, and their history.

Those considering Columbia need to understand that it is a highly selective and competitive Ivy League college which has the advantage of being small and fairly liberal (although a few years ago a racial incident on campus led to arrests by New York City police). Students say that you will find both tolerance and intolerance here—but overall, a solid academic program at an institution whose name will go a long way to help you meet your future goals.

New York University
22 Washington Square North
New York, New York 10011
212-998-4500

Type: **Private**
Overall campus environment: **Urban, Creative, Intellectual**

Total enrollment: **12,153**
African-American students: **1,008**
Graduate students: **8,711**
African-American graduate students: **N/R**
Percentage of applications accepted: **63%**
Average SAT score: **N/R**
Special admissions programs: **Higher Education Opportunity Program, C-Step Program**
Percentage of African-American graduates: **60%**
Percentage receiving financial aid: **66%**
Average amount of award: **$10,500**
Percentage in ROTC programs: **N/A**
Number of faculty: **1,226**
Number African-American faculty: **N/A**
Student/faculty ratio: **13 to 1**
Tuition: **$16,750**
Scholarship programs: **NYU Scholars Program**
Academic programs: **160 majors in 7 Undergraduate Schools: Tisch School of the Arts, College of Arts and Sciences, Stern School of Business, School of Education, Health, Nursing and Arts Professions, School of Social Work, School of Continuing Education, Gallatin Division**
Most popular majors: **Pre-Med, Journalism, Business, Arts**
Prominent African-American graduates: **Fritz W. Alexander II; Lou Gossett, Jr., actor; Dr. Lorraine Hale; Carol Jenkins, television anchor, New York City; Spike Lee, independent filmmaker; Constance Baker Motley, judge, civil rights lawyer; Congressman Charles Rangel (New York)**
Prominent African-American faculty: **N/A**
African-American student organizations/activities: **Black Business Students Association, Black Dance Collective, Black Science Students Organization, Black Student Service Center, Organization of Black Women**
Administrative services: **Office of African-American Student Services**

The Big Apple is the home of New York University, a private university offering undergraduate and postgraduate degrees and known as one of the finest universities in the country. The big question for most students considering NYU is whether they can adapt to the New York City lifestyle; adapting is necessary if a student is to take full advantage of what NYU and the city have to offer. For all of its problems, New York City remains the arts and cultural capital of the nation and a financial and business center. There are few aspects of business and industry on which the city does not have some influence, including advertising, publishing, music and fashion. Few places offer as much excitement as New York City.

NYU is in the midst of this excitement and as such offers students a unique opportunity to experience life among a community of students and faculty who come from all over the country and the world, attracted by the city itself. NYU faculty are world-famous scholars, researchers, artists, Nobel laureates and Pulitzer prize winners. Its student body is international and represents a wealth of cultures and perspectives.

A highly selective university, NYU offers a wide range of academic study, with more than 2,500 courses and 160 major fields from which to choose in the arts and sciences, business, education, health, fine arts and performing arts, natural sciences and technology. Admissions are based on a combination of standard test scores, high school grades, recommendations, talent and ability, as well as a student's social and economic background. NYU's academic program is rigorous, and students are expected to develop the ability to think and apply ideas from a wide range of sources to excel academically. Vast resources are available to students, including the Bobst Library, one of the largest open-stack research libraries in the world and the myriad other resources available in New York City itself. The payoff for students is a successful college experience; more than 75 percent of NYU graduates go on to obtain postgraduate degrees, many of them in medicine and law.

The international flavor and urban setting of NYU provide African-American students with a comfortable environment in which to learn and grow. African-American students at NYU follow a legacy of successful graduates, the best known of whom are filmmaker Spike Lee, actor Louis Gossett, Jr., Congressman Charles Rangel and judge and civil rights lawyer Constance Baker Motley. Many students believe that the cultural composition of the university places less emphasis on race, thereby removing a barrier to a successful academic experience. "Attending NYU is a 'real world' experience, far from the sheltered environment of many colleges," said one student. "Here you learn as much from your surroundings and the many cultures on campus as you do from professors." A number of African-American student organizations provide academic and social support; the Black Business Students Association, Black Dance Collective and Black Science Students Organization offer support in particular fields of interest.

The administration strongly encourages participation in all aspects of college life, including the more than 250 clubs, the two radio stations, six newspapers, twelve journals and magazines, instrumental and vocal groups and numerous sports teams.

Generally, students seem to get along with each other at NYU. "It would be unrealistic to think that there aren't differences in opinions that occur at NYU," said one student. "However, that's not a NYU thing, it's a life thing. NYU is not perfect, but it brings out the best in its students."

**Sarah Lawrence College
1 Mead Way
Bronxville, New York 10708
914-395-2510**

Type: **Private liberal arts**
Overall campus environment: **Unconventional/artistic/literary**
Total enrollment: **1,000**
African-American students: **85**
Graduate students: **150**
African-American graduate students: **N/R**
Percentage of applications accepted: **49%**
Average SAT score: **1160**
Average SAT African-Americans: **1030**
Special admissions programs: **N/A**
Percentage of African-American graduates: **80%**
Percentage receiving financial aid: **69%**
Average amount of award: **$10,130**
Percentage in ROTC programs: **N/A**
Number of faculty: **211**
Number of African-American faculty: **15**

Student/faculty ratio: **6 to 1**
Tuition: **$17,280**
Scholarship programs: **N/A**
Academic programs: **Creative and Performing Arts, Natural Sciences and Mathematics, Humanities, History and the Social Sciences**
Most popular majors: **Writing, Literature, Psychology, Theater, History, Studio Arts, Philosophy, Women's Studies, Music**
Prominent African-American faculty: **N/R**
Prominent African-American graduates: **Robin Givens, actress; Holly Robinson, actress; Alice Walker, Pulitzer prize–winning author**
African-American student organizations/activities: **Harrambee-African-American Union, Common Ground, Gospel Choir**
Administrative services and programs: **N/R**

Sarah Lawrence College is clearly not a typical liberal arts college. There are no grades, no conventional majors and no tests. But if you think that this less structured environment means an easy curriculum, think again. At Sarah Lawrence, you design your own program of study under the close supervision of a faculty member, who acts as your adviser or "don." You can choose to study virtually any subject, and you will get to know the subject well through a tremendous amount of reading, writing and special projects. Grades are given for transcript purposes, but your academic performance is primarily assessed by written faculty evaluations. Beginning students are required to take some coursework in the sciences, mathematics, history, social science, the humanities and the arts. Once the requirements are fulfilled, students are free to proceed with research projects and independent study.

For students at Sarah Lawrence, education means supervised independent study, so you need to be able to succeed in an unstructured environment. Your faculty adviser will virtually become your partner and guide in the educational process, but what and how much you learn will largely depend on how well you apply yourself. You are in essence responsible for your own education, and that freedom can be both liberating and overwhelming.

Whatever your field of study, one thing that all Sarah Lawrence students do plenty of is writing. If you are interested in becoming a writer or have a passion for literature, Sarah Lawrence will not disappoint you. The college has one of the strongest programs in the country and has graduated a number of prominent writers, including Pulitzer prize winner Alice Walker.

Sarah Lawrence generally appeals to the artisan student—one who is interested in writing, performing or the visual arts. Its educational philosophy seems to work best for students whose talents flourish when freed from the constraints of a traditional academic environment. Indeed, Sarah Lawrence has produced some of the nation's most renowned literary and performing arts figures and continues to attract some of the most talented students.

Until 1968 Sarah Lawrence was a women's college. The school's original goal of providing an alternative to mainstream higher education remains intact. A liberal administration whose free-flowing style has given the college its bohemian image has not changed much either. Tolerance and mutual respect are advocated in all aspects of campus life, whether racial, sexual or religious. There is an active gay and lesbian community on campus. Despite a growing conservatism and trend toward "pre-professionalism" in college, Sarah Lawrence is popular, and the administration reports that applications have increased substantially in recent years.

Sarah Lawrence is unconventional in almost every way, including its climate for African-American and other minority students. The college's advocacy of tolerance creates a fairly comfortable setting; however, the still small number of African-Americans is of concern to many students. The administration supports efforts to organize activities and events of specific interest to African-American and other minority students, such as the African-American Union, and the Gospel choir.

Most of the social life at Sarah Lawrence revolves around the arts—theater, dance and ethnic social affairs. However, many students opt for the social life of New York City instead of the suburban environs of Bronxville.

Sarah Lawrence offers students a unique educational experience with freedom unmatched on any campus, as well as an opportunity to work almost one-on-one with a renowned member of the faculty. If you are an independent thinker who is self-motivated and want to study in an unconventional environment of artistic freedom, take a serious look at Sarah Lawrence College.

State University of New York at Purchase
735 Anderson Hill Road
Purchase, New York 10577
914-251-6312

Type: **State university**
Overall campus environment: **Suburban, Culturally Diverse**
Total enrollment: **2,540**
African-American students: **164**
Graduate students: **37**
African-American graduate students: **N/R**
Percentage of applications accepted: **N/A**
Average SAT score: **1000**
Average SAT African-Americans: **N/A**
Special admissions programs: **Minority Access Program (MAP), Educational Opportunity Program (EOP)**
Percentage of African-American graduates: **50%**
Percentage receiving financial aid: **75%**
Average amount of award: **N/R**
Percentage in ROTC program: **N/A**
Number of faculty: **129**
Number of African-American faculty: **6**
Student/faculty ratio: **19 to 1**
Tuition: **$2,650 in state/$6,000 out of state**
Scholarship programs: **N/A**
Academic programs: **Arts and Sciences; Divisions of Natural and Social Sciences, Humanities, Science, Dance, Theater Arts and Film, Music, Visual Arts**
Most popular major: **Biology, Chemistry, Performing Arts, Literature, Social Sciences**
Prominent African-American faculty: **N/R**
Prominent African-American graduates: **Wesley Snipes, Actor**
African-American Student organizations/activities: **Organization of African People in America (OAPIA); BlackFest; Black History Month**
Administrative services and programs: **Minority**

Recruitment/Retention, Minority Access Program (MAP), Academic Support Center, LINKS, Counseling Center, Educational Opportunity Program (EOP)

The State University of New York at Purchase is one of the campuses of New York State's vast university system. Known primarily for its liberal arts and fine arts programs, SUNY Purchase provides a solid curriculum on a campus small enough to give students a chance to know the professors and administrators, yet large enough to offer the kinds of academic programs and resources available on much larger campuses. "I have found faculty and administrators to be helpful and, on the whole, very accessible," said one student. "My program, Letters and Science, offers a wide curriculum to choose from and has allowed me, as a literature major, to explore areas of study from medieval to African-American literature."

One feature that stands out at SUNY is its interest in the African-American and other minority communities on campus. With about 2,500 students, SUNY Purchase has a small population of African-American and other minority students but has been working to increase that population. Besides ongoing recruitment efforts, the administration has established specific programs targeted to previously ignored segments of the minority population. Recently the administration established MAP (Minority Access Program), which targets students with potential but who traditionally would not be admitted to SUNY. These students are provided peer counselors and are followed closely by faculty, who meet with them monthly to resolve any problems. Finally, these students are matched with a faculty member or administrator who acts as a mentor, meeting with the student individually on a regular basis. Students who are selected to participate in MAP must be interested in obtaining a college degree and be committed, assertive and willing to adhere to program rules that set standards for class attendance, coursework and tests.

The university provides minority career counseling to students, as well as a variety of other services. From counseling services to academic advising, mentoring and tutoring, SUNY Purchase helps all of its students succeed. "SUNY Purchase taught me how hard work was an essential factor in becoming successful," said one student. "I've learned that being a minority has its obstacles and that those of us raised in the poor areas of cities have to see these obstacles and with hard work and dedication overcome the barriers that stand before us."

SUNY Purchase is in Westchester County, just thirty miles from New York City. Many students take advantage of the university's proximity to New York for additional research, job and internship opportunities, as well as social life. The city is accessible both by train and by student vans, which run on the weekend.

While African-American students at SUNY Purchase constitute less than 10 percent of the student body, they report that they get along with all students and that they appreciate the diversity of students on campus. "The Purchase community as a whole is varied and colorful, consisting of a wide range of students from different cultural backgrounds," said another minority student. "Interaction between students of different backgrounds is encouraged, and I believe it promotes a better understanding and appreciation for others' beliefs and cultures."

SUNY Purchase has a good reputation for producing successful graduates. More than 85 percent of natural science graduates who apply to medical school are accepted, and many graduates have gone on to prestigious graduate schools such as Yale, Columbia and New York University. Among the university's most notable areas of study is its performing and visual arts programs, including dance, acting, film, photography, graphic design and printmaking. One of the most noted graduates of the performing arts program is actor Wesley Snipes, who has appeared in a number of highly successful films, including *White Men Can't Jump* and *Jungle Fever*.

Students who are looking for a solid academic program in a supportive and culturally aware university setting, and at an affordable cost, will find SUNY Purchase worthy of serious consideration.

Syracuse University
201 Tolley Administration Building
Syracuse, New York 13244-1100
315-443-3031

Type: **Private**
Overall campus environment: **Cordial**

Total enrollment: **15,892**
African-American students: **1,025**
Graduate students: **4,500**
African-American graduate students: **N/R**
Percentage of applications accepted: **72%**
Average SAT score: **1000**
Average SAT African-Americans: **N/A**
Special admissions programs: **Higher Education Opportunity Program**
Percentage of African-American graduates: **N/A**
Percentage receiving financial aid: **75%**
Average amount of award: **$11,850**
Percentage in ROTC programs: **0**
Number of faculty: **955**
Number of African-American faculty: **32**
Student/faculty ratio: **9 to 1**
Tuition: **$13,480**
Scholarship programs: **Merit and need-based scholarships**
Academic programs: **Schools of Architecture, Computer and Information Science, Engineering, Management, Public Communications, Arts and Sciences, Education, Nursing, Performing Arts; Graduate Law School, School of Social Work, College of Environmental Science and Forestry, Liberal Arts**
Most popular majors: **Public Communications, Visual and Performing Arts, Architecture, Engineering, Liberal Arts**
Prominent African-American faculty: **Bruce Hare, Director, African-American Studies; Howard Johnson, Writer, Professor of Mathematics Education**
Prominent African-American graduates: **Darryl Bell, actor, *A Different World*; Dave Bing, former NBA star, entrepreneur; Vincent Cohen, Sr., attorney, Hogan & Hartson; Suzanne DePasse, former president, Motown Records, now President/Producer, DePasse Productions; Robert E. Johnson, Executive Editor, *Jet* magazine; Jacqueline Jones, Commissioner, Public Safety Commission; Angela Robinson, news anchor, Fox Broadcasting; Vanessa Williams, actress/singer**
African-American student organizations/activities: **Afro-American Society, national Black Greek sororities and**

fraternities, Black Celestial Choral Ensemble, professional organizations
Administrative services and programs: **Office for Multicultural Resources, Bridge, Focus in Science, Minority Engineering Program, Mentoring Program, Faculty and Peer Advising, Freshman Forum, Freshman Advocacy Network**

Syracuse University is one of the nation's top private institutions. The university is best known for its Newhouse School of Communications, named for the owners of Condé Nast publishing *(Glamour, Mademoiselle, Self, Vogue)*, and its schools of architecture, engineering and management.

People often mistake Syracuse for a state university because of its size and the sheer number of its program offerings. SU offers 200 major fields of study through its twelve colleges. Besides specialized programs like communications, engineering and management, SU has a challenging liberal arts major that gives students an opportunity to explore humanities, social and natural sciences, mathematics, writing and foreign languages. The program is diverse and offers students many choices. One criticism is that there is so much from which to choose that a less self-directed student may be overwhelmed.

To assist minority students, the administration has established several academic advising programs, including Bridge, which sponsors the Focus in Science and Minority Engineering Program. Both of these programs are designed to provide academic and personal support to students interested in the sciences and engineering. In addition, students receive academic advising support through the Office of Multicultural Resources, a Mentor Program, peer and faculty counseling and a Freshman Advocacy Network.

At Syracuse, the administration strives for inclusion of all students in university-wide programs. SU sponsors more than 300 student organizations and activities and claims that nearly a quarter of those are devoted to students from multicultural backgrounds. Sports are very big here, especially basketball and football, and SU's Carrier Dome stadium, said to be one of the largest enclosed facilities in the country, seats more than 30,000 fans and is filled to capacity for every home game.

While the ideal is to have all students participate equally in

224 / Syracuse University

campus organizations, the reality is that students still socialize primarily within their own racial groups. The national Black Greek sororities and fraternities have chapters on campus, and organizations such as the Afro-American Society sponsor guest speakers and bring other forms of entertainment to SU. African-American professional organizations such as the Society of Black Engineers also provide support to students. "When African-Americans constitute such a small percentage of the student population, there is a bond that forms," said one student. "You feel compelled to get to know someone, if for no other reason than they are Black."

The administration has established an African-American studies program with thirty-nine course offerings. The program combines history, literature, culture and socioeconomics. It also recognizes the link between African and Caribbean countries.

Although students who attend SU tend to be from middle-class families (including African-Americans), the university offers a Higher Education Opportunity program for New York State residents who are economically or academically disadvantaged. It also awards athletic scholarships and need-based and merit scholarships as part of its regular financial aid program.

Besides campus activities, many students participate in the community through the local Urban League or through volunteer work. Some students get involved in local politics. One of the strongest links between school and community is the Black Celestial Choral Ensemble, which sings in local churches and during cultural events such as Black History Month.

One reason many students cite for coming to SU, besides academics, is the "real world" experience that the university offers. "The main reason I chose not to attend an all-Black college is because I wanted a taste of reality," one student said. "At Syracuse I found a university where the African-American student body is small but diverse and powerful, and the entire student population eager, ambitious and supportive." The school is not perfect. Classes are often overcrowded and taught by teaching assistants; some students believe the university should provide a better system of advising; and though the administration can do nothing about it, the weather in Syracuse is less than pleasant in winter. Still, when all is said and done, SU is an excellent school and one at which many African-Americans have excelled. "If I had to reconsider where to pursue my college education," another student said, "I would choose Syracuse again."

North Carolina State University
Raleigh, North Carolina 27695-7103
919-515-2434

Type: **Land-grant**
Overall campus environment: **Cordial**
Total enrollment: **27,236**
African-American students: **2,380**
Graduate students: **4,391**
African-American graduate students: **216**
Percentage of applications accepted: **62%**
Average SAT score: **1070**
Average SAT African-Americans: **950**
Special admissions programs: **N/R**
Percentage of African-American graduates: **13% (over 4 years)**
Percentage receiving financial aid: **20%**
Average amount of award: **$3900**
Percentage in ROTC programs: **N/R**
Number of faculty: **1,462**
Number of African-American faculty: **67**
Student/faculty ratio: **14 to 1**
Tuition: **$7,930**
Scholarship programs: **Dean's Minority Scholarships, Athletic Scholarships**
Academic programs: **Majors in Colleges of Engineering, Agriculture, Textiles, Forestry, Education, Physical and Mathematical Sciences, Humanities and Social Sciences, Management**
Most popular majors: **Computer Science, Business Administration, Electrical Engineering, Pre-Med**
Prominent African-American graduates: **Philip G. Freelon, architect; James W. Gwyn, Jr., pilot, American Airlines**
Prominent African-American faculty: **Dr. Lawrence R. Clark, Professor of Mathematics; Dr. A. M. Witherspoon, Professor of Botany**
African-American student organizations: **More than 30**

including Black Greek organizations, Black Repertory Theater, Dance Visions, Society of Black Engineers, Society of Afro-American Culture, NAACP, Black Accountants Association, Heritage Society
Administrative services and programs: **African-American Cultural Center, African-American Coordinator/Peer Counselors, African-American Symposium, African-American Job Fair**

African-American students attending North Carolina State University at Raleigh will face many challenges. The academic program can be downright difficult; sports, particularly basketball, get a top priority, and many African-American athletes are under pressure to perform as well as keep up with academics; interaction between African-Americans and white students is improving, but each group primarily socializes apart. Yet African-American students report they have made great achievements at NC State and are generally pleased with the school. A graduating senior confided, "NC State gave me a stronger will and drive to work hard for what I want out of life, and provided me with a quality education in the process."

With a student body of more than 27,000, NC State boasts an African-American student population of about 10 percent, higher than on most predominantly white campuses. The university's success in attracting these students is due in part to its aggressive recruitment program, which makes use of community resources such as Black Greek fraternities and sororities and African-American alumni. Recruiters visit junior as well as senior high schools. NC State also holds an African-American Symposium, which brings prospective students to campus in the summer to experience college life in and out of the classroom. During the summer program, an African-American peer counselor from each of the university's nine colleges helps students learn the ropes. These counselors are also available to students once they're on campus.

The academic program at the highly selective NC State is largely technical; the colleges of engineering, agriculture, life sciences and management are among the most popular. Students admitted to NC State have an average SAT score of 950 to 1150, as well as a B average in high school. Although academics are not the only criterion, students need to have a college-prep background, including some mastery of a foreign language. Financial aid is available through the traditional sources, as well as scholarships from the university, which are generally based on academic achievement—unless you are an athlete. In that case, you may be eligible for a substantial portion of the $1 million in scholarships the university awards to support fewer than 300 male and female athletes. Athletes are treated royally by the administration and students alike, who are always hoping to win another NCAA championship.

Besides its strong academic program, NC State offers a cooperative education program, which allows students to work and go to school in alternate semesters. Students can also take advantage of international exchange programs. NC State is in what's known as the Research Triangle Park along with Duke University and UNC–Chapel Hill, and NC State students can take courses at these schools and participate in their student organizations and activities. This arrangement has proved beneficial to each institution and has spawned several cooperative efforts, including Feed Raleigh, a tutorial program for local high school students, gospel choir and a theater and dance company.

Students can participate in a number of student groups, including the national Black Greek fraternities and sororities, a Black repertory theater, Dance Visions, the Society of Black Engineers, the Society of Afro-American Culture, the NAACP, the Black Accountants Association, the Heritage Society and more than thirty other African-American organizations. African-American students also enjoy the campus radio station, which plays gospel, jazz and popular music daily.

Many students do volunteer work in the community, take advantage of local entertainment, attend local churches and generally become involved with Raleigh's African-American community. Indeed, many students who attend NC State have roots in North Carolina or live in the state. The fact that North Carolina has a large number of colleges, particularly predominantly African-American colleges, is also of interest. St. Augustine's College, a small African-American college, for example, is in Raleigh.

Overall, NC State offers African-American students an opportunity to receive a sound education in a reasonably comfortable environment. There is a very active social life on campus, a sub-

228 / Marietta College

stantial number of African-American faculty and students, and an academic program (particularly in the technical fields) that is considered among the best in the country. If you are looking for a top-notch education, consider NC State.

Marietta College
215 Fifth St.
Marietta, Ohio 45750
1-800-331-7896

Type: **Private liberal arts**
Overall campus environment: **Cordial**
Total enrollment: **1,304**
African-American students: **11**
Graduate students: **73**
African-American graduate students: **N/R**
Percentage of applications accepted: **51%**
Average SAT/ACT score: **1025/23**
Average SAT/ACT African-Americans: **N/R**
Special admissions programs: **N/A**
Percentage of African-American graduates: **N/R**
Percentage receiving financial aid: **90%**
Average amount of award: **$9,265**
Percentage in ROTC programs: **N/A**
Number of faculty: **112**
Number of African-American faculty: **1**
Student/faculty ratio: **13 to 1**
Tuition: **$12,370**
Scholarship programs: **College scholarships, need-based grants**
Academic programs: **Bachelor of Arts, Fine Arts, Science, Science in Petroleum Engineering, Master of Arts in Education, Master of Arts in Liberal Learning**
Most popular majors: **Business, Mass Media, Education**
Prominent African-American faculty: **N/R**
Prominent African-American graduates: **Charles Nelson, Trustee, Marietta College, and Manager, Marketing Division, Aetna-Easton, Pennsylvania; Alva Rogers, actress** *(Do The Right Thing, Daughters of the Dust)*

African-American Student organizations/activities: **Minority Affairs Task Force**
Administrative services and programs: **Awareness Society, faculty advisers**

Are you looking for a college where you will receive individualized attention from faculty and advisers? One that has great facilities like computer labs equipped with MacIntosh and IBM computers and state-of-the-art broadcast stations that are available to you even as a freshman? Are you interested in studying abroad or perhaps interning at the seat of government in Washington, D.C.? Would you like to attend a school that has among its graduates a U.S. vice president, a NASA astronaut, a Nobel Peace Prize winner and an actress in a Spike Lee film? Are you the type of student who can flourish on a college campus where you are one of about only ten other African-Americans? If the answer is yes, consider Marietta College.

In Marietta, Ohio, about fifteen miles north of the West Virginia line, Marietta is a hands-on college. From your arrival on campus, you are assigned a faculty member to serve as academic adviser and counselor from your freshman through your senior year. Student housing is provided for your entire four years. There are few restrictions on using the college's many laboratories and facilities, and qualified students (including freshmen) are given access to the professional production equipment in the campus's two FM radio stations and television station. Marietta has study abroad options, and you can earn degrees from Marietta and other universities through a cooperative program. Those developing the skills to become leaders in community affairs or in a particular subject or discipline can participate in internships and volunteer services through the McDonough Leadership program. Finally, a Senior Career Development Office not only arranges for job interviews but assists students in mapping out a career strategy, which may include postgraduate or other additional training. Marietta boasts that its graduates have been successful in landing jobs at major corporations and agencies and have obtained entrance into top graduate schools, including Harvard, Northwestern, Columbia and William and Mary.

Though their numbers are small, African-American students are not completely forgotten at Marietta. An Awareness Society offers academic support and raises consciousness about African-American culture and history. In addition, a Minority Task Force provides support and discussion of issues of concern to women and minorities. The Minority Task Force also plans cultural events for Black History Month and Martin Luther King, Jr., birthday celebrations. Aware that it needs to do more to attract African-American students, Marietta has begun working with Stillman College, a predominantly African-American school in Alabama, to establish a cooperative program through a satellite link.

The small numbers of African-American students who have attended Marietta have been fairly successful in their careers, and current students seem happy. Clearly, Marietta College is not for everyone, but students who fit the school's profile may find that the small proportion of minorities is not a hindrance to their success. One African-American student, for example, expressed little concern over the fact that she is one of only a handful of African-Americans on campus. "From my perspective," she said, "being an African-American student here is no different than anywhere else. Faculty and advisers are very helpful and I find the academic program to be fairly accommodating. I am comfortable with the fact that Marietta is a small, quiet college and I associate with students of many ethnic backgrounds. I like Marietta and look forward to my next four years here."

Oberlin College
101 North Professor Street
Oberlin, Ohio 44074
216-775-8411/1-800-622-OBIE

Type: **Private liberal arts**
Overall campus environment: **Excellent**
Total enrollment: **2,843**
African-American students: **215**
Graduate students: **18**
African-American graduate students: **N/R**
Percentage of applications accepted: **61%**
Average SAT/ACT score: **1250/28**
Average SAT/ACT African-Americans: **1090/24**
Special admissions programs: **N/A**

Percentage of African-American graduates: **75%**
Percentage receiving financial aid: **60%**
Average amount of award: **$16,150**
Percentage in ROTC programs: **N/A**
Number of faculty: **241**
Number of African-American faculty: **14**
Student/faculty ratio: **13 to 1**
Tuition: **$23,093**
Scholarship programs: **National Achievement Scholarships, Multicultural Grants, Need-Based Financial Aid**
Academic programs: **College of Arts and Sciences, Conservatory of Music**
Most popular majors: **English, Biology, History, Politics, Psychology, Music**
Prominent African-American faculty: **Calvin Hernton, Professor of Black Studies; Wendell Logan, Professor of Afro-American Music; Gloria Watkins, Professor of English and Women's Studies**
Prominent African-American graduates: **Avery Brooks, actor and college professor; Johnnetta B. Cole, President, Spelman College; Charlene Drew Jarvis, Washington, D.C., City Councilperson; Gilbert Moses, Emmy Award-winning producer of *Roots*; Carl Rowan, award-winning syndicated columnist; Niara Sudarkasa, President, Lincoln University**
African-American student organizations/activities: **ABSUA, Afrikan Heritage House, *Rain* magazine, *Eclipse* yearbook, Black Arts Cooperative, *Nommo* newspaper, SOAR (Students Organized Against Racism)**
Administrative services and programs: **Office of Developmental Services, Student Support Services Center**

Oberlin College began its rich history of educating African-Americans and fighting injustice and inequality long before it was popular to do so. It was among the first predominantly white institutions of higher education to admit African-Americans; those first students went on to become the earliest influential black educators, religious leaders, professionals and politicians in this country. Graduates like John Mercer Langston, ancestor of poet Langston Hughes, earned three degrees from Oberlin and became a lawyer and the first African-American to hold elective office, as a congressman from Virginia. Langston also served as U.S. Minister to Haiti.

Oberlin was also a leader in feminism and educated the first African-American female class to attend college anywhere in the United States. These women went on to become educators themselves and were leaders in the women's suffrage movement. Among the college's most notable historical female leaders was Mary Church Terrell, educator and charter member of the NAACP.

Oberlin's attractions for African-Americans go well beyond these pioneering admissions policies. Throughout its history the college has shown a commitment to fostering an open dialogue about the problems of discrimination and racism. From its participation in freeing slaves as a stop on the Underground Railroad, to its refusal to adhere to Jim Crow policies and its support of the civil rights movement, to fighting racism in society today, Oberlin has remained true to its founders, who sought equality of opportunity for all people no matter what their racial origin. As Oberlin entered the twentieth century, it had graduated nearly half of all African-American college graduates in the United States—an achievement that led W.E.B. Du Bois to write, "Oberlin was the great pioneer in the work of blotting out the color line in colleges."

Today Oberlin graduates nearly 75 percent of its African-American students, who represent about 7 percent of the student population. Offering a solid program of liberal arts, Oberlin is a highly regarded institution and is especially known for its programs in the fine and performing arts, science, education and Black Studies. Besides its major programs of study, the college has a conservatory of music, offers access to computers at sixty-two terminals and microcomputers across the campus, and maintains state-of-the-art scientific laboratories, music facilities, a top art museum and an athletic complex.

Special programs abound at Oberlin. The comprehensive Black studies program, which offers an undergraduate degree as well as a minor, is recognized as one of the best in the country. A paid business internship program exposes students to some of the top companies and career areas such as advertising, high-tech fields, management, and journalism. "Last summer I worked as an intern at the Cleveland *Plain Dealer*," reported an African-

American English major. "The experience was both exciting and rewarding, and it has led me to pursue a career in journalism."

Oberlin continues to support African-American students through its aggressive recruitment efforts and programs to assist students academically and financially. Oberlin has established ethnic houses, including the Afrikan Heritage House, which serves as a cultural center and residence for African-American students. The college has also established extensive academic advising and counseling programs.

As one of the institutions selected for the Mellon Minority Undergraduate Fellowship program, Oberlin awards a stipend up to $3,000 and repayment of loans up to $10,000 to eligible Ph.D. candidates. The program was launched by the Mellon Foundation in an effort to increase the number of African-American Ph.D.'s and to encourage them to pursue careers in higher education.

Oberlin continues to provide all of its students with an excellent education and to instill a sense of social responsibility. One of its most noted graduates, columnist Carl Rowan has said, "There is something special about an educational institution that class after class inculcates so many of its graduates with a commitment to fight injustice whatever the economic, political, social and other risks. That is why, as I travel from city to city, I get such pleasure from meeting people who are fighting for good causes for a better society, especially when they come up to me and say, 'Carl, I'm Oberlin too.' "

If you want a solid education in an atmosphere in which social and moral responsibility counts for a great deal, and where you will be part of an extraordinary legacy, Oberlin may be for you.

Ohio University
Athens, Ohio
614-593-4100

Type: **4-year public**
Overall campus climate: **Cordial**
Total enrollment: **17,500**
African-American students: **742**
Graduate students: **2,500**
African-American graduate students: **61**

Percentage of total applications accepted: **76%**
Average SAT/ACT score: **870–1080/21–25**
Average SAT/ACT African-Americans: **N/R**
Special admissions programs: **N/R**
Percentage of African-American graduates: **74% (over 5 years)**
Percentage receiving financial aid: **81%**
Average amount of award: **$4,546**
Percentage in ROTC programs: **Less than 1%**
Number of faculty: **760**
Number of African-American faculty: **41**
Student/faculty ratio: **21 to 1**
Tuition: **$6,880**
Scholarship programs: **John Newton Templeton Scholarship, Minority Incentive Grant, Departmental Scholarships**
Academic programs: **More than 250 majors in fields including Liberal Arts, Arts and Sciences, Business, Communications, Health and Human Services, Education, Fine Arts, Engineering**
Most popular majors: **Zoology, Biomedical Sciences, Journalism, Telecommunications, Accounting/Marketing/Management, Elementary Education, Electrical and Computer Engineering, Political Science**
Prominent African-American graduates: **Clarence Page, Columnist, *Chicago Tribune*; John Newton Templeton, 1828 graduate, first Black Ohio university graduate and fourth Black in U.S. to earn college degree**
Prominent African-American faculty: **N/A**
African-American student organizations/activities: **African-American Student Union, Black Student Cultural Programming Board, Black Student Union Communication Caucus, Mercedes Modeling Troupe, Romeo Club, Black Student Business Caucus, Delta Sigma Theta, Zeta Phi Beta, Alpha Kappa Alpha, Sigma Gamma Rho, Phi Beta Sigma, Alpha Phi Alpha, Kappa Alpha Psi, Homecoming Pageant, Kwanzaa Celebrations, Black Film Series, *Shades of Color* radio program**
Administrative Services and programs: **Office of Minority Student Programs, Office of Affirmative Action, Lindley Arts and Cultural Center, LINKS Summer Program**

Ohio University is a good example of the new "liberal education" philosophy that many institutions of higher education have adopted. This sprawling campus with more than 17,000 students now aggressively recruits African-American and other minority students with a number of incentives, including generous financial aid packages and programs specifically designed to meet special academic, social and cultural needs. Still, despite these efforts, students remain socially and culturally segregated. According to one student, "There is little interaction between minority and white students outside of the classroom and resident halls at OU. Most minority students tend to socialize within their own race." Like many large predominantly white universities, OU has experienced some backlash from the perceived special treatment of African-American students, and there have been some racially motivated incidents. The administration's response has been to take a proactive role in race relations through programs and workshops designed to promote better understanding and communication among racial groups and to improve social interaction. The campus judicial network, consisting of the Office of Affirmative Action, Omsbudsman, Dean of Students and Judiciaries, sets up an extensive grievance procedure for students and investigates any allegations of discrimination.

Admission into OU is fairly competitive, with major emphasis placed on high school class rank, grade point average, curriculum and SAT scores. Although the administration says its admissions decisions are not guided by affirmative action programs or policies, it has established a number of programs to assist African-American and other minority students in adjusting to life at this large, often overwhelming institution. Students admitted to Ohio University can choose among more than 250 majors, the most popular being zoology and biomedical sciences, journalism, telecommunications, business, education, electrical and computer engineering and political science. According to the administration, these areas are "centers of excellence on campus with outstanding faculty, facilities, and superior reputations."

Besides excellent academic programs, OU has more than 500 campus organizations, including its famous Marching 110 Band and award-winning student newspaper, *The Post*. The university's sports events are a main attraction. Athletic facilities include a

13,000-seat Convocation Center, a newly renovated football stadium and one of the nation's top aquatic centers. The university also boasts an extensive intramural sports program, with more than 400 registered teams on campus and approximately 60 percent of students participating in sporting events.

African-American students are challenged both academically and socially at OU. Students say many faculty and administrators are caring and helpful, "going beyond the call of duty to help African-Americans strive to achieve their goals." A junior journalism student said, "Most African-American students know which administrators and professors they can go to for help by the end of the second quarter at OU. Extra office hours, late-night calls at home and attendance at student programs are the norm for these dedicated administrators and faculty. They are genuinely interested in the welfare of all students." Although students feel "connected" in this way, many shun interaction with the majority population on campus. African-American students who socialize with white students may find themselves on the outside as well. "Most African-American students seem to socialize with their own race," said another student. "Those who socialize only with white students are ridiculed and are often called 'sellouts.' "

OU has much to offer, and students believe that there is a sincere effort to include African-Americans in all aspects of campus life. The sheer number of African-American student and campus organizations and events attests to the level of commitment. Besides an Office of Minority Student Programs which sponsors a lecture series, homecoming pageant, variety show, Kwanzaa celebration and Black film series, there is the Lindley Arts and Cultural Center, where students hang out; all the major Black Greek organizations; and special-interest groups such as the Black Student Communication Caucus, the Society of Black Engineers, Faces Modeling Club and the Black Student Business Caucus.

Ethnic bonding is an important element of campus life for many students. However, one student warned African-Americans against allowing perceived racial intolerance to become a barrier to their success and cautioned them not to retreat from the realities of a world in which they must learn to live. "African-American students need to recognize that not everyone welcomes you with open arms, including townspeople, professors, administrators, staff and students. But once you leave OU, not everyone will welcome you in the outside world either. Students must be willing to work to find their niche and strive for excellence. By taking the best classes offered by the best teachers, an African-American student exiting Ohio University's gates will be sought after by employers all over the country."

University of Toledo
2801 West Bancroft Street
Toledo, Ohio 43606-3398
419-537-2696

Type: **Public**
Overall campus environment: **Pleasant**
Total enrollment: **24,969**
African-American students: **1,835**
Graduate students: **3,349**
African-American graduate students: **117**
Percentage of applications accepted: **95%**
Average ACT score: **20**
Average ACT African-Americans: **20**
Special admissions programs: **N/A**
Percentage of African-American graduates: **N/A**
Percentage receiving financial aid: **56%**
Average amount of award: **$2,124**
Percentage in ROTC program: **N/R**
Number of faculty: **721**
Number of African-American faculty: **27**
Student/faculty ratio: **18 to 1**
Tuition: **$2,788 in state/$6,531 out of state**
Scholarship programs: **John H. Anderson Scholarship, 50 Men and Women of Toledo Scholarship, Joseph and Edith Friedman Memorial Scholarship, Le Maxie Glover Scholarship, National Achievement Scholarship, Northwest Ohio Black Media Association Scholarship, William W. Stewart Scholarship, William N. Thomas Memorial Scholarship, University of Toledo Black Community/Girlfriends, Inc., Scholarship**
Academic programs: **Colleges of Arts and Sciences, Business**

Administration, Education and Allied Professions,
Engineering, Pharmacy; University Community and Technical
Programs, University College, additional special programs
Most popular majors: **Communications, Elementary
Education, Pharmacy, Engineering**
Prominent African-American graduates: **Michael Bell, Fire
Chief, City of Toledo; Virgis Colbert, Vice President, Miller
Brewing Company; Dr. Thomas Hutton, Physician, Toledo;
Dr. Brenda Henry Leake, Professor of Education, University
of Wisconsin; Dr. Donald Leake, Professor of Education,
University of Wisconsin; Keith Mitchell, Executive Director,
Board of Community Relations, Toledo**
Prominent African-American faculty: **N/A**
African-American student organizations/activities: **Black
Student Union, Society of Black Professionals, National
Society of Black Engineers, Black Student Law Association,
Gospel Choir, Kappa Alpha Psi, Alpha Phi Alpha, Phi Beta
Sigma, Alpha Kappa Alpha, Delta Sigma Theta, Omega Psi
Phi**
Administrative services and programs: **Office of Multicultural
Student Development, Minority Mentoring Program**

Described as the fastest-growing state university in Ohio, the University of Toledo enrolls more than 24,000 students from around the country, including students from many racial and ethnic backgrounds and nearly 2,000 African-Americans. The university has six campuses, including the Toledo Museum of Art and the Medical College of Ohio at Toledo. The University College is designed for students who require a more flexible study program or who want to design their own major; it is popular with students seeking an associate degree or those who cannot study full-time. In addition, the University Community and Technical College (referred to as ComTech) offers technical training in a number of fields, including business, health care, engineering, science, social work, public service, data processing and information management. There are also colleges of law, engineering, business administration, and arts and sciences and numerous cooperative programs with other schools, such as Case Western Reserve's School of Dentistry and Bowling Green State University. However, UT is perhaps best known among sports enthusiasts for its sports program (it is an NCAA school) and newly renovated $18-million Glass Bowl Football Stadium, as well as its newly constructed $17-million Student Recreation Center, which is touted as the premier leisure facility in the country.

The mere size of UT can be overwhelming; however, each of the six colleges forms its own insular environment creating the feeling of a small campus. Many students find that they can have the best of both worlds—the special programs and facilities of a large university and the personal attention of a small college. African-American students who may already feel a bit isolated on such a large campus will be comforted by this. And while many African-American students believe more can be done to accommodate their needs, UT has established many special programs and support systems for them and other minorities. Its Student Development Program, for example, provides tutoring and counseling to incoming students, and the university has established a minority mentoring program. It also has an outreach program to local schools, encouraging students to visit and apply; a large majority of UT students come from Ohio. African-American student organizations on campus include the Black Student Union, Society of Black Professionals, National Society of Black Engineers, Black Student Law Association, Gospel Choir and a number of fraternities and sororities.

Many Black students socialize primarily with other African-Americans, although the more outgoing will find it comfortable to spend time with those of all racial backgrounds. "I realized that you can socialize with students from different racial backgrounds without losing your identity as an African-American," remarked a senior business student and president of the Black Student Union. "The most rewarding feeling I have as a student is to know who I am and use that knowledge to teach others through programs and speakers about African-American heritage, and, at the same time, learn about the culture of other ethnic groups. I have met many international students at the University of Toledo, and it has truly been educational."

The many support systems for African-American students are not always enough to keep students at UT. More than 40 percent of African-American students who enroll drop out after freshman year. But those who stay often go on to great things. Among the more prominent graduates are a vice president of Miller

Brewing Company and professors of education at the University of Wisconsin.

UT offers excellent academic programs in a variety of disciplines as well as many hands-on experiences. For the student who is self-assured and self-directed, learning here can be a rewarding experience, but some African-American students suggest that students get involved if they want to succeed at UT. "There are numerous resources available here, but a student will not realize it if he or she chooses not to get involved," one student said. Another said, "Student involvement is the key to fitting in in college. Getting involved has given me the feeling that I am not only attending UT, but I am a functioning part of this university."

University of Oklahoma
Norman, Oklahoma 73019
405-325-0311

Type: **Public**
Overall campus climate: **Diverse, Sports Oriented**
Total enrollment: **19,650**
African-American students: **1,094**
Graduate students: **4,965**
African-American graduate students: **161**
Percentage of applications accepted: **85.9%**
Average ACT score: **23.5**
Average ACT African-Americans: **19.5**
Special admissions programs: **Alternative Admissions**
Percentage of African-American graduates: **31.4**
Percentage receiving financial aid: **86%**
Average amount of award: **$4,224**
Percentage in ROTC programs: **5% Air Force/4.5% Navy**
Number of faculty: **829**
Number of African-American faculty: **25**
Student/faculty ratio: **16 to 1**
Tuition: **$4,941**
Scholarship programs: **Alpha Kappa Alpha Sorority–Kappa Psi Chapter Scholarship; Alpha Phi Alpha Fraternity Scholarship; Black Alumni Scholarship Award; Black Scholarship (Star Supporters); College of Engineering National Achievement**

Scholarship; David Hall Scholarship; Dart & Kraft/National
Urban League Scholarship and Intern Program for Minority
Students; Delta Sigma Theta Sorority–Kappa Alpha Chapter
Scholarship; Kappa Alpha Psi Achievement–Zeta Omega
Chapter and Norman Alumni Scholarship; National
Achievement Scholarship; Oklahoma Metro Area Black
Officers Association Inc. Scholarship; Omega Psi Phi
Fraternity–Pi Delta Chapter Scholarship; Phi Beta Sigma
Fraternity Scholarship; Wyatt F. and Mattie M. Jeltz Memorial
Scholarship

Academic Programs: **More than 120 undergraduate majors in
Colleges of Architecture, Arts and Sciences, Business
Administration, Education, Engineering, Fine Arts,
Geosciences, Liberal Studies; graduate and pre-professional
programs**

Most popular majors: **Management, Accounting, Journalism,
Psychology, Marketing, Political Science, Finance**

Prominent African-American graduates: **Ada Lois Sipuel
Fisher, first African-American graduate of a professional
school; University of Oklahoma Board of Regents; Derrick
Minter, dancer, Alvin Ailey Dance Company; Waymon
Tisdale, NBA basketball player; J. C. Watts, Oklahoma
Corporation Commission Member**

Prominent African-American faculty: **Anita Hill, Professor of
Law**

African-American student organizations/activities: **8 national
Greek organizations; National Society of Black Engineers,
Society of Black Journalists, National Business League, Public
Administration and Political Science College Organization,
Know Thyself Society, Black Student Association, National
Pan-Hellenic Council, Society of African-American Men,
Black Law Student Association, Henderson-Tolson Cultural
Center**

Administrative services and programs: **Alternative Admissions
program, Minority Engineering program, African-American
Student Services, Minority Recruiting Services**

Recovering from negative publicity in the 1980's that arose from
improper behavior by members of its football team, the University
of Oklahoma is attempting to shed its "sports college" image and

refocus attention on its fine academic programs. Indeed, as the largest public institution in Oklahoma, the university provides the state with the majority of its engineers, architects, geologists, doctors, educators and other professionals and business executives. The University of Oklahoma is known nationally as a major research university that offers undergraduate and graduate study in more than 100 fields of interest, as well as doctoral programs in 71 fields and professional degrees in medicine, dentistry, pharmacy, law and business administration.

The University of Oklahoma is a state institution and has a moderately competitive admissions policy. More than 85 percent of applicants, most of them Oklahomans, are admitted each year. African-American students represent about 8 percent of enrollment. The university maintains a number of special efforts to recruit and retain minority students, including its Alternative Admissions program. Through this program, underrepresented minority students with ACT or SAT scores in the upper third of their ethnic group who demonstrate the ability to succeed academically are offered admission to the university. Needy students receive adequate financial aid through the standard aid packages and individual minority scholarships. African-American students can also take advantage of free tutorial services, writing workshops and peer counseling through the Office of Student Support Services.

Entering freshmen begin their studies at the University College before selecting a major field of interest from one of the other seventeen colleges of the university. Each of the colleges operates fairly autonomously, with its own academic requirements. With fewer than 1,000 faculty members for nearly 20,000 students, the atmosphere at Oklahoma is often impersonal, and African-American students, like others, may often feel they are just another number. For camaraderie and social and cultural support, African-American students can choose from myriad social organizations and cultural outlets. The Henderson-Tolson Cultural Center is a favorite hangout for many, with meeting rooms and other facilities to accommodate the programs of the Black Student Union. The center is a short distance from residence halls, and there's usually something of interest going on there. Oklahoma is traditionally a Greek campus, and several national Black Greek organizations make their homes here, as do other organizations such as the Society of Black Journalists, the National Business League, the Public Administration and Political Science College Organizations, Know Thyself Society, the Black Student Law Association and the Society of African-American Men.

All students at the University of Oklahoma get along well, despite isolated racial incidents. However, students of all racial groups are increasingly more comfortable socializing in class and at campus-wide social events. This is a trend that the administration is encouraging, although it also supports specific cultural organizations such as the Black Student Union. There is also a great deal of administrative support for African-American students. Currently 25 percent of Student Services staff, who serve as academic and constituency support for students, are minority.

Oklahoma has long been known for its prowess in football (the team won the national championship in 1985), and the games bring thousands of spectators. Indeed, some say that football at OU is almost a religious experience. One benefit of this distinction is that Oklahoma is able to offer generous athletic scholarships to talented players, many of whom are African-American. But administrators point out that the real mission of the university is to give talented athletes an opportunity to obtain a good education.

For students who believe they can make it at a large university and who thrive in an atmosphere where sports is a favorite pastime, the University of Oklahoma is a school to think about.

Willamette University
900 State Street
Salem, Oregon 97303
503-370-6303

Type: **Private liberal arts, affiliated with Methodist Church**
Overall campus environment: **Good/not culturally diverse**
Total enrollment: **1,623**
African-American students: **17**
Graduate students: **705**
African-American graduate students: **8**
Percentage of applications accepted: **80%**

Average SAT/ACT score: **1110/26**
Average SAT/ACT African-Americans: **N/A**
Special admissions programs: **N/A**
Percentage of African-American graduates: **N/A**
Percentage receiving financial aid: **100%**
Average amount of award: **$10,500**
Percentage in ROTC: **N/A**
Number of faculty: **179**
Number of African-American faculty: **1**
Student/faculty ratio: **15 to 1**
Tuition: **$13,030**
Scholarship programs: **Minority Achievement Scholarship, National Achievement Scholarships**
Academic programs: **American Studies, Art, Biology, Business Economics, Chemistry, Computer Science, Economics, English, Environmental Science, French, German, History, Humanities, International Studies, Mathematics, Music Education, Performance and Therapy, Philosophy, Exercise Science, Physics, Political Science, Psychology, Religious Studies, Sociology, Spanish, Speech, Theater**
Most popular majors: **History, Biology, English, Political Science**
Prominent African-American graduates: **Mel Henderson, management executive, Microsoft; Donna Tyner, Administrator, State of Oregon**
Prominent African-American faculty: **N/R**
African-American student organizations: **Black Student Group**
Administrative services and programs: **Office of Multicultural Affairs**

Being one of a scattering of African-American students on any campus can be a difficult and lonely experience, even when the institution has a lot to offer academically and socially. At Willamette University, a private liberal arts school in Salem, Oregon, African-American students will need to be emotionally secure and already knowledgeable about their cultural heritage. This university, which has its roots in the Methodist Church, is fairly selective, with students scoring, on the average, over 1000 on the SAT. Willamette has a fine reputation as a strong liberal arts college, and students are drawn to it because of the outstanding faculty and the opportunity to develop close relationships with professors.

Most students here are from the Northwest, particularly Oregon, Alaska and Canada; although the majority of students are white, there are a fair number of Asian, Hispanic and students of other races on campus. Administrators indicate they would like to see more minorities apply, especially African-Americans, and have become more conscious of the need to create an environment that is attractive to them. Willamette has established support organizations for African-American students including the Office of Multicultural Affairs, and the Black Student Group. The administration also offers generous financial aid and scholarships to lure top students to the institution.

Social life for African-American students is fairly limited at Willamette. Most activities revolve around white students and Greek organizations. These organizations dominate because there is so little to do off campus. Outside of the social realm, Willamette students do interact with the community. Each year Willamette offers a number of internship opportunities for students to work in the state capitol, in downtown Salem across the street from the university.

African-American students who can adjust to the limited social and cultural life at Willamette can have a wonderful academic experience. The academic program, small classes and caring faculty create an environment in which students can learn and excel. More than 60 percent of students who complete undergraduate work at Willamette continue to graduate school. Generally, students do well, and African-Americans have gone on to become business executives, state officials and university administrators. "Willamette's small, supportive, friendly environment allows a student to obtain a first-rate education," said one student. However, minority students should not expect to get much chance to express their culture or heritage.

Students who come here must be prepared to work, as academics take priority over other aspects of campus life. That coupled with the small number of minority students makes Willamette a campus for the most serious and self-disciplined student.

**Albright College
P. O. Box 15234
Reading, Pennsylvania 19612-5234
215-921-7512/1-800-252-1856**

Type: **Private liberal arts, affiliated with United Methodist Church**
Overall campus environment: **Cordial**
Total enrollment: **1,253**
African-American students: **50**
Graduate students: **zero**
African-American graduate students: **zero**
Percentage of applications accepted: **71%**
Average SAT score: **1000–1200**
Average SAT African-Americans: **N/R**
Special admissions programs: **N/A**
Percentage of African-American graduates: **N/R**
Percentage receiving financial aid: **75%**
Average amount of award: **$8,700**
Percentage in ROTC programs: **N/A**
Number of faculty: **93**
Number of African-American faculty: **N/A**
Student/faculty ratio: **10 to 1**
Tuition: **$13,400**
Scholarship programs: **Jacob Albright Scholar Awards, Presidential Awards**
Academic programs: **Accounting, Art, Biology, Business Administration, Chemistry, Computer Science, Economics, English, Environmental Science, French, German, History, Home Economics, Mathematics, Nutrition, Philosophy, Physics, Political Science, Psychology, Religion, Sociology, Spanish, Textile and Design, Visual and Apparel Merchandising; Interdisciplinary Programs; Pre-professional Programs**
Most popular majors: **N/A**
Prominent African-American faculty: **N/R**
Prominent African-American graduates: **N/R**
African-American student organizations: **African-American Society, BASE (Brother and Sister Exchange)**
Administrative services and programs: **Counseling Center**

Albright College takes liberal arts education seriously. A college with a strong academic program that emphasizes the development of critical thinking and writing skills, as well as the ability to think creatively and make educated choices, Albright is committed to developing the total student. An important aspect of learning is being exposed to more than just academics. All freshmen and sophomores are required to participate in The Experience, a cultural awareness program of concerts, lectures, exhibits and performances.

Besides programs like this, Albright also provides students with a variety of academic options. Among the programs that it is most proud of is the Alpha Program for students undecided about their major. Alpha allows students to defer selection of a major to the end of the sophomore year. It gives them an opportunity to explore their options with individual advisers, attend departmental presentations and participate in career development seminars.

For students who have decided on a field of study, Albright offers thirty-two majors and ten pre-professional programs, and has three cooperative programs in engineering, forestry and environmental management, and natural resources at the University of Pennsylvania, Duke and the University of Michigan, respectively. Albright also offers study abroad programs and field study opportunities to research special interests such as humpback whales and Hindu religion and culture.

A small, highly selective private liberal arts college, Albright is in the suburban area of Reading, Pennsylvania. Founded in the late 1800s and reformed through a series of mergers to its present relationship with the United Methodist Church, Albright has a philosophy built on student self-governance and leadership development. Though the school has a religious affiliation, students are not required to be Methodists or to attend religious services or classes.

Besides a great academic program, one advantage of attending a school like Albright is the personal contact with faculty and administrators. There is a 10 to 1 student-to-faculty ratio, and professors are so involved in students' lives they are considered mentors. More than 80 percent of the faculty have doctoral degrees, and many are published and renowned in their fields.

African-American students can expect to find a friendly and largely cordial faculty and student body at Albright, as well as the one-on-one attention often absent from large universities. African-Americans represent about 4 percent of the student body, and Asians and other minorities comprise about another 10 percent. While not perfect, the administration of Albright seems to understand the need for African-American students to have a fair opportunity to participate in the academic and social setting but also to be free to "be united, to share in and understand their common history and culture," said one student. The administration demonstrates this understanding by encouraging students to participate in all campus events as well as supporting minority organizations such as the African-American Society. In addition, Albright has affirmed its commitment to promote a better understanding between the races and to recruit, retain and graduate successful African-American students. The administration has developed a Peer Counseling program, and its five-day orientation program gives students more than a cursory look at campus life. "My advice to any prospective freshman is to relax and enjoy," said an African-American administrator. "Albright is such a busy place, you won't have time to feel confused or worried, especially during orientation. There are so many things going on you won't be able to sit still."

If a first-class liberal arts or pre-professional program is what you're looking for, Albright is a college to consider. More than 50 percent of its students go on to graduate and professional schools immediately after graduation. About 10 percent go on to medical school, with the largest numbers enrolling at Lehigh, Temple and the University of Pennsylvania. African-American students will find a supportive environment here in which attempts are made to treat all students equally.

Allegheny College
Meadville, Pennsylvania 16335
1-814-332-4351/1-800-521-5293

Type: **Liberal arts**
Overall campus environment: **Cordial/conservative**
Total enrollment: **1,858**
African-American students: **110**
Percentage of applications accepted: **N/A**

Average SAT/ACT score: **940–1160/21–27**
Average SAT/ACT African-Americans: **N/R**
Special admissions programs: **N/A**
Percentage of African-American graduates: **N/A**
Percentage receiving financial aid: **83%**
Average amount of award: **$15,200**
Percentage in ROTC programs: **N/A**
Number of faculty: **160**
Number of African-American faculty: **N/R**
Student/faculty ratio: **11 to 1**
Tuition: **$7300**
Scholarship programs: **Allegheny College Scholarships, National Merit Scholarships**
Academic programs: **More than 30 majors in Liberal Arts; 31 minors including Black Studies, Latin American/Carribean Studies, Women's Studies**
Most popular majors: **English, Psychology, Economics, Political Science, History**
Prominent African-American faculty: **N/A**
Prominent African-American graduates: **N/A**
African-American student organizations/activities:
Advancement of Black Culture, Ad Hoc Committee on Racial Issues, Black History Month
Administrative services and programs: **Office of Multicultural Affairs**

Nestled in the Allegheny mountains of Pennsylvania, this small liberal arts college is typical of many in the state. Emphasis is placed on developing students' writing, communications, reasoning and mathematical skills as a basis for their education in any major field of study. Allegheny offers a limited number of majors (about thirty-three) and about the same number of minors in areas including Black, Latin American and Caribbean, and women's studies. It augments these with a number of special academic programs which allow students to design their own majors and participate in off-campus programs in the sciences, arts and government. Allegheny has cooperative programs in engineering, environmental management, forestry, nursing and other health-related programs with Columbia University, Case Western Reserve, Duke, the University of Pittsburgh and Washington University. The college prides itself on its ability to respond to students' needs and touts its 11 to 1 ratio of students to faculty as well as its average class size of sixteen or less. Generally, students seem pleased with their access to faculty, and many have developed longstanding relationships with professors.

African-American students will find that Allegheny is a conservative institution in an environment that has few cultural outlets for students of color. There is a ban on alcohol in the dorms, and there are a number of religious groups on campus and in the town of Meadville. Social life for all students is limited and is dominated by Greek organizations. The administration reports no such organizations for African-American students, although its Office of Multicultural Affairs sponsors programs and activities of special interest to African-Americans. However, these activities tend to be one-time events. All students are encouraged to participate in campus organizations without regard to their racial origin. Allegheny is a school with a social conscience, supporting a number of volunteer efforts such as Head Start, Big Brothers/Big Sisters and special projects like the South African Scholars Fund and Soup Kitchen Volunteers. Still, African-Americans may find themselves fairly isolated on this campus, not only in their numbers but also in terms of the lack of emphasis on any special academic and cultural organizations. In reviewing the college's recruitment literature, for example, African-American students will have to read carefully to find programs and services directed to their needs.

However, the small size and nurturing environment of Allegheny may well outweigh a student's need for more cultural outlets. After all, academic offerings and ability to succeed at an institution must be a student's first concerns, and Allegheny gets high marks for its academic programs. Allegheny is a fairly competitive college, with students averaging about 1000 on the SAT and 21 to 27 on the ACT. The college has a good record in preparing students for graduate school, with about 30 percent enrolling right after college in top schools, including Harvard, Yale, Case Western Reserve, Cornell, NYU, Penn State and UCLA.

Students who attend Allegheny will find a personal yet challenging institution with a flexible academic program and faculty who are interested in helping them succeed.

Bryn Mawr College
Bryn Mawr, Pennsylvania 19010
215-526-5152

Type: **Private liberal arts**
Overall campus environment: **Traditional, Liberal**
Total enrollment: **1,150**
African-American students: **50**
Graduate students: **550**
African-American graduate students: **30**
Percentage of applications accepted: **50%**
Average SAT score: **1250**
Average SAT African-Americans: **1190**
Special admissions programs: **N/R**
Percentage of African-American graduates: **80%**
Percentage receiving financial aid: **95%**
Average amount of award: **$16,000**
Percentage in ROTC programs: **N/A**
Number of faculty: **209**
Number of African-American faculty: **6**
Student/faculty ratio: **6 to 1**
Tuition: **$16,165**
Scholarship programs: **Mellon Scholars**
Academic programs: **Africana Studies, Anthropology, Astronomy, Biology, Chemistry, Classical and Near Eastern Archaeology, Classical Languages, Classical Studies, Comparative Literature, Computer Sciences, East Asian Studies, Economics, English, Feminist and Gender Studies, Geology, German and German Studies, Greek, Growth and Structure of Cities, Hispanic and Hispanic American Studies, History, History of Art and Religion, Human Development, International Economic Relations, Italian, Latin, Mathematics, Music, Neural and Behavioral Studies, Peace Studies, Philosophy, Physics, Political Science, Psychology, Religion, Romance Languages, Russian, Sociology, Spanish, independent majors**
Most popular majors: **English, Psychology, Chemistry, Political Science, Economics**
Prominent African-American graduates: **Linda A. Hill, Associate Professor, Harvard Business School, Member Bryn**

Mawr College Board of Trustees; Christine Philpot, entertainment attorney, Yale graduate, Washington, D.C.; Mindy Thompson-Fullilove, M.D., Associate Professor of Clinical Psychiatry, New York State Psychiatric Institute
Prominent African-American faculty: **Bronhilde Ridgway, Ph.D., Professor, highly published and world-renowned in classical archaeology; Charles Swindel, Ph.D., Professor, chemistry**
African-American student organizations/activities: **Minority Women in Science, Sisterhood, Black Cultural Center, Perry House, Gospel Choir, Delta Sigma Theta, COLOR, African Dance Group**
Administrative services and programs: **Minority Alumni Mentoring Program, Tri-College Summer Institute, Seminars in Social Change, Minority Affairs Newsletter**

Bryn Mawr is a college rich in endowments and special programs that expose students to a variety of multicultural events, speakers and scholars, but its greatest strength is the development of a student's self-image. "I've made some incredible discoveries about myself here," said one student. "I no longer accept other people's image of me as Black. My ideas come from inside me now, and they will never come from outside again. I'm viewing the world in an entirely different way, and I can construct that view of myself, without relying on anyone else."

Founded as a Quaker college for women, Bryn Mawr is still an institution where students can retreat from the realities of racial tensions into a world where sincere efforts are made toward cultural peace and understanding. Bryn Mawr's efforts to inculcate African-American and other cultural interests and scholarship into its academic and social program are admirable. The school offers, among other things, the Mellon Scholars program, which provides financial support to African-American students to encourage them to become college faculty; Minority Women in Science which seeks to increase the numbers of African-American women on science and math faculties; mentoring programs and study groups to assist freshmen; a TriCollege program in which nearby Haverford and Swarthmore colleges collaborate in seminars on issues of race, ethnic identity and cross-cultural communication, and an Exchange Program with Spelman College, which provides students an opportunity to attend the predominantly African-American women's school for up to one year.

Bryn Mawr's small size and concerned faculty and administrators are responsive to students' needs. All students are assigned deans who provide academic and personal counseling, and African-American students receive additional support from a minority affairs director, who reviews their academic progress as well as how they are adjusting emotionally to campus life. Administration and faculty team up to help resolve any problems a student may encounter. Special attention is also given to providing a fair number of extracurricular programs that are sensitive to the needs of African-American students and other minorities. The college brings a variety of African-American scholars, political figures, entertainers and authors to campus. It also supports other cultural programs sponsored by groups like Sisterhood, a campus organization of African-American, African-Caribbean and African women. Sisterhood also coordinates Perry House, a Black cultural center and small student residence. Each year seven active upperclass members of Sisterhood may live in Perry House, but for no more than two years.

Although opportunities abound here, students can feel overwhelmed and out of place. In its upperclass Pennsylvania suburb, Bryn Mawr has the reputation of being an elite school for "supergenius" or "super-rich" (white) kids. It is not an image that is easily shaken among young African-Americans, and many who attend the school shun the administration's attempts to include them in campus life. Students who seem to fare best here are those who have found a balance between their cultural identity and individual achievement. A male student in the TriCollege Program had this to say to students: "Bryn Mawr has a lot going for it. The academics are incredible, and you'll get a great education. You'll make good contacts and meet great people. But if you're looking to be politically active or make a real statement, you'll be frustrated. Not because of the administration, but because students who come here put their priorities on academics and not on extracurricular concerns."

Bryn Mawr's combination of academic excellence and cultural and social awareness has had a positive impact on its ability to graduate African-American students. The administration reports that 80 percent of its African-American students graduate, many of them going on to graduate school and successful careers. Among its graduates are a number of very successful African-American women, including Christine Philpot, a Washington, D.C., attorney and Yale graduate who represents some of the top African-American entertainers in the country, and Linda A. Hill, an associate professor at the Harvard Business School. Administrators also proudly point out that almost no students drop out after the first year—an incredible accomplishment. One reason that the school may have such great success is that it is working with "cream of the crop" African-American students whose SAT scores average nearly 1200. These students would probably do well at almost any school. But there is much to be said for Bryn Mawr's ability to hold on to these students and the rich experiences which many claim have helped them to grow. "I'm a Mellon Fellow, in part at the urging of an administrator that I apply and because of the kind of research I'd been able to do after my freshman year," said a biology and math student. "I don't believe my abilities are rare here, but opportunities just keep popping up at Bryn Mawr." That is an attitude held by many students. "At Bryn Mawr, students get the opportunity to develop real leadership skills," another student pointed out. "I'm involved with the GTE Minority Women in Science program, Sisterhood, and the Student Government Association. These are real leadership roles, not just interacting with students, but with administrators, faculty and staff; and I am respected as an individual who can get the job done."

Carnegie Mellon University
5000 Forbes Avenue
Pittsburgh, Pennsylvania 15213-3890
412-268-2123

Type: **Private**
Overall campus environment: **Highly academic**
Total enrollment: **6,997**
African-American students: **187**
Graduate students: **2,712**
African-American graduate students: **25**
Percentage of applications accepted: **65%**

Average SAT score: **1207**
Average SAT African-Americans: **1071**
Special admissions programs: **N/A**
Percentage of African-American graduates: **52% (3-year avg)**
Percentage receiving financial aid: **47%**
Average amount of award: **$15,824**
Percentage in ROTC programs: **N/R**
Number of faculty: **544**
Number of African-American faculty: **6**
Student/faculty ratio: **8 to 1**
Tuition: **$15,250**
Scholarship programs: **University scholarships**
Academic programs: **College of Fine Arts, College of Humanities and Social Sciences, Carnegie Institute of Technology, Mellon College of Science, School of Industrial Management**
Most popular majors: **Computer & Electrical Engineering, Communication Arts, Architecture**
Prominent African-American faculty: **N/R**
Prominent African-American graduates: **N/R**
African-American student organizations/activities: **SPIRIT, National Society of Black Engineers**
Administrative services and programs: **Academic and Student Affairs Office**

Students who attend Carnegie Mellon University need to have a clear vision of their career goals and be prepared to work hard to achieve them. At CM students are serious about academics, and even as freshmen many have selected a major field of study. Generally, student interest is split between two areas, the arts and technology, and CM programs in both fields are renowned. The engineering program here is outstanding. The drama department is highly regarded and its faculty are working professionals. The university offers programs through its five undergraduate colleges: Fine Arts; Humanities and Social Sciences; Carnegie Institute of Technology; Mellon College of Science, and the School of Industrial Management.

Each school has its own admission requirements and separate character, but all share a commitment to giving students a liberal arts base. Administrators call it "liberal professionalism" and believe the liberal arts are necessary to prepare students for the real world of work. Admission to CM is selective; students need to score about 1100 on the SAT. But the greatest challenge to students is keeping up with the workload and coping with the stress of academic life. Many students report pulling all-nighters to get good grades.

Life at CM is like life at no other campus in the country. Here, the computer reigns supreme. Students will need to use one, though it is not required that they purchase a computer. Those who do will find the university computer store offers incredible discounts to students. The administration prides itself on being automated, and it does everything from teaching courses in logic and conducting research to handling ticket sales at the campus box office using its massive computer system, called Andrew for CM's founder, Andrew Carnegie. Students who are uncomfortable with computers may want to think twice about this university. In order to succeed at this school, you must be on a first-name basis with a keyboard and monitor.

The desire to succeed overrides most other concerns at CM, including issues of race and politics. Students are more interested in their studies and are generally apathetic about these issues. Although interaction between African-American and white students as groups is limited, individual students seem to have no problem developing positive relationships. The campus is somewhat diverse, with minorities comprising about 20 percent of the student body; Asians are the majority, and less than 3 percent are African-American.

The administration provides extensive academic counseling and tutorial services which minority students say are very helpful. Campus professional organizations such as the National Society of Black Engineers also provide workshops and seminars in their fields and keep students abreast of career opportunities. In addition, African-American CM alumni are involved with the student body and often help arrange summer jobs and internships. While social life for African-Americans is limited, a student group called SPIRIT sponsors social, educational and cultural events. Of course, all students are invited to participate in all campus activities, but even among the majority students, activities are limited because of the overwhelming emphasis on academics. An alternative for many students is a visit to downtown Pittsburgh, a booming metropolis that offers a fair amount of cultural and social activity. Students can get around the city fairly easily on public transportation.

Students seeking careers in engineering and other high-tech fields, or interested in the performing arts, the humanities and the social sciences, will find Carnegie Mellon University a challenging yet rewarding experience. The curriculum is rigorous and the workload is constant and may sometimes be overwhelming. The payoff for students who tough it out is tremendous. CM graduates obtain good job offers and are generally successful in their fields.

Haverford College
Haverford, Pennsylvania 19041
215-896-1350

Type: **Private liberal arts**
Overall campus environment: **Liberal, Culturally supportive**
Total enrollment: **1,113**
African-American students: **60**
Percentage of applications accepted: **43%**
Average SAT score: **400–800**
Average SAT African-Americans: **400–800**
Special admissions programs: **N/A**
Percentage of African-American graduates: **90% (over 5 years)**
Percentage receiving financial aid: **45%**
Average amount of award: **$10,580**
Percentage in ROTC programs: **None**
Number of faculty: **91**
Number of African-American faculty: **7**
Student/faculty ratio: **11 to 1**
Tuition: **$16,960**
Scholarship programs: **Ira Reid Scholarship**
Academic programs: **Majors in 26 departments including special study programs in African-American Studies, Comparative Literature, Religion, Computer Science, Education and Child Development, Gender and Women's Studies, General Studies, Intercultural Studies, Latin American Studies, Peace Studies**

Most popular majors: **Science, Math, Social Sciences, Humanities**
Prominent African-American graduates: **Juan Williams, columnist** *Washington Post* **and author,** *Eyes On the Prize*
Prominent African-American faculty: **N/R**
African-American student organizations/activities: **Black Student League**
Administrative services and programs: **Minority Scholars Program**

It's said that Haverford is among the best colleges in the country for African-American students. Founded by Quakers in the early 1800s, Haverford is a highly selective institution that places a great deal of emphasis on academic and social integrity. At the core of its philosophy is an Honor Code established as a means of promoting trust and respect between students and the faculty and administrators at the college. The system, in place since 1897, is administered by students and allows them a great deal of academic and social freedom, including proctoring of student exams (without the presence of a faculty member). A student board is responsible for administering the Honor Code and meets regularly to discuss changes in the system.

The philosophy of mutual respect and freedom practiced here sets Haverford apart from many other colleges and spills over into the attitudes and campus climate experienced by African-Americans and other minorities. The number of minorities at Haverford alone says something about the school. More than 22 percent of students are minority, with African-Americans representing about 5 percent of that number. Students come from all over the country, from Puerto Rico and from twenty-seven foreign countries. Moreover, African-American students report they truly feel a part of the campus even though Haverford does not place a great deal of emphasis on separate minority student organizations. The administration is supportive of the Black Students' League, which provides a majority of the social and cultural events for African-American students. However, students also play a substantial role in campus life. Over the past decade, at least two African-American students have headed the student government organization, and they have also held key roles on a number of policy-setting committees and councils—this despite their small numbers on a predominantly white campus. Perhaps one of Haverford's strongest selling points is its outstanding faculty and the close relationships between students and faculty. African-American students report that faculty are not only accessible to them but very helpful and supportive, and the small student-to-faculty ratio of 11 to 1 creates a friendly and comfortable environment in which students can learn and grow.

Admission to Haverford is highly competitive and is based on high SAT scores, students' ranking in their class (90 percent are from the top fifth of their class), a minimum grade point average of 3.0 (B), consideration of personal qualities, recommendations and accomplishments. Once students are admitted, they need not be concerned about financial aid, as the college has ample resources. According to the administration, "no able student should hesitate to apply to Haverford because of financial circumstances."

Overall, a spirit of student autonomy exists at Haverford College. With the help of a faculty adviser and established guidelines, students plan their own academic programs. Certain requirements must be met before a student can begin work on a major field of study, but students are encouraged to experiment within the confines of the many opportunities available. Besides study abroad programs, for example, Haverford has a special cooperative relationship with Bryn Mawr College. Students at Haverford may take courses at either school, live on either campus and eat their meals on either campus. They may use the facilities of both schools; a free bus service connects the two campuses, which are about a mile apart. Haverford students may also take courses at Swarthmore College and the University of Pennsylvania. In addition, African-American students can take advantage of the Minority Scholars program, whose workshops help to create a strong base in the natural sciences and humanities and social sciences. The program is designed to introduce students of color to these fields and thereby encourage and support their selection of these subjects as major fields of study. Students work closely with faculty on research projects, and some have participated in summer medical programs at Harvard and Cornell. Others have attended such programs as Princeton's Woodrow Wilson Minority Access Program in Public Policy and International Affairs and the University of Chicago's Business Fellows Program. The Minority Scholars program is responsible for a number of student successes: over the past five years more than 97 percent of Haverford Minority Scholars who applied to graduate schools were accepted into programs in medicine, business and law.

Clearly, Haverford College provides students of all colors a rich and satisfying college experience and helps builds leaders in the process. If you're looking for a good school and a great environment for learning and growing, Haverford is among the best.

Lafayette College
Easton, Pennsylvania 18042
215-250-5100

Type: **Private liberal arts**
Overall campus environment: **Conservative**
Total enrollment: **2,000**
African-American students: **80**
Graduate students: **0**
African-American graduate students: **0**
Percentage of applications accepted: **58%**
Average SAT score: **1070–1300**
Average SAT African-Americans: **N/A**
Special admissions programs: **N/A**
Percentage of African-American graduates: **80%**
Percentage receiving financial aid: **100%**
Average amount of award: **$12,900**
Percentage in ROTC programs: **N/A**
Number of faculty: **175**
Number of African-American faculty: **2**
Student/faculty ratio: **10 to 1**
Tuition: **$21,985**
Scholarship programs: **Simon Scholarships; Marquis Regional Scholars Program; African-American and other minorities guaranteed financial aid in amount of need**
Academic programs: **American Studies, Anthropology and Sociology, Art, Biochemistry, Biology, Chemistry, Computer Science, Economics and Business, Engineering, English, French, Geology, German, Government and Law, History,**

International Affairs, Mathematics, Mathematics/Economics, Music History and Theory, Philosophy, Physics, Psychology, Religion, Russian, Spanish
Most popular majors: **Economics and Business, English, Engineering, Government, International Affairs**
Prominent African-American faculty: **N/A**
Prominent African-American graduates: **Ronald B. Brooks, Senior Vice President, Bechtel Co.; Terence L. Byrd, CEO, Blue Cross/Blue Shield of New Jersey; Dr. Eugene M. Deloatch, Dean, School of Engineering, Morgan State University; Michael Newsome, Controller, Armstrong World Industries; Leroy D. Nunery, Vice President, Swiss Bank Corp.; Jon Davis Smith, Assistant Treasurer, Hearst Foundation; Riley Temple, Chairman of the Board, Whitman-Walker Clinic**
African-American Student organizations/activities: **Association of Black Collegians, Black Alumni Network, Black Children Can, Black Cultural Center, Black Women's Support Group, Brothers of Lafayette, *CHANGE* Newsletter, Society of Black Engineers, Apartheid Awareness Organization, Black History Month, Martin Luther King, Jr., Tribute, Minority Senior Recognition and Awards Banquet, Sleeping Bag Weekend**
Administrative services and programs: **Counseling Center, Focus on Study Skills, Orientation for Academic Success, Peer Counseling, Tutoring**

One benefit of a well-endowed institution is the ability of its administration to establish innovative programs and turn into reality its vision for the future. Such is the case of Lafayette College, a highly selective private liberal arts and engineering college in the small city of Easton, Pennsylvania. With a student body of just 2,000, Lafayette is ranked among the top national liberal arts colleges in the country.

Lafayette's commitment to strong academics, service to the world community and cultural diversity is noteworthy. The college boasts a prestigious faculty who are well published and nationally recognized in their fields; and the administration's concern for the disenfranchised of the nation and world is evidenced by Lafayette's volunteer and relief programs. Its innovative Hands Together, a Peace Corps-like program, has focused recent efforts on helping those living in the most impoverished areas of Haiti. The interest in Haiti is led by Lafayette's president, Robert I. Rotberg, who was among the international team of observers, led by former president Jimmy Carter, assigned to ensure the integrity of Haiti's democratic elections in 1987. President Rotberg has written extensively on Africa and Haitian affairs.

Lafayette seeks the most intellectually able African-American students. Once admitted, these students are almost guaranteed financial assistance, largely in scholarships or grants, and they are provided with a bevy of support systems including counseling services, study skills training, time management and test-taking workshops and individualized academic assessments. Students of color are also matched with similar students as peer counselors, who provide much-needed support to many students who are uncomfortable with life on a predominantly white campus. In addition, African-American students can take advantage of the support of professional organizations such as the Society of Black Engineers as well as the Association of Black Collegians, the Black Women's Support Group and Brothers of Lafayette. "I'm a member of the Association of Black Collegians, the Lafayette Christian Fellowship, the Latin American Club," said one student. "I work on the Black campus newspaper and I spend a lot of time with younger students as a peer counselor, making sure they feel connected to campus. Academically, no one will hand you anything— you have to work—but if you make an effort, your professors will reach out to you, and so will the rest of the community."

At this largely residential college (98 percent of students live on campus), African-American students may find additional support by living in Lafayette's Black Cultural Center residence or on a special-interest floor in one of the other residential facilities.

Lafayette encourages all students to participate in a wide variety of recreational and cultural programs. The administration has sponsored a campus-wide retreat to the Pocono Mountains for students, faculty and administrators for sensitivity training. It also provides leadership training to the heads of larger campus organizations, including resident assistants, fraternity and sorority presidents and peer counselors.

Beyond the administration's commitment to a culturally diverse campus is its excellent academic program, from which all students can benefit. Lafayette's engineering program is outstanding; students have worked on innovations such as a mechanical prosthetic hand. Lafayette's program in the visual arts is equally challenging and has produced graduates like Berrisford Boothe, an African-American student whose works captured the attention of Walters Museum of Art in Baltimore and eventually led to his receiving a traveling fellowship. "Lafayette provided me with an arena for encounter with fundamental moral, social, economic and political issues that shape and affect my art," Boothe said. "My undergraduate work expanded my view of the world."

Lafayette has a study abroad program which, unlike those of many other colleges, offers the chance to study in Africa and Haiti. There are several honors programs, including the Marquis Scholars and EXCEL program, that provide scholarship funds and research grants to students. In addition, programs such as the Ben Franklin Partnership, Technology Clinic and various internship and independent study programs provide students the opportunity for real-life work experiences in their field of interest.

Social life for African-American students at Lafayette is fairly limited and centers largely around the African-American cultural and social organizations such as the Black Cultural Center. There are no Black Greek organizations on campus, and many activities center around the interests of majority students. However, groups like Sweet Honey in the Rock have also made appearances at the college. The campus also has excellent facilities such as the Farinon College Center, which houses a video arcade, movie theater and snack bar with live entertainment.

Although Lafayette clearly is a predominantly white "prestige" college, there is evidence that the administration has become more flexible with regard to meeting minority students' needs. "As a minority population, it's impossible for us to separate ourselves from white students," said one student. "Prospective students need to understand that and to be ready to work toward keeping this dialogue going and learning from each other."

African-American students looking for a rich social life in a college with lots of parties should look elsewhere. Students say that academics is one of the overwhelming reasons to come here. "The support I received from my peers, the faculty and administration allowed my personal qualities to develop so I could succeed," said a recent graduate. "I tell visiting students that they have to go where they feel comfortable. Lafayette was where I fit."

Lehigh University
Bethlehem, Pennsylvania
215-758-3100

Type: **Private 4-year**
Overall campus environment: **Academically challenging, Supportive, Friendly**
Total enrollment: **4,500**
African-American students: **97**
Graduate students: **2,000**
African-American graduate students: **N/R**
Percentage of applications accepted: **60%**
Average SAT/ACT score: **1050–1250/30–31**
Average SAT/ACT African-Americans: **N/A**
Special admissions programs: **Challenge for Success**
Percentage of African-American graduates: **N/R**
Percentage receiving financial aid: **75%**
Average amount of award: **$13,500**
Percentage in ROTC program: **N/A**
Number of faculty: **407**
Number of African-American faculty: **N/R**
Student/faculty ratio: **11 to 1**
Tuition: **$15,650**
Scholarship programs: **Trustee Scholars, Lehigh University Scholarships, Sponsored Scholarships, Endowed Scholarships (geographic restrictions apply), Merit Scholarships, Athletic Awards, Loan-Cancellation Awards, ROTC Scholarships**
Academic programs: **Arts and Sciences, Business and Economics, Engineering and Applied Science**
Most popular majors: **Engineering**
Prominent African-American graduates: **N/A**
Prominent African-American faculty: **N/A**
African-American student organizations/activities: **Black Student Union, Association of Minority Business Students, National Society of Black Engineers, STEM (Society of Together Ebony Men), Minority Programming Committee, Gospel Choir, Kappa Alpha Psi, Omega Psi Phi, Peer Counselors**
Administrative services and programs: **Challenge for Success, Learning Center, Minority Connection, Umoja House**

Lehigh University is among the top-rated universities in the country. Yet this private university of about 4,500 undergraduates is both small enough to give students a feeling of support and belonging, and academically challenging enough to be a powerful institution. Lehigh students study under expert professors who combine their knowledge and experience with hands-on projects that allow students to put theory into practice. Students do market research, design and build products, compose music, publish articles; they benefit from internships and summer jobs that expose them to real-life problems. Lehigh is fairly successful at graduating its students; 85 percent of students earn their degree within five years, compared to a national average of 33 percent. An unusually high proportion of these graduates succeed in the business world, according to the administration; 75 percent of its alumni are employed in business, and 25 percent are officers in their firms. According to Standard & Poor's, Lehigh also ranks fourteenth among colleges and universities in the percentage of graduates who hold high-level positions in major firms. Perhaps one reason for the university's success in educating students is its academic philosophy, which combines some of the components of a strong liberal arts education. Lehigh encourages all students, regardless of major, to develop skills in critical thinking, communication and technology, and an awareness of cultural diversity, the global economy and its impact on society. Lehigh also encourages research through cooperative efforts between faculty and students.

African-American students will find that the university's philosophy spills over into its dealings with all minority students. Once admitted, Lehigh is committed to seeing that a student succeeds. It does this by guaranteeing financial aid to meet demonstrated need, and through a number of support programs such as the six-week Challenge for Success (CFS) summer program. Here new students attend mini-classes that help them adjust to campus life while earning three credits toward graduation. Once on campus, each African-American student is matched with a peer counselor (usually an upperclass student) who helps the student learn the ropes and acts as a sounding board. The university also has a counseling service called the Minority Connection, which gives students an opportunity to speak openly about sensitive issues such as interracial dating and male-female relationships. All of this takes place against a backdrop of a close-knit African-American and Hispanic campus community. One student wrote, "Compared to what I've seen and heard, Lehigh's African-American students are comparatively well taken care of, but they still have a long way to go. The academics are very challenging at Lehigh, but there are many ways to get help. While I do feel part of the school community, I admit to a bit of self-imposed isolation because I choose to interact mostly with other African-American students. I get along fine with students of other ethnic backgrounds but most of my friends are people of color."

Although the number of African-American students on campus is small, there are a number of student organizations and activities designed for them. There are a Black Student Union, gospel choir, fraternities and business and engineering groups, in addition to annual ethnic activities such as Kwaanza celebrations, a student-coordinated "Night at the Apollo" talent show, Minority Prospectives' Weekend and numerous athletic and social events. African-American students say they feel "connected" to the faculty and administration and can freely ask for help. One student said, "Because classes are relatively small here, I have found it easy to get to know professors on an individual basis. This has helped me not only in learning for their course but in other courses I took at a later date." Students who choose Lehigh University will get a degree from a school whose graduates are sought after in a variety of fields. At the same time, they'll enjoy learning at a college whose administration and faculty are concerned about their needs and want to help them succeed.

Swarthmore College
500 College Avenue
Swarthmore, PA 19081-1397
215-328-8300

Type: **Private liberal arts**
Overall campus environment: **Intellectual, Culturally supportive**
Total enrollment: **1330**
African-American students: **95**
Graduate students: **zero**

African-American graduate students: **zero**
Percentage of applications accepted: **32%**
Average SAT score: **1300**
Average SAT African-Americans: **N/A**
Special admissions programs: **N/R**
Percentage of African-American graduates: **N/R**
Percentage receiving financial aid: **60%**
Average amount of award: **$7000**
Percentage in ROTC program: **N/A**
Number of faculty: **135**
Number of African-American faculty: **N/R**
Student/faculty ratio: **9 to 1**
Tuition: **$15,490**
Scholarship programs: **Mellon and Pew Fellowships**
Academic program: **Arts and Sciences and Engineering**
Prominent African-American graduates: **Mary Schmidt Campbell, Dean, NYU Tisch School of the Arts; Christopher F. Edley, Jr., Professor of Law, Harvard University; Dr. Sara Lawrence Lightfoot, Professor, Harvard School of Education; Rupa Redding-Lallinger, medical school professor, Tanzania**
Prominent African-American faculty: **Dr. Asmarom Legesse, Professor of Sociology and Anthropology, first Black professor at Swarthmore**
African-American student organizations/activities: **Black Cultural Center, Swarthmore African-American Student Society, Gospel Choir, Sophisticated Gents, Sistahs**
Administrative services and programs: **N/R**

Make no mistake, Swarthmore is a college for students who are highly intelligent and self-directed and seek a challenging education. Referred to as the quintessential liberal arts college, Swarthmore is also known for its engineering and technical programs, which have served as the educational foundation for some of the nation's finest scientists, doctors and engineers. Swarthmore has produced three Nobel laureates, thirty-six members of the National Academy of Sciences and nine members of the National Academy of Engineering. Its alumni include Pulitzer prize–winning author James Michener; former Massachusetts governor Michael Dukakis; Mary Schmidt Campbell, former New York City commissioner of cultural affairs and now dean of the Tisch School of the Arts at New York University; philanthropist Eugene M. Lang, founder of the "I Have A Dream" program; and Alice Paul, legendary suffragist and author of the Equal Rights Amendment. In addition, Swarthmore has graduated nineteen current or former college and university presidents, and claims distinguished professors at most of the nation's major universities.

Such a reputation could be intimidating to even the most academically accomplished student; but Swarthmore is not interested in admitting only "smart" students, but those who can best succeed in its unique environment. Students who qualify should not be deterred by the college's selectivity, but be encouraged by the college's celebration and support of its diversity.

Those who do apply and are accepted, need to be prepared for a challenge. Swarthmore is a truly intellectual college where academics reign supreme and "going honors" is a coveted achievement. (At Swarthmore, the honors program requires the recommendation of faculty and students, and courses are taught in small seminar groups. Students do not receive a grade until the end of the course. The grade is the result of a five-hour final exam.) "The liberal arts education I took with me from Swarthmore has been an invaluable, dynamic, ever-growing treasure," said one African-American alumnus. "It gave substance to my confidence that I could do and be anything I wanted, and it has kept my intellect free, young and active."

The challenge at Swarthmore is real; but so is the tremendous support that students receive from an outstanding and caring faculty and administration. At Swarthmore, students report that faculty are involved in their social lives as well as in the classroom. It is not unusual for faculty members to attend student social gatherings or to hold classes at their homes. As an intellectual institution, Swarthmore is sensitive to the realities of the African-American plight in this country. "Students, faculty and administration are aware of the consistent underrepresentation of African-Americans on college campuses nationwide, and agree with the college's commitment to encourage more students to attend Swarthmore," said one student. There is also a great deal of support for student organizations and cultural institutions such as the Black Cultural Center; the Swarthmore African-American Student Society; the Gospel Choir; Sistahs, an a cappella singing group, and a male group called The Gents. "Swarthmore, I gotta hand it to the school, really goes out of its way to provide everything imaginable," said another student.

In recent years Swarthmore has increased its efforts to attract African-American students and has established a generous financial aid policy that enables students to attend regardless of ability to pay. The college is able to do this, in part, because of its more than $300-million endowment.

Once on campus, students receive a great deal of academic and counseling support and are especially encouraged by the growing number of African-American teachers, who now represent more than 10 percent of the faculty. However, students will still find that there are adjustments to be made. "Being Black at Swarthmore requires that you demand a lot of yourself," said one student. "You have to be prepared to be the only Black in a class and yet feel comfortable; to be the only dissenter in a sea of conformity and still hang on to your beliefs. This does not mean that being Black at Swarthmore requires that you cut yourself off from the rest of the community, but rather that you can maintain your identity in all of your relationships."

Students who are up to the challenge will join the ranks of illustrious alumni, most of whom have gone on to receive postgraduate degrees and have made great strides in their careers. From successful engineers to college faculty, medical doctors and businesspeople, Swarthmore prepares great leaders. If academics are a priority and social life takes a back seat to what you want out of a college experience, Swarthmore should be at the top of your list.

University of Pittsburgh
Pittsburgh, Pennsylvania
412-624-PITT

Type: **Public**
Overall campus environment: **Academically Challenging, Supportive, Progressive**
Total enrollment: **27,973**
African-American students: **1,796**
Graduate students: **9,723**
African-American graduate students: **397**

Percentage of applications accepted: **81.5%**
Average SAT score: **980**
Average SAT African-Americans: **N/A**
Special admissions programs: **UCEP, QUEST, Upward Bound Transitional Educational Programs**
Percentage of African-American graduates: **47% (in 6 years)**
Percentage receiving financial aid: **73%**
Average amount of award: **$4,200**
Percentage in ROTC programs: **N/R**
Number of faculty: **2,674**
Number of African-American faculty: **93**
Student/faculty ratio: **13 to 1**
Tuition: **$9,690**
Scholarship programs: **University, Chancellor, Provost and athletic scholarships available to all students who qualify; for African-American students grants provided through the University Challenge for Excellence (UCEP) program**
Academic programs: **More than 100 majors in the Colleges of Arts and Sciences, Engineering, Nursing, Pharmacy, Education; Center for International Studies; Schools of Health and Rehabilitation Sciences, Library and Information Science, Social Work**
Most popular majors: **Psychology, Communications, Political Science, Nursing, Pharmacy, Economics, Engineering**
Prominent African-American faculty: **Brenda Berrian, Chairman and Associate Professor, Black Studies; Dennis Brutus, Professor, Black Studies Department, internationally renowned poet, South African activist and former political prisoner; Nathan Davis, Professor of Music and jazz musician; David E. Epperson, Dean and Professor of Social Work; Donald Henderson, Provost of the University and Professor of Sociology; E. J. Josey, Professor, School of Library and Information Science**
Prominent African-American graduates: **Derrick A. Bell, Jr., Dean and Professor of Law, University of Oregon School of Law; Monoseta Covington-Burwell, D.M.D., first female oral and maxillofacial surgeon in Pennsylvania; Mildred Glenn, M.B.A., President, New World National Bank; Frederick S. Humphries, Ph.D, President, Tennessee State University**
African-American student organizations/activities: **Black Action**

Society, Pre-Med Organization for Minority Students, Black Engineering Council, Black American Law Students, Black MBA Association, Black Students Psychological Association, Kuntu Repertory Theater and Writing Workshop, Black Greek fraternities and sororities
Administrative services and programs: University Challenge for Excellence Program, Office of Minority Affairs, QUEST Program

The University of Pittsburgh (Pitt) is one of the best universities in the country and, under the leadership of its president, is clearly committed to increasing educational opportunities for African-American students. The university has an above-average rate of retention of African-American students and has numerous programs and services to attract students to campus and help them succeed once they enroll. This is particularly true of its graduate- and doctoral-level programs, which strongly encourage African-American students to consider entering higher education. The university can point to a specific recruitment program for African-Americans and other minorities (such as women and disadvantaged students) in each of its professional schools. However, the schools of engineering, medicine, education and law have the most extensive programs. These schools provide financial support and academic and peer counseling programs and, in many cases, embark on aggressive recruitment efforts to attract students to their postgraduate schools.

Equally aggressive is Pitt's recruitment effort for undergraduate students. Its Summer Information program reaches out to 10,000 African-American students each year who are identified through the College Board Student Search Service. These students, from states in the Mid-Atlantic region as far west as Ohio and as far south as Florida, are invited with their families to spend two days on campus. The university provides lodging in a residence hall, and students eat in the cafeteria and get an extensive tour. Afterward, they are closely monitored through all stages of the admissions process to ensure they are not overlooked by campus bureaucracy; easy enough considering that this is a campus of nearly 30,000 students.

In addition, the university maintains a continuing recruitment effort through traditional channels of college fairs and high school visitations (especially within the Pittsburgh public schools) and participates in the Upward Bound, In Roads and Investing Now programs, which target disadvantaged students with academic potential. Recognizing that students need to be made aware of college opportunities as soon as possible, the university has established an Outreach Program aimed at middle-schoolers.

Finally, the university has begun to merge its efforts with those of predominantly and historically African-American institutions to bring students into its graduate-level programs and to encourage their consideration of careers in which minorities are underrepresented. Relationships exist between the university and Florida A&M University and South Carolina State College. A number of other departments are now developing summer programs that bring undergraduates from schools like Lincoln University and Cheyney State University to the campus to expose them to careers in public health, international affairs and library and information science.

The programs offered at Pitt for African-American students (particularly at the graduate level) are too numerous to mention, but clearly there is a strong commitment to increasing enrollments in all of them.

Perhaps one of the biggest challenges for students at Pitt is wading through the many academic, social and cultural opportunities available at the university. Pitt is one of the most renowned research institutions in the country; Pitt's laboratories produced the Salk polio vaccine and synthetic insulin and are responsible for the identification of vitamin C. Pitt is known worldwide for research on organ transplants and has a good reputation in such fields as anthropology, art history, behavioral science, business, chemistry and public administration. To help inform students about its many opportunities, the university has developed a publication titled *How to Choose the College or University That's Right For You.* This is highly recommended reading for African-Americans or any student.

Pitt is one of the few universities with a Department of Black Studies and an undergraduate degree-granting social science department that creates a link among African-American, African and Caribbean affairs and explores their impact on the society at large. Pitt's Kuntu Repertory Theatre is well known and its Kuntu

Writing Workshop has among its founders Pulitzer prize-winning playwright August Wilson.

The university's commitment to African-Americans goes beyond recruitment and special programs. About 100 members of the faculty are African-American, and 20 hold key positions in the administration, including Provost, Vice Provost, Dean, Associate Dean, Department Chair and Assistant Department Chair positions.

Located near downtown Pittsburgh, the university is accessible to the city by public transportation. About 100,000 African-Americans call Pittsburgh home, and their presence here is noted in several media, including a newspaper, *The New Pittsburgh Courier;* radio station WAMO, and talk shows on several local television stations. There are two African-American-owned banks here and four restaurants. Campus organizations include several Black Greek fraternities and sororities, the Black Action Society and professional organizations.

Students who consider the University of Pittsburgh need to be open-minded and willing to take advantage of all that the institution has to offer. Clearly, at Pitt, the sky is the limit.

Clemson University
Clemson, South Carolina 29634
803-656-2287

Type: **Public research**
Overall campus environment: **Conservative/athletic**
Total enrollment: **17,295**
African-American students: **1,240**
Graduate students: **4,010**
African-American graduate students: **188**
Percentage of applications accepted: **74%**
Average SAT score: **1028**
Average SAT African-Americans: **928**
Special admissions programs: **N/A**
Percentage of African-American graduates: **N/R**
Percentage receiving financial aid: **95%**
Average amount of award: **$3,300**

Percentage in ROTC programs: **16%**
Number of faculty: **1,223**
Number of African-American faculty: **40**
Student/faculty ratio: **19 to 1**
Tuition: **$2,778 in state/$7,394 out of state**
Scholarship programs: **Clemson Scholars Program, R. C. Edwards Scholarship, a variety of other minority programs**
Academic programs: **Colleges of Agriculture, Architecture, Forest Recreation Resources, Liberal Arts, Commerce and Industry, Nursing, Engineering, Sciences**
Most popular majors: **Engineering, Architecture, Commerce and Industry**
Prominent African-American faculty: **N/A**
Prominent African-American graduates: **Harvey Gantt, former mayor, Charlotte, North Carolina, and first African-American graduate of Clemson**
African-American student organizations/activities:
African-American Alliance, Gospel Choir, Minority Committee Organizing Resources and Events, NESBE (National Society of Black Engineers), TWSPA (Third World Programming Alliance), Panhellenic Greek sororities and fraternities, Minority Council, NAACP
Administrative services and programs: **BEST (Black Educational Support Team), PEER (Program for Engineering Enrichment and Retention)**

If you are a sports enthusiast you are already familiar with Clemson University. This championship-winning university is best known for its football and basketball teams and, unfortunately, for the scandals in 1990 surrounding its less than prudent practices behind the scenes. Yet Clemson has more than sports to offer. A research university, Clemson offers top-notch training in agricultural and technical fields. The university also boasts a nationally ranked engineering program that is a leader in computer circuitry as well as robotics; and a popular agricultural program that dates to the university's founding and continues to bring forth innovations.

A large university with nearly 18,000 students, Clemson is in the foothills of the Blue Ridge Mountains. This Southern university is fairly conservative. The drinking age is twenty-one; most dorms are single-sex, and although the university is not affiliated with any religion or church, there is a preponderance of Southern Baptists on campus. However, the overall environment is relaxed and friendly, and even students who are not from the South find it easier to fit in here than on most campuses of this size.

African-American students generally find campus life comfortable and report that their interaction with faculty and administrators is one of the major benefits of campus life. "What I like most about Clemson is its relaxed learning atmosphere and its promotion of a close relationship between students and faculty," said one student. "I often go one-on-one with my professors to clear up any problems that I might have in the classroom. Administrators are equally helpful and willing to provide me with insight and information to help me solve a problem." Indeed, Clemson's faculty is a good reason to attend the university. Among the many well-known professors at this university is a NASA researcher.

It's no surprise that many African-American students are here because of generous athletic scholarships (the university awards about 400 such scholarships each year). At Clemson sports is *big!* Nearly everyone identifies with the Tiger fever that overshadows campus life, and home games usually draw capacity crowds. However, even if you're not an athlete you stand a good chance of getting the financial aid you need or of winning one of the scholarships available to African-American students.

Clemson's Big School image and athletics can be intimidating, but the administration has made an effort to ease the transition by providing a number of peer counseling and academic support programs for African-American students. It also supports a number of student organizations, including the African-American Alliance, Minority Council, Third World Programming Alliance and Minority Committee Organizing Resources and Events, which provide cultural and social activities.

Even before students begin classes here, some care is taken to introduce them to faculty and staff as well as to campus life. "African-American students have an opportunity to meet faculty and staff through a minority reception given each fall semester, and parents get a chance to do the same during freshmen orientation," says one administrator.

Clemson has the benefits of a successful college athletic program as well as a solid academic program in the much sought-after fields of engineering and the sciences. Students are more likely to come here from South Carolina; however, this school is a good bet no matter what part of the country you come from. "I'm from a small town of about 800 people and was concerned about the racial tensions that exist at other predominantly white universities across the nation," said one student. "After a few months at Clemson many of the fears I had disappeared and I found that Clemson was a very nice place to be."

Sports enthusiasts and those who have an interest in technical fields but who are not prepared for the high-pressure academics of a school like Georgia Tech will find Clemson a good choice.

University of South Carolina
Columbia, South Carolina 29208
803-777-7323

Type: **Public**
Overall campus environment: **Cordial**
Total enrollment: **26,133**
African-American students: **3,298**
Graduate students: **10,074**
African-American graduate students: **815**
Percentage of applications accepted: **78–83%**
Average SAT score: **954**
Average SAT African-Americans: **827**
Special admissions programs: **N/A**
Percentage of African-American graduates: **66% (over 6 years)**
Percentage receiving financial aid: **21%**
Average amount of award: **$3,000**
Percentage in ROTC programs: **N/R**
Number of faculty: **1,514**
Number of African-American faculty: **51**
Student/faculty ratio: **17 to 1**
Tuition: **$7,046**
Scholarship programs: **Merit Scholarships**
Academic programs: **Colleges of Business Administration, Engineering, Education, Journalism and Mass Communications, Humanities and Social Sciences, Science**

and Math, Health, Applied Professional Sciences; School of
Hotel, Restaurant and Tourism Administration
Most popular majors: **Business and Management, Political
Science, Psychology, Graduate International Business
Program, Government and International Studies**
Prominent African-American faculty: **N/R**
Prominent African-American graduates: **Bruce Caughman,
former personal aide to President George Bush; Alex English,
professional basketball player; I. S. Leevy Johnson, attorney,
former director, South Carolina Bar Association; Frank L.
Matthews, Co-Publisher, *Black Issues in Higher Education*;
George Rogers, Heisman Trophy winner; Sterling Sharpe,
professional football player**
African-American student organizations/activities: **Umoja,
NAACP, Touch of Faith Gospel Choir, Association for
African-American Students, National Society of Black
Engineers, Sigma Gamma Rho, Delta Sigma Theta, Alpha
Kappa Alpha, Zeta Phi Beta, Alpha Phi Alpha; Kappa Alpha
Psi, Omega Psi Phi, Phi Beta Sigma**
Administrative services and programs: **Minority Student Affairs
Office, Minority Assistance Peer Team (MAP)**

The University of South Carolina is one of the best schools in the
country for a number of reasons, not the least of which are its
top-rated business, engineering and medical schools. Each has
received national recognition from the public and private sectors
as well as research funding in the millions. What is most impressive about USC, however, is that it seems to have so many good
programs. Whether it's the School of Hotel, Restaurant and Tourism Administration (one of four such accredited programs in the
nation), the marine sciences department (ranked fourth nationally), or the International Business Program, with more than
1,300 graduates working in fifty-one countries around the world,
USC seems to do everything well, including promoting itself.

USC is a public university that until recently had the image of
being a party school and a Greek-dominated campus whose students were not serious about academics. For some students this
remains the view of the college. However, for African-Americans
seeking an opportunity to obtain a good, affordable education in

programs that will help them become marketable after graduation, USC is definitely a school to consider. African-American students largely come from within the state, and those who are serious about their studies seem to do well. Over a six-year period, the administration reports that more than 65 percent of African-American students graduated.

Located in the state capital, Columbia, USC has more than 26,000 students, with African-Americans representing more than 12 percent of enrollment (an admirable number considering this is a predominantly white campus). Not surprisingly, African-Americans at USC are comforted by their numbers and have made their presence known by their involvement on campus and in the community. All the major sororities and fraternities are represented, and many are involved in community service projects such as Big Brothers/Big Sisters and the Boys Clubs. "There are many opportunities for intellectual growth and personal development at USC," said one student. "African-American students will find myriad organizations to become involved with to get their voices heard." Other African-American student organizations include Umoja, which promotes cultural awareness; the NAACP; Touch of Faith Gospel Choir, and the Association for African-American Students.

USC's interest in increasing the number of African-American students on campus has spawned a number of support organizations, such as the Minority Assistance Peer Team (MAP), which provides upperclass peer counselors to freshmen, and the Minority Student Affairs office, which assists students with academics and counseling. One responsibility of this office is to help with the recruitment of African-American students, and it has developed a formal campus visitation program called Carolina Tip-Off. Programs such as these get students into USC and help them over the hurdles of beginning campus life. Those who successfully withstand the rigors of college life here can also find help in planning their careers after college through USC's Career Center. Besides getting help with employment, students can learn about internships and cooperative education opportunities at a variety of companies and agencies. Students can also participate in the annual Minority Career Day Fair, a joint project of the Minority Affairs Office and Career Center. No doubt USC is on the right track—its

African-American graduates have had success in law, business, sports and government, as well as other fields. Some of its more prominent graduates are sports figures (largely because of the school's emphasis on sports and its recruitment of African-American athletes), among them Heisman Trophy winner George Rogers.

Generally, African-Americans report they are satisfied with the academic and social environment at USC and recommend the university to other students. "I thought I was selling myself short by going to USC," said a resident of South Carolina. "Instead I found an administration and faculty who were quite receptive and helpful and an academic experience that was rewarding."

Middle Tennessee State University
208 Cope Administration Building
Murfreesboro, Tennessee 37132
615-898-2111/1-800-331-MTSU

Type: **State**
Overall campus environment: **Traditional**
Total enrollment: **15,691**
African-American students: **1,443**
Graduate students: **1,600**
African-American graduate students: **N/R**
Percentage applications accepted: **78%**
Average ACT score: **20.1**
Average ACT score African-Americans: **N/R**
Special admissions programs: **N/A**
Percentage of African-American graduates: **N/R**
Percentage receiving financial aid: **62%**
Average amount of award: **$3,600**
Percentage in ROTC programs: **N/R**
Number of faculty: **615**
Number of African-American faculty: **46**
Student/faculty ratio: **25 to 1**
Tuition: **$1,480 in state/$5,000 out of state**
Scholarship programs: **Willie Brown, Ken Tony and Matching Scholarship Programs for Minority Scholars, INROADS**

Academic programs: **More than 75 majors in 33 departments of Colleges of Basic and Applied Science, Business, Education, Liberal Arts and Mass Communications**
Most popular majors: **Accounting, Aerospace, Education, Music, Recording Industry Management**
Prominent African-American faculty: **Terry Weeks, Assistant Professor, Education, 1988 National Teacher of the Year**
Prominent African-American graduates: **N/R**
African-American student organizations/activities:
African-American Student Association, NAACP of MTSU, Organization for African-American Unity, Erudite Emancipators, United Greek Council, Alpha Kappa Alpha, Alpha Phi Alpha, Delta Sigma Theta, Sigma Gamma Rho, Kappa Alpha Psi, Zeta Phi Beta, Phi Beta Sigma, Omega Psi Phi, African-American History Month
Administrative services and programs: **Office of Minority Affairs, National Alumni Association**

Middle Tennessee State University, one of the larger public institutions in the state, offers a variety of academic programs in its five colleges. Like many public institutions, MTSU is committed to providing a solid education to as many of the state's residents as possible and works closely with them to achieve that goal. Although admissions policies take into consideration that some young people are economically or academically disadvantaged, they hold to stringent requirements that include completion of courses in English, a foreign language, science and the arts. As one administrator put it, "The ideal student at MTSU arrives ready to be challenged academically and enlightened socially. No student is denied admission who meets our requirements, but it becomes a very competitive process for those who do not meet our standards."

Located in the small town of Murfreesboro, MTSU enjoys a close relationship with the community, and African-American students attend nearby churches, participate in social events and recently began a student chapter of the NAACP.

More than 80 percent of students who attend MTSU are from Tennessee, and about 10 percent of them are African-American. The administration encourages all students to take an active role in college life. Students are asked to serve on committees, assist in the development and implementation of campus programs and lead student organizations.

For African-American students, the primary student organization on campus is the African-American Student Association, which is responsible for many of the social and cultural events. In addition, the Office of Minority Affairs plays a key role in helping African-American students get used to campus life. There are nineteen minority organizations at MTSU, including the African-American Student Association and chapters of all the national Black Greek fraternities and sororities.

A special program, INROADS, has been established by the administration for minority youth to train and develop their talents in corporate and community leadership. Students are awarded scholarships through this program and provided summer internships, year-round counseling and training workshops. In addition, students will find an active African-American Alumni Association whose members serve as mentors and professional contacts to introduce students to various careers and to pave the way for their entrance into the field.

Among the extensive academic offerings at MTSU is a Recording Industry Management program that is touted as having the best college recording facility in the country. The university also has a top-rated aerospace program that offers state-of-the-art equipment and a nationally ranked flight team, and majors in historic preservation and animal science, as well as more traditional studies such as business, communications and the applied and natural sciences.

Overall, the relationship between majority and minority students is good. In addition, students report that they find faculty members (particularly African-American professors) helpful and supportive. "I feel this is due more to the type of student we recruit than to efforts on the part of the administration," says an administrator.

MTSU offers a solid academic program in an environment that recognizes a changing world in terms of cultural, social and work force needs. It is particularly well suited to students who live in Tennessee or in the Ohio Valley and any student who would enjoy the pace and friendliness of the South. With an in-state tuition less than $5,000, MTSU also offers good value.

African-American students will find that although they are just

10 percent of the student population at MTSU, their influence on campus exceeds their numbers, and this experience can prepare them for a future in a world much the same.

Tennessee Technological University
Box 5006
Cookeville, Tennessee 38505
615-372-3888

Type: **Public**
Overall campus environment: **Cordial**
Total enrollment: **8,160**
African-American students: **280**
Graduate students: **899**
African-American graduate students: **34**
Percentage of applications accepted: **95%**
Average ACT score: **20.94**
Average ACT African-Americans: **18.75**
Special admissions programs: **N/A**
Percentage of African-American graduates: **N/A**
Percentage receiving financial aid: **75%**
Average amount of award: **$1,400**
Percentage in ROTC programs: **10% (Army and Air Force)**
Number of faculty: **375**
Number of African-American faculty: **15**
Student/faculty ratio: **21 to 1**
Tuition: **$3,360**
Scholarship programs: **Tennessee Tech Scholarships for African-Americans, Athletic Scholarships**
Academic programs: **Colleges of Education, Arts and Sciences, Business, Engineering, Agriculture and Home Economics**
Most popular majors: **Engineering, Business, Computer Science, Education**
Prominent African-American graduates: **N/R**
Prominent African-American faculty: **N/R**
African-American student organizations/activities: **Black Student Organization, National Society of Black Engineers, Alpha Phi Alpha, Omega Psi Phi, Kappa Alpha Psi, Alpha Kappa Alpha, Delta Sigma Theta, Black Cultural Center**

Administrative services and programs: **University 101 Program, Black Cultural Center, Young Scholars Program**

Tennessee Technological University is a public institution in the small town of Cookeville about eighty miles outside Nashville. A moderately selective university, TTU has a good academic reputation, particularly in the sciences, engineering and other technical fields. The university draws the largest majority of its students from inside the state and has a minority population of about 6 percent, most of whom are African-Americans. Considering its size, the university also has a fair number of African-American professors—far more than many schools that strongly advocate cultural diversity. About 4 percent of the faculty is African-American, and the majority hold doctoral degrees.

Like many universities, TTU has an established program to recruit and retain more African-American students. Its scholarship programs include the traditional financing of tuition but also, in some cases, include a housing allowance; spending money, which it calls "maintenance fees," and a $300 credit. Not all students are eligible for all of these allowances. Some get only one, or a combination, depending on financial need. TTU also attracts minority students through its Young Scholars Program and through Summer Camps for high school students which incorporate activities like basketball, cheerleading and band to give students a taste of campus life. For many students, sports is an attraction, since TTU is a member of the NCAA Division I and Ohio Valley Conference; the university awards sports scholarships. There are fourteen intercollegiate sports on the campus and more than 100 intramural teams in softball, basketball and volleyball, as well as football and a number of other sports. Aside from sports, many African-American students are drawn to TTU's ROTC program, which pays for a student's college education in return for service in the military as a commissioned officer. About ten percent of the students enrolled in the Army and Air Force ROTC programs are African-American.

Although the administration provides some academic support for students through an orientation class, most of the advising and support of African-American students comes through the Black Cultural Center, which conducts workshops as well as social activities. Students also rely on the faculty, especially African-American professors, for guidance and support.

Social life revolves around campus organizations and involvement in the community of Cookeville, where many students attend church and tutor schoolchildren. The university is in a rural area where there is little to do for entertainment, so campus life is important. African-American students tend to socialize with one another through campus organizations like the Black Student Organization, National Society of Black Engineers and several national Black Greek organizations.

If you are a resident of Tennessee, TTU is a college to consider because of its academic offerings, financial aid and low tuition, and fairly significant number of African-American students and faculty.

Southern Methodist University
P.O. Box 296, Dallas, Texas 75275-0296
1-800-323-0672

Type: **Private**
Overall campus climate: **Cordial**
Total enrollment: **8,746**
African-American students: **403**
Graduate students: **3,275**
African-American graduate students: **158**
Percentage of applications accepted: **68%**
Average SAT score: **950–1160**
Average SAT African-Americans: **N/R**
Special admissions programs: **N/R**
Percentage of African-American graduates: **N/R**
Percentage receiving financial aid: **72%**
Average amount of award: **$11,780**
Percentage in ROTC programs: **N/R**
Number of faculty: **482**
Number of African-American faculty: **N/R**
Student/faculty ratio: **13 to 1**
Tuition: **$11,768**
Scholarship programs: **National Achievement Scholarships for African-American Students, SMU Diversity Scholarships, SMU Minority Awards, Meadows Scholars, University Major Scholarships**

Academic programs: **Dedmond College, Cox School of Business, Meadows School of the Arts, Center for Communication Arts, School of Engineering and Applied Science**
Most popular majors: **Fine Arts, Humanities, English, Accounting, Marketing, Finance, Engineering**
Prominent African-American faculty: **N/A**
Prominent African-American graduates: **N/A**
African-American student organizations/activities: **Association of Black Students, Total Success Paraprofessional Program, STARS (Steps to Academic Rewards and Success), Mentoring Program**
Administrative services and programs: **Department of Intercultural Education and Minority Affairs**

If the name of this university has you thinking that this is a religious institution, think again. Although about 20 percent of the students who attend Southern Methodist University are Methodists, religion is not what attracts students to SMU. A visit to SMU's campus will give you some idea why this is a popular university, especially among more affluent students. The campus looks like a country club, and SMU's facilities, including its own health club complete with heated pool, Nautilus equipment and racketball and handball courts, will have you convinced you're at a plush resort instead of a college.

Despite appearances, however, SMU has outstanding academics. All students are required to demonstrate a strong foundation in the liberal arts and must enroll in the Common Educational Experience program for the first two years. After that they may enroll in a major field of study at one of the university's five schools. SMU has notable fine arts, humanities and English programs, as well as a solid business school which offers majors in finance, marketing and accounting. Other popular programs include an engineering school and center for communication arts.

The university administration seems to go out of its way to accommodate students' needs with innovations such as the wellness program, in which all students must participate. This health-oriented, noncredit program essentially analyzes the state of your health and suggests a personal fitness, nutrition and lifestyle regimen.

For African-American students a strong academic advising program, including personalized counseling, a mentoring and peer support program and tutoring, is administered by SMU's Intercultural Education and Minority Student Affairs department.

Such programs serve a real need. African-American students at SMU represent less than 5 percent of the student body, Hispanics make up about another 5 percent. Although the campus is moderate in size, minority students can feel isolated, primarily because of the social and class differences. A majority of students here are very affluent, with BMWs, Saabs, Mercedes and other luxury cars and Rolex watches. This, coupled with their lack of exposure to members of minorities, can make an African-American student feel uncomfortable and out of place.

Still, many students are able to get past these issues and instead deal with the high-quality education and opportunities SMU offers. "The campus is predominantly white but SMU still offers opportunities for other ethnic groups if they want to get involved and help make a change to more cultural diversity," said one student. It also does not hurt that SMU can offer minority students generous financial aid and scholarship packages because it is so well endowed.

While social activity centers around Greek life (there are no predominantly African-American Greek organizations at SMU), students can get involved with one of the more than 140 student organizations on campus, including the Association of Black Students, which is the focus of most cultural activities. The administration strongly encourages African-American students to participate in other campus events. According to one student, the administration also does what it can to help familiarize students with campus and city life. "The Intercultural Education department is a good place to get advice on making the transition into SMU and to find out what's happening in the minority community in Dallas," the student said. That SMU is located a short ride from downtown Dallas is worth noting, as is the fact that many of the African-American alumni of SMU have remained in the area and now serve as mentors and advisers to new students.

SMU is making an effort to become more culturally diverse, and its new president seems committed to this effort and to that of making the university one of the best academically in the country. This is not the school to attend if you need the nurturing, comfort and reinforcement of a strong African-American presence. On the other hand, if you are self-directed, want a solid education in a luxurious campus environment with a strong possibility of a good financial aid package, and can handle being one of very few African-American students, SMU may be a good choice.

Southwestern University
University at Maple
Georgetown, Texas 78626
512-863-1200

Type: **Private liberal arts, affiliated with United Methodist Church**
Overall campus environment: **Pleasant**
Total enrollment: **1,231**
African-American students: **37**
Graduate students: **N/A**
African-American graduate students: **N/A**
Percentage of applications accepted: **65%**
Average SAT/ACT score: **1040–1200/24–26**
Average SAT/ACT African-Americans: **1000/24**
Special admissions programs: **N/R**
Percentage of African-American graduates: **64%**
Percentage receiving financial aid: **94%**
Average amount of award: **N/A**
Percentage in ROTC program: **N/A**
Number of faculty: **83**
Number of African-American faculty: **1**
Student/faculty ratio: **12 to 1**
Tuition: **$10,300**
Scholarship programs: **Presidential Scholarship Program, Jesse H. and Mary Gibbs Jones Scholars Program for minority scholars**
Academic programs: **Brown College of Arts and Sciences, School of Fine Arts, Divisions of Humanities, Social Sciences, Natural Sciences and General Education Program**

Most popular majors: **Business, Psychology, Biology, Communications, International Studies**
Prominent African-American graduates: **N/R**
Prominent African-American faculty: **N/R**
African-American student organizations/activities: **Black Student Union**
Administrative services and programs: **Office of Multicultural Affairs**

Southwestern University has a rich history and committed alumni and friends who support it philosophically and financially. It was the first institution of higher learning in Texas and is now among the best-endowed universities in the nation (more than $136 million), with numerous sports facilities and other buildings named for its generous benefactors. The university offers a fair number of scholarships each year (two of the programs are for minorities). Located in rural Georgetown about thirty miles outside Austin, Southwestern provides a traditional liberal education "that teaches communication skills, sharpens decision-making capacities, and develops analytical abilities," says one administrator. In addition, students must demonstrate competence in the use of computers and their major field of study. Southwestern offers thirty-one major programs of study as well as a study abroad program and cooperative relationships with schools in South Korea, France, Germany, Spain, Japan, England and Thailand. It also has a community outreach program in the local school district of Georgetown.

The university sits on more than 500 beautifully landscaped acres, which include a 75-acre nine-hole golf course. More than 70 percent of students live in residence halls; those who live off campus have cars. Although there are other minorities and internationals on campus, African-Americans comprise only 3 percent of the more than 1,200 students. It's not surprising, then, that many students feel isolated. But according to one student, the small size of the university compensates. "I feel there is a family atmosphere among the Black students at Southwestern. We're concerned about each other and the issues that affect us as African-Americans. I don't think that sense of family can be found so easily in larger universities." There are a Black Student Union and Office of Multicultural Affairs, but there is a stronger attempt to include African-Americans in the mainstream of campus life. The administration has also made it clear that it is working toward a more culturally diverse campus. When questions about affirmative action policies arose recently, the administration held an open forum and explained its policy to the student body. But Southwestern has a long way to go. Besides its small minority student population, the university reports having only one faculty member who is African-American. "If I could change one thing about Southwestern, I would have more minority—particularly African-American—faculty," says one student, "not only to benefit African-Americans but for all students to see them in non-stereotypical roles."

Still, students have found that Southwestern is a good choice if you are looking for a good liberal arts college where faculty and administrators care about you. "I have nothing but positive experiences from faculty and administrators at Southwestern," one student said. "The faculty are committed to student excellence and are always available and willing to help students of all races, and the administration is cooperative and supportive. They recognize that African-American students at a racially unbalanced school have special needs and concerns."

University of North Texas
P. O. Box 13797
Denton, Texas
817-565-3926

Type: **Public**
Overall campus environment: **Cordial**
Total enrollment: **27,020**
African-American students: **1,643**
Graduate students: **6,805**
African-American graduate students: **232**
Percentage of applications accepted: **62%**
Average SAT/ACT Score: **971/23**
Average SAT/ACT African-Americans: **809/19**
Special admissions programs: **N/A**
Percentage of African-American graduates: **5%**
Percentage receiving financial aid: **16%**

Average amount of award: **$3,500**
Percentage in ROTC programs: **7%**
Number of faculty: **831**
Number of African-American faculty: **20**
Student/faculty ratio: **19 to 1**
Tuition: **$4,474**
Scholarship programs: **Data Bank of outside scholarships maintained by the Office of Multicultural Affairs**
Academic programs: **More than 150 majors through the College of Arts and Sciences, College of Business Administration, School of Community Service, College of Education, School of Library and Information Sciences, School of Merchandising and Hospitality Management, College of Music, Robert B. Toulouse School of Graduate Studies**
Most popular majors: **Art, Music, Accounting, Psychology**
Prominent African-American graduates: **N/R**
Prominent African-American faculty: **N/R**
African-American Student Organizations/activities: **Progressive Black Student Organization (PBSO), National Association of Black Accountants (NABA), National Association of Black Journalists (NABJ), NAACP, Ujima, Alpha Kappa Alpha, Delta Sigma Theta, Zeta Phi Beta, Sigma Gamma Rho, Kappa Alpha Psi, Alpha Phi Alpha, Omega Psi Phi, Phi Beta Sigma**
Administrative services and programs: **Intercultural Services Division, STAR (Skills, Training, and Academic Retention) Program, Dr. Martin Luther King, Jr., Candlelight Service, Multicultural Scholarship Awards Banquet, Sharing and Growth Conference**

The University of North Texas is a public university in the small town of Denton, just outside Dallas-Fort Worth. Academic standards here are high, and admission has become increasingly competitive as the institution attempts to slow the enormous growth that increased enrollment by several thousand in the past decade. University of North Texas has reason to be competitive. Among its more than 150 degree programs, the university has the largest school of visual arts at a U.S. public university, as well as the second-largest college of music and a variety of other widely respected academic programs. University of North Texas's faculty are highly regarded, with more than 80 percent holding doctoral degrees; all are full professors published and nationally recognized in their fields. University of North Texas does an admirable job of providing students with an understanding of liberal arts, business and sciences through its Academic Core Programs. Its Great Books Program guides students through the classics of Western thought; and the Honors Program, reserved for fifty of the brightest freshmen each year, leads to a bachelor's degree "with University Honors."

Built into this highly competitive academic environment is a number of tutorial and skill-building services for majority and minority students. Free and paid tutors can be found through individual academic departments, through the NT Connection, which provides free tutorial service, and through the Student Employment Service, which maintains a file on graduates and undergraduates who seek employment as tutors. The University Writing Center provides free tutoring and workshops in an effort to improve all students' writing and composition skills. African-American and minority students will find additional help through the STAR (Skills, Training and Academic Retention) program, which teaches note-taking, study and test-taking skills.

Additionally, African-American students will find a host of academic, social and cultural programs designed to help them adjust to life on campus and succeed through graduation. The majority of these programs are administered through the Dean of Students' office, which has set up a department to handle multicultural affairs. Recruitment of African-American students is conducted by this office, as is planning for special events such as Black History Month, Martin Luther King, Jr., birthday celebrations and the annual Multicultural Scholarship Awards banquet, which honors African-American and Hispanic students who have achieved excellence in their majors.

Overall, African-American students report that life at UNT provides an equitable atmosphere for all students that is conducive to learning. "The faculty and administrators throw opportunities my way and I catch them," said one student. At times, she said, the underlying attitudes of racism emerge. "Many of my friends have criticized me for attending a predominantly white university, but I feel like I can make a difference on this campus." If you are self-aware and confident of your ability to succeed at a large university, and if you are seeking a degree in visual arts, music or psychology, University of North Texas may be worth including in your list of prospective choices.

Utah State University
Logan, Utah 84322-0160
801-750-1000

Type: **Public**
Overall campus environment: **Cordial**
Total enrollment: **15,000**
African-American students: **100**
Graduate students: **2500**
Percentage of applications accepted: **66%**
Average ACT score: **23**
Average ACT African-Americans: **20**
Special admissions programs: **N/R**
Percentage of African-American graduates: **N/A**
Percentage receiving financial aid: **65%**
Average amount of award: **$2500**
Percentage in ROTC programs: **N/R**
Number of faculty: **678**
Number of African-American faculty: **N/R**
Student/faculty ratio: **11 to 1**
Tuition: **$1,485 in state/$4700 out of state**
Scholarship programs: **N/A**
Academic programs: **Colleges of Agriculture, Business, Education, Engineering, Family Life, Humanities, Arts and Social Science, Natural Resources, Science**
Most popular majors: **Business Administration, Elementary Education, Computer Science, Art, Humanities, Math, Sciences, Engineering, Social Science, Education, pre-professional programs**
Prominent African-American faculty: **N/A**
Prominent African-American graduates: **N/A**
African-American student organizations/activities: **Black Collegiates and Associates United, Black Greek organizations**
Administrative services and programs: **N/R**

Utah State University is a research university offering a wide variety of majors, as well as preprofessional degrees in law, medicine, dentistry and veterinary medicine. Among its more popular offerings are programs in high-tech fields, including majors in acoustics, agronomy, aviation technology, bioengineering, blood bank technology, conservation, geosciences and industrial hygiene. The university's facilities include laboratories for research and study of agriculture, water research and space exploration. In addition, the university offers dual majors, independent study programs, internships and cooperative programs with nearby Weber State College.

It's probably no surprise that Utah State University only enrolls a small percentage of African-American students. This four-year public institution reports that minority students in general comprise just over 10 percent of its student body, and African-Americans represent about one percent of that number. In fact, the largest minority on this campus are Native Americans.

Utah State attracts students primarily from inside the state. More than half commute either from nearby off-campus housing or because they live within a short distance of the university. Only 20 percent live on campus. Whether students choose to live on or off campus, however, has little impact on campus life, as Logan (population 30,000) is primarily a college town, about eighty miles from Salt Lake City.

African-American students cannot help feeling somewhat isolated here, as the African-American community is very small and estranged from college life. For most students, social activities revolve around the Black Collegiates and Associates United, which sponsors most of the cultural and social events. There are also two African-American fraternities, which students find a more comfortable alternative to the majority Greek organizations which dominate campus life.

Student interaction is reportedly good, although the administration admits that majority students tend to be standoffish and hesitant to approach African-American students outside the classroom. "Some white students have a tendency to hesitate to interact with minority students," says one administrator. "Generally, minority students have to make the first step."

Utah State is moderately selective, although the administration does have a provisional program that is geared toward enrollment of minority students. Besides test scores, the administration looks for students who are well rounded, have good grades and are motivated to achieve.

Although Utah State does not have a religious affiliation, there is a preponderance of religious clubs and organizations on campus, including the Mormons, who dominate in this part of the country.

Students who consider Utah State need to keep in mind that they will be in an environment with few other African-Americans either on campus or in Logan. There are signs that the administration is working to make life more comfortable for African-Americans and other minorities, but a student who is unfamiliar with this part of the country may feel isolated and out of touch. However, if you are strong-minded, self-directed and willing to deal with these realities to reap the academic benefits Utah State provides, you can succeed at this school.

Hampden-Sydney College
Hampden-Sydney, Virginia 23943
804-223-6120/1-800-755-0733

Type: **4-year men's liberal arts, affiliated with Presbyterian Church**
Overall campus environment: **Good/conservative**
Total enrollment: **950**
African-American students: **28**
Graduate students: **N/A**
Percentage of applications accepted: **75%**
Average SAT score: **1066**
Average SAT African-Americans: **N/R**
Special admissions programs: **N/R**
Percentage of African-American graduates: **85%**
Percentage receiving financial aid: **100%**
Average amount of award: **$14,500**
Percentage in ROTC programs: **Coop Program offered at nearby Longwood College**
Number of faculty: **77**
Number of African-American faculty: **1**

Student/faculty ratio: **13 to 1**
Tuition: **$11,882**
Scholarship programs: **Numerous scholarships, none specifically for minorities**
Academic programs: **Liberal Arts, Pre-Law and Pre-Medical Programs, Business Preparation and Internships, Dual Degree Programs in Engineering with Georgia Tech and Virginia Tech, Washington Semester in Government, Honors Program, Foreign Study Program**
Most popular majors: **Economics, History, Political Science**
Prominent African-American graduates: **Maurice Jones, Rhodes scholar, Truman Fellow; Rodney Ruffin, Administrative Law Judge, Department of Employment Services, Washington, D.C.**
Prominent African-American faculty: **N/R**
African-American student organizations/activities: **N/R**
Administrative services and programs: **Minority Affairs Committee, Admissions Office, Student Support Group**

Hampden-Sydney College is one of the oldest private liberal arts colleges in the country, and one of the few still serving an all-male population. Founded in the 1700s with the help of statesmen Patrick Henry and James Madison, Hampden-Sydney carries on a tradition of preparing young men for leadership through a rigorous liberal arts program which includes courses in the humanities, natural sciences, mathematics and social sciences as well as English composition, rhetoric and at least one foreign language. Over its 200 years of continuous operation Hampden-Sydney has become known, according to its administration, as a college that produces strong leaders: 12 senators, 33 congressmen, 12 governors, 8 ambassadors, 120 state representatives, and numerous doctors, lawyers and leaders of business and industry. This small college of nearly 1,000 students with a student-to-faculty ratio of 13 to 1, provides young men an opportunity to focus on their studies without many of the distractions present at larger, less traditional institutions. Since the campus is all-male, activities seem to be less centered on partying and more around sports, leadership development and participation in campus organizations. The college sits on a 650-acre wooded campus in Hampden-Sydney, Virginia, a rural community of 6,000 about sixty miles from Richmond. More than 90 percent of students live on campus, as do most faculty members, which provides students the opportunity to get to know their professors on a first-name basis and to form lasting relationships. "Faculty are not only teachers but mentors and friends," said a senior. "The number of African-American professors is small; however, African-American students can and do have close relationships with various professors."

The focus at Hampden-Sydney is clearly on academics; expectations are high for all students. Admission is highly selective; applicants are expected to have had strong college preparatory training and score around 1000 on the SAT. Once students are admitted, the college becomes dedicated to helping them academically and financially. Students benefit from a huge endowment of more than $34 million, which allows the school to provide 100 percent of a student's financial need, mostly through grants and scholarships. Faculty and administrators are demanding but helpful. "Part of the challenge of Hampden-Sydney is the expectation of professors," a student said. "A student is expected to express his ideas and defend them in speech and in writing." This formula seems to work for the African-American students enrolled at Hampden-Sydney, which reports no dropouts in the freshman year and an 85 percent graduation rate. Some graduates have gone on to great achievements, including an administrative law judgeship and a Rhodes scholarship.

Currently, African-American students represent just under 3 percent of students enrolled at Hampden-Sydney, and there is a push to attract more students to the school. The college has employed several strategies, including a program which brings prospective students to campus. Recruitment also relies heavily on the testimonials of successful alumni. While there are no special campus organizations to support minority students, the college has formed a Minority Affairs Committee to address concerns of African-American students, and the admissions staff works closely with students to plan events and activities. The administration encourages African-American participation in all campus organizations. In addition, Hampden-Sydney sponsors a summer liberal arts program which provides African-American students enrolled in community colleges an opportunity to attend summer school and investigate a liberal arts college. This is another way of attracting potential students, as many African-Americans come to four-year institutions from community colleges.

Hampden-Sydney is not a college for everyone, as even the college's admissions materials will attest. However, a student who wants a challenging academic environment, is self-directed and goal-oriented, and who is not "political," may want to consider this college. One student said, "Hampden-Sydney is a college for any young man who wants to learn and be challenged. Its mission is to form good men and good citizens, which is of vital importance in a time when good African-American men are considered rare, endangered and extinct."

Hampton University
Hampton, Virginia 23668
804-727-5688

Type: **private predominantly African-American**
Overall campus environment: **Supportive**
Total enrollment: **5,700**
African-American students: **5,000**
Graduate students: **400**
Percentage of applications accepted: **30%**
Average SAT score: **800**
Average SAT African-Americans: **800**
Special admissions programs: **N/A**
Percentage of African-American graduates: **54%**
Percentage receiving financial aid: **64%**
Average amount of award: **$2500**
Percentage in ROTC program: **N/R**
Number of faculty: **355**
Number of African-American faculty: **N/R**
Student/faculty ratio: **15 to 1**
Tuition: **$10,126**
Scholarship programs: **Numerous private and corporate scholarships**
Academic programs: **Schools of Business, Liberal Arts and**

298 / Hampton University

Education, Nursing, Pure and Applied Sciences; Graduate College; College of Continuing Education
Prominent African-American faculty: **N/R**
Prominent African-American graduates: **Judy A. Johnson, Director, Profit Management Systems, IBM Corp., Mid-Atlantic Area**
African-American student organizations/activities: **More than 50, including Black Greek organizations**
Administrative services and programs: **Student Services Office, Learning to Learn program, Student Support Services, Educational Talent Search, Upward Bound**

Until performer Bill Cosby donated an unprecedented $20 million to Spelman College in Atlanta, Hampton University was the best-endowed African-American college in the country. Hampton's endowment is still among the largest, and it has a long history of receiving public and private support. Begun to provide education to freed slaves during Reconstruction, Hampton has historically been supported by religious groups, individuals and the federal government through land grants. Its purpose then was to provide African-Americans with an "education for life," which encompassed teaching such virtues as character and usefulness to society—a philosophy Hampton still supports.

Today Hampton has grown to five schools offering majors in business, liberal arts, education, nursing and pure and applied sciences; a graduate college, and a college of continuing education. Admission to Hampton is fairly selective; students must have had college-preparatory courses in high school. "The academic program at Hampton is rigorous and faculty have high expectations of students who come here," says one student. The administration does provide academic assistance to students who need it. Hampton has a variety of resources including academic and personal counseling services and the Learning to Learn course, which teaches time management skills, reading comprehension and test-taking. Two tutorial programs are also available for students who need help with a specific course or area of study.

In keeping with its historical mission, Hampton is very community-minded and does a great deal of outreach to the local African-American community through a variety of volunteer programs as well as recruiting of students through local high schools.

The college's Educational Talent Search program targets high school students with potential, helps them complete their high school education and facilitates their entrance into college. Hampton is also an active participant in Upward Bound, which provides motivational assistance and enrichment to students with college potential but who may not otherwise have an opportunity to attend college.

Besides its strong academic program, Hampton offers students the supportive environment that distinguishes predominantly African-American colleges. All of the more than fifty student organizations are African-American, and there's always something to do, whether it's attending a party or a performance of the Hampton Jazz Ensemble. Besides the many clubs on campus, students also have the benefit of a campus radio station and television studio, which invite student participation. There is, however, a predominance of Greek organizations on campus, which concerns some students who do not like the way they separate themselves from others. Overall, students find that the positives of being on a predominantly African-American campus outweigh the negatives.

Students will find that the benefits of attending Hampton continue after graduation. Hampton has a strong and active alumni association that not only visits the campus during homecoming weekend and helps with recruitment, but is ever present. The National Hampton Alumni Association gives each senior a "Black Family" kit which includes the name and number of a contact person who will serve as a career mentor. Since the early 1960s, Hampton has encouraged loyalty and unity in its students through the Pre-Alumni Council and has taught the importance of passing on knowledge, expertise and influence to help others achieve. As one student put it, "When you attend Hampton you are forever bound to the college."

Perhaps the only drawback of attending a college like Hampton is its insular environment, which tends to shields students from the "real world" of racial interaction (although Hampton does have a small white population). On the other hand, many students find that this kind of environment helps them acquire the confidence and self-awareness they need to take on the world.

Hollins College
P.O. Box 9523
Roanoke, Virginia 24020
703-362-6407/1-800-456-9595

Type: **Women's liberal arts**
Overall campus environment: **Traditional/Friendly**
Total enrollment: **1,000**
African-American students: **30**
Graduate students: **200**
African-American graduate students: **N/R**
Percentage of applications accepted: **80%**
Average SAT/ACT score: **890–1110/21–26**
Average SAT/ACT African-Americans: **N/A**
Special admissions programs: **None N/A**
Percentage of African-American graduates: **N/R**
Percentage receiving financial aid: **100%**
Average amount of award: **$12,250**
Percentage in ROTC programs: **N/A**
Number of faculty: **92**
Number of African-American faculty: **1**
Student/faculty ratio: **10 to 1**
Tuition: **$17,150**
Scholarship programs: **College scholarships and need-based grants**
Academic programs: **American Studies, Art, Art History, Biology, Chemistry, Classics, Communication Studies, Computational Sciences, Economics/Business, Education, English/Creative Writing, French, German, History, Mathematics/Statistics, Music, Philosophy, Physics, Political Science, Religion, Sociology, Spanish, Theater Arts/Drama, Film**
Most popular majors: **Dance, Education, International Relations, Pre-Law, Pre-Medicine, Russian**
Prominent African-American faculty: **N/A**
Prominent African-American graduates: **N/A**
African-American student organizations/activities: **Black Student Alliance, Multicultural Club**
Administrative services and programs: **Student Services, Freshman Year Experience, Task Force on Diversity**

Young women who are looking for a college experience in which they will be challenged to go after their dreams will find that Hollins College offers them the academic training and the emotional support to make those dreams a reality. Hollins is one of the few remaining women's colleges in the country that offers a sound liberal arts education on a small campus. One of Hollins's strong points is its small enrollment of about 1,000 and the resulting close interaction with faculty. Students get a lot of one-on-one attention here. Moreover, the atmosphere promotes individual achievement rather than competitiveness. "Every student here has a voice, and if you don't, Hollins helps you find one," said one student.

Young women looking to build their self-confidence will find that Hollins will stretch them academically and creatively. Students are encouraged to take on any task in which they have an interest. "I have always been one of the strongest in my high school classes, yet because I was a girl, I wasn't even allowed the option to use my strength in the class to help lift boxes or move a desk or table," said one student. "Here in the theater, I learned and applied skills that I would have had to fight to learn in coed institutions. I know my way around a shop; power tools are now my good friends. At Hollins being a woman is not an excuse, reason, explanation, or an apology. It's something to be proud of."

This can-do spirit pervades Hollins and is credited with helping its many prominent graduates achieve success. Some of its better-known graduates include Pulitzer prize–winning author Annie Dillard and *Time* magazine publisher Lisa Valk. Numerous others have found their way into leaders' positions in government, politics, medicine, engineering, business and international service.

The diversity of alumni career fields is a direct result of the preparation they receive at Hollins. Typically, students opt for career internships that take them into the White House, Congress, the diplomatic corps; major corporations such as IBM, AT&T, NBC News, and Paramount Pictures; government agencies such as the Environmental Protection Agency; international organizations like the Peace Corps, and study abroad programs in Paris, London, Japan, Rome, and Jamaica. "I have learned things that have already assisted me in my forays in the 'real world,' said one

African-American student. "I spent my Short Term internship in New York working on the production crew of Eddie Murphy's movie *Boomerang* and had many opportunities to express my opinions. I found myself teaching these men that there is a large difference between girls and women."

More than 50 percent of students spend a semester or year studying abroad, and more than 30 percent pursue career internships each year. "While interning in journalism at the *Gaithersburg Gazette*, I spent a day with Ann Compton, a Hollins graduate and ABC News White House correspondent," said one student. "Talking to her and many other alums, it seems that Hollins has produced some pretty amazing women who don't shy away from a challenge."

Although African-American students represent a small percentage of the student body, their needs are not overlooked. The Black Student Alliance and Multicultural Club provide programs promoting diversity on campus and sponsor social and cultural events. Recently the president of Hollins appointed a Task Force on Diversity composed of students, faculty and administrators to implement programs and provide services that will help African-American students and other minorities settle in at Hollins. Task Force events have included a series of "Celebrating Diversity" workshops, and discussion groups on current books such as Terry McMillan's *Waiting to Exhale.* An African-American student services director also provides assistance to freshman students.

Students are comforted by the fact that Roanoke has a substantial African-American community, including its mayor of the past sixteen years. There is a great deal of interaction with the African-American community, students teach at local schools, volunteer at the African-American Museum, receive discounts from local businesses that cater to African-American students and are generally involved with community life, though most live on campus.

If you are a serious-minded student who wants an opportunity to study at a college that not only provides a good education but also offers exposure to leading roles in government, business, politics and the international arena, Hollins College can help you make your dreams a reality.

University of Virginia
P.O. Box 9017
Charlottesville, VA 22901
804-982-3200

Type: **Public**
Overall campus environment: **Congenial**
Total enrollment: **11,000**
African-American students: **1,400**
Total graduate students: **6,000**
African-American graduate students: **200**
Percentage of applications accepted: **48%**
Average SAT score: **1220**
Average SAT African-Americans: **1090**
Special admissions programs: **Jefferson Scholars Program,**
University Achievement Awards
Percentage of African-American graduates: **78%**
Percentage receiving financial aid: **75%**
Average amount of award: **N/A**
Percentage of African-Americans in ROTC programs: **4%**
Faculty: **986**
African-American faculty: **25**
Student/faculty ratio: **12 to 1**
Tuition: **$3,888 in state, $10,800 out of state**
Scholarship programs: **Jerome Holland Scholarship, Jefferson**
Scholars Program, School of Engineering Scholarships,
University of Virginia Scholarships, National Achievement
Program for Outstanding Negro Students Scholarships
Academic programs: **College of Arts and Sciences, School of**
Architecture, School of Engineering and Applied Science,
School of Nursing, Curry School of Education, McIntire
School of Commerce
Prominent African-American Graduate: **Ralph Sampson,**
former NBA basketball star
Prominent African-American faculty: **Rita Dove, Professor of**
English and 1987 Pulitzer prize–winning poet
Student organizations: **Black Student Alliance, Alpha Phi**
Alpha, Kappa Alpha Psi, Phi Beta Sigma, Alpha Kappa Alpha,
Delta Sigma Theta, Zeta Phi Beta, Sigma Gamma Rho
Administrative services and programs: **Office of Afro-American**

**Affairs, Office of Career Planning and Placement, Luther
Porter Cultural Center, Nat Turner Library**

The first thing you notice about UVA is the enthusiasm and
excitement its administration, students and alumni share. Besides
being ranked among the best institutions that provide the equiva-
lent of an Ivy League education, UVA has gained a reputation as
being a good school for African-Americans.

This university aggressively recruits African-Americans and
works at retaining them once they're admitted. Like many colleges, it has placed special emphasis on providing African-
American students with academic advising, tutoring, counseling
and career planning services. While there is a clamoring for more
African-Americans in key areas of the administration and faculty,
UVA has placed African-American administrators in admissions
and other areas of student services. It has an Office of African-
American Affairs, a special summer orientation program for high
school students, and other special recruitment efforts. It boasts a
78 percent graduation rate for African-Americans—a success that
eludes many majority colleges in the country.

Founded in 1819 by Thomas Jefferson, UVA quietly integrated
its campus in the early 1950s. Several of the original students went
on to receive advanced degrees, some at the university's law
school, and have enjoyed successful careers. In recent years many
of those alumni have become involved with the school's efforts to
recruit African-Americans and to raise money for scholarships.
That connection has been bolstered through a special Black
Alumni Weekend that has grown into a major fund-raising event
as well as a time for graduates to reconnect and encourage current
students to pursue their goals.

UVA has six undergraduate schools, including a school of
engineering and applied science, a school of architecture, a
school of nursing and a college of arts and sciences, to which
freshmen can apply. Two other schools—Curry School of Education and McIntire School of Commerce—are available to students in their third year. UVA also administers the Echols Scholars
Program, which offers flexible course choices and exemption
from the customary course requirements for the Bachelor of Arts
degree; a special dean supervises students' academic progress.
Only 7 percent of the entering first-year class are invited to partici-

pate in this prestigious program, whose graduates have gone on to top graduate schools, including Harvard law and medical schools and the University of Virginia's Law School.

The environment at UVA is pleasant, and relations between African-American and white students are congenial. As is the case on many large, predominantly white campuses, an African-American student can feel cut off from the rest of the student body, particularly if he or she is not confident and outgoing. There is interaction between races, but African-American students tend to socialize with each other through campus organizations or one of the many fraternity or sorority chapters.

The UVA campus with its historic buildings sits on beautiful grounds in the rural community of Charlottesville. Its architecture is world-famous and has won many design awards. The buildings and landscape were designed by Thomas Jefferson himself, and many of the original features such as housing for faculty, are still in use. There is also guaranteed housing for first-year students, and adequate housing for a student to live on campus the entire four years. UVA has an active sports program and is a Division I Atlantic Coast Conference school, but enforces strict academic requirements for players. In addition to varsity sports, the school reports that 85 percent of students are involved in intramurals. Athletic facilities include three swimming pools (open year-round), basketball courts, tennis courts, playing fields and racquetball courts.

Admission to UVA is highly selective, and successful candidates have usually graduated in the top 10 percent of their high school class. But academics are not the only criteron used for selection. A student's proven leadership ability, social and personal achievements, and future goals are all considered in the decision, which is still made by the college admissions staff and the dean, not by computer formula. In keeping with the tradition and vision of Thomas Jefferson, UVA prides itself on being a diverse institution with students from all backgrounds, cultures, racial groups and geographic areas. This highly selective process and UVA's academic offerings, accomplished faculty and administration and tradition of excellence have won it the distinction of being called a "public Ivy League" college.

Virginia Polytechnic Institute and State University
104 Burruss Hall
Blacksburg, Virginia 24061-0202
703-231-6267

Type: **Public land-grant**
Overall campus environment: **Cordial/culturally aware**
Total enrollment: **23,912**
African-American students: **1,092**
Graduate students: **4,297**
African-American graduate students: **124**
Percentage of applications accepted: **60–70%**
Average SAT/ACT score: **1000–1200**
Average SAT/ACT African-Americans: **N/R**
Special admissions programs: **Student Transition Program (STP)**
Percentage of African-American graduates: **47%**
Percentage receiving financial aid: **90%**
Average amount of award: **$5,447**
Percentage in ROTC programs: **7%**
Number of faculty: **1,909**
Number of African-American faculty: **36**
Student/faculty ratio: **17 to 1**
Tuition: **$8,986**
Scholarship programs: **National Achievement Scholarship Program (ranked 14th in the nation in enrollment of scholars); Virginia Transfer Grants for Black Students, numerous scholarships for African-American students**
Academic programs: **76 majors in 7 undergraduate colleges: Agriculture and Life Sciences, Architecture and Urban Studies, Arts and Sciences, Business, Education, Engineering, Human Resources**
Most popular majors: **Biology, Accounting/Business, Engineering**
Prominent African-American graduates: **Dell Curry, NBA player, Charlotte Hornets**
Prominent African-American faculty: **Nikki Giovanni, Professor of English, poet and writer**
African-American student organizations/activities: **Black Student Alliance, National Society of Black Engineers, Alpha**

Phi Alpha, Kappa Alpha Psi, Omega Psi Phi, Phi Beta Sigma, Alpha Kappa Alpha, Delta Sigma Theta, Zeta Phi Beta, Sigma Gamma Rho, Ujima Dance Theatre, Gospel Experience singers; Black History Month Committee, Black Student Weekend, Black Cultural Center, NAACP

Administrative services and programs: **Summer Pre-College Awareness program, Student Transition Program, Virginia Tech Peer Group Leader program, Virginia Tech Academic Success program, tutoring program, Support Program for Juniors and Seniors, Distinguished African-American Students, Multicultural Awareness Program, Minority Career Advancement Program**

Once an agricultural school for young men, Virginia Tech is quickly moving into the twenty-first century as a leader in technology and cultural diversity. Nationally recognized for its professional and technical programs in engineering and computer technology as well as the life sciences, Virginia Tech in recent years has been successful in achieving a greater African-American presence. It has increased the numbers of African-American students and faculty as well as supported academic, cultural and social organizations that benefit minority students. African-American students represent only 5 percent of the student population, but the administration is aggressively recruiting students through a targeted effort which reaches out to local high schools, promoting a career in the sciences. Among Virginia Tech's myriad recruitment and retention efforts is the Partnership Program, which is designed to increase the number of minority high school students who enroll in college-preparatory curriculums in Virginia's schools; the summer Pre-College Awareness Program, which motivates middle-school students to prepare for higher education, and the Spring Black Student Weekend, which brings prospective African-American students and their parents to campus for a weekend orientation.

Once they are enrolled at Virginia Tech, a number of support programs help African-American students succeed through graduation. The Student Transition Program (STP), for example, provides incoming students an opportunity to begin their freshman year during the summer and provides instruction in study methods, counseling and academic support services. Students who participate in STP earn six credit hours. The Virginia Tech Academics Success Program (VTASP), the Virginia Tech Peer Group Leader Program, and Tutoring Programs all provide academic assistance, counseling, and in some cases just friendship to incoming students, who may be overwhelmed by the environment and academic rigors of campus life. All of these programs are provided by the Office of Academic Enrichment, whose responsibility it is to increase the numbers of African-American students enrolling in college-prep courses and to provide academic and other support services to these students once enrolled.

Besides these academic supports, Virginia Tech has also increased its hiring of African-American faculty. Among its faculty are world-renowned African-American poet Nikki Giovanni and former Dance Theatre of Harlem dancer and choreographer Carol Ann Crawford, director of the Ujima Dance Theatre.

African-American students will find that in addition to academics Virginia Tech is supportive of cultural and social activities. There are Black Greek fraternities and sororities on campus, as well as organizations such as the Black Student Alliance, NAACP and National Society of Black Engineers. There is also a popular singing group, the Gospel Experience, and the *Black Voices* newspaper published by African-American students. In the fall of 1992, Virginia Tech opened a Black Cultural Center to bring a variety of programs, exhibits and cultural events to campus and become home to many of these organizations. In addition, plans are under way to establish an Afrocentric residence hall. This is significant, since a large majority of students live on campus and all freshmen are required to do so. Residential life is an important social feature at Virginia Tech, which has 8,500 undergraduates living on campus and maintains the fifteenth-largest residence hall system in the country.

Sports are also important on this campus; the university is in the Division I level of the NCAA and a member of the Metro Conference and the Big East Conference in football. Many of the athletes are African-American; one alumnus is basketball star Dell Curry, who now plays for the Charlotte Hornets. Virginia Tech prides itself on the fact that Curry was drafted by the Utah Jazz in 1986 and returned to school during the off-season to earn his degree in sociology in 1990.

Many African-American students have flourished here and feel a part of the university. One student said, "I love Virginia Tech! Faculty and administrators are very helpful and I am comfortable with the academic program. The only time I deal with the issue of my race is when someone else brings it up. Otherwise it is not an issue I deal with." Other students find that being one of a few African-Americans on campus is a tough position to be in but admit that their experience here has helped them to grow and prepare for the imperfect world in which we live.

For African-American students who can stay the course, Virginia Tech is a fine school that is putting forth great efforts to make life for all students academically and socially satisfying.

Virginia Union University
Richmond, Virginia 23220
804-257-5856

Overall campus environment: **Traditional/Supportive**
Type: **Private—Affiliated with Baptist Church**
Total enrollment: **1,077**
African-American students: **1,066**
Graduate students: **150**
African-American graduate students: **130**
Percentage of applications accepted: **98%**
Average SAT/ACT score: **665/15**
Special admissions programs: **None**
Percentage of African-American graduates: **N/A**
Percentage receiving financial aid: **75%**
Average amount of award: **$4,634**
Percentage in ROTC program: **N/R**
Number of faculty: **79**
Number of African-American faculty: **60**
Student/faculty ratio: **16 to 1**
Tuition: **$3,071 in state/$5,774 out of state**
Scholarship programs: **College Assistance Program, Departmental and Academic Scholarships, VUU/St. John's Law School Program**
Academic programs: **College of Liberal Arts and Sciences (Divisions of Education and Psychology, Humanities, Natural Sciences and Mathematics, Social Sciences); Sydney Lewis**

School of Business Administration; Graduate School of Theology
Most popular majors: **Business, Management, Education, Social Sciences, Biological Sciences, Communications, Public Affairs and Services**
Prominent African-American faculty: **N/R**
Prominent African-American graduates: **N/A**
African-American student organizations/activities: **Student government association, drama group fraternities and sororities, VUU Informer newspaper**
Adminstrative services and programs: **Counseling Center, Office of Student Affairs**

Founded in the late 1800s to give newly emancipated slaves an opportunity to obtain a formal education, Virginia Union University today is providing hope to a new generation of African-Americans. An urban institution, VUU is very much a part of the community of Richmond, sharing its resources with the community as part of the legacy begun more than 100 years ago.

Begun as a Christian college merged from the Wayland Seminary and Richmond Theological Institute, VUU later merged again with two other colleges (Hartshorn Memorial College of Richmond and the Storer College of Harpers Ferry in West Virginia) to form the "union" of educational institutions it is today. Its mission then and now is based on Christian principles, and the university continues to require students to complete one course in religion. VUU is not only concerned with educating its students but seeks to enlighten and convince them of the benefits of committing themselves to service in an effort to better mankind. This philosophy pervades the entire university, and many students are attracted to the university because of the dedication and supportive, nurturing environment that results.

Given its history, it is no surprise that VUU is the home of a well-known school of theology, which offers Master of Divinity and Doctor of Ministry degrees. The School of Theology also has a cooperative relationship with the Union Theological Seminary in Virginia and the Presbyterian School of Christian Education in Virginia.

Thanks to a $2-million endowment, VUU is often able to offer opportunities for needy students to attend college. Students may qualify for one of many scholarship, grant, college work-study or other financial aid opportunities. The College Assistance Program, for example, provides need-based financial aid to Virginia residents. In addition, there are departmental and academic scholarships for which other students may qualify.

The university also participates in programs like Upward Bound, an effort to motivate African-American high school students from low-income families to consider going to college. Its Student Early Entrance (SEE) program gives high school students an opportunity to take college courses while still in high school; and the Special Opportunity Program guides students through six-weeks of intensive study emphasizing the fundamentals of math, reading and the development of good study skills.

VUU programs in the liberal arts and humanities are strong, and its education programs are considered good. Its most popular major is business, with nearly 40 percent of recent graduates receiving degrees in the field. In addition, the university has cooperative 3–2 (three years at VUU and two years at coop school) programs in engineering with Howard University, Michigan University and the University of Iowa. The university faculty, half of whom have doctoral degrees and who are mostly African-American and multiracial, also get high marks from students, who rate the student-teacher relationship "good and very supportive."

As for social life, there are eight national chapters of fraternities and sororities on campus and more than forty-five student organizations, a student newspaper, the *VUU Informer,* and numerous cultural and social activities. Because VUU is such an integral part of the Richmond community, the university is the focus of many events and activities. Sports is big here and the college boasts a 10,000-seat stadium among its facilities. Homecoming is one of the biggest events each year.

Students who are considering a predominantly Black college will find VUU's history and continuing commitment to "good teaching and enlightened guidance," and its honest concern for young people and their future, appealing.

Marlboro College
College Road
Marlboro, Vermont 05344
802-254-4333

Type: **Private liberal arts**
Overall campus environment: **Liberal**
Total enrollment: **275**
African-American students: **N/R**
Graduate students: **N/A**
Percentage of applications accepted: **62%**
Average SAT score: **950–1200**
Average SAT African-Americans: **N/R**
Special admissions programs: **N/A**
Percentage of African-American graduates: **N/R**
Percentage receiving financial aid: **65%**
Average amount of award: **$7000**
Percentage in ROTC programs: **N/A**
Number of faculty: **40**
Number of African-American faculty: **N/R**
Student/faculty ratio: **7 to 1**
Tuition: **$16,110**
Scholarship programs: **College scholarships and need based grants**
Academic programs: **American Studies, Anthropology, Astronomy, Biology, Ceramics, Chemistry, Classics, Computer Science, Creative Writing, Dance, Economics, Environmental Studies, Film/Video Studies, History, Languages, Literature, Mathematics, Music, Philosophy, Physics, Political Science, Psychology, Religion, Sculpture, Sociology, Teacher Certification, Theater, Visual Arts, Woodworking, World Studies Program**
Most popular majors: **Humanities, Environmental Studies, Science, Writing**
Prominent African-American faculty: **N/R**
Prominent African-American graduates: **N/R**
African-American student organizations/activities: **N/R**
Administrative services and programs: **N/R**

Being a student at Marlboro College is like being a "real life" participant in any community. At Marlboro students become a working part of the college community and participate in the running of the college, sharing in the decision-making process and taking responsibility for the decisions that are made. Obviously, Marlboro is unique, and the college experience a student receives here is not likely to be found at any other liberal arts institution in the country. However, to appreciate Marlboro you must first understand its purpose.

Marlboro is a small college of just over 200 students in the quiet rural town of Marlboro, Vermont. Situated atop a small mountain with a view of southern Vermont, Marlboro College has picture-postcard beauty and serenity. The 400 acres of land on which the college sits make a perfect environment for the mind-expanding and soul-searching study that goes on here.

At Marlboro students not only receive a degree, they develop the knowledge and skills to pursue an interest. A primary goal is to help students develop the ability to think—to analyze, deduce, form opinions and defend them—and to write with precision and clarity. Through one-on-one interaction between faculty and students in small classroom groups as well as informal settings, the administration slowly achieves this goal. At first a great deal of emphasis is placed on the study of humanities, arts and the natural and social sciences. By the junior year, students are ready to undertake more vigorous study of their major field of interest under the close supervision and tutelage of a faculty adviser. Underlying this style of teaching is a simplistic philosophy that says that the only thing really necessary for education to take place is a student, a teacher and a log for them to sit on. The academic program is not that simple, however; the faculty work closely with the student to develop an individualized program that will be most beneficial to the student.

By providing students with such a supportive framework, Marlboro prepares them for the challenge of taking control of their own lives and careers. Students are encouraged to "learn by doing" through independent study and internships such as the World Studies program, in which a student lives and works in another culture. Student internships have spanned the globe; students have worked with CARE in Uganda, and with the Wilderness Society in Tasmania, and have spent stints at London's *International Management Magazine.* Experiences obtained through these programs help to set Marlboro students apart and speak to their interest in social issues and their motivation to make a difference in society. "I can understand why people feel on the national level that they don't have any power to change things," said one student. "At Marlboro, you do." "Marlboro is a do-it-yourself kind of place," said another. "If you want something to happen, you've got to make it happen yourself."

All students are expected to participate in campus life equally. Because of its community spirit, Marlboro does not separate its students out racially, and African-American or other minority student issues are dealt with as part of the concerns of the campus at large. Indeed, the small numbers of these students support such a decision.

African-American students report that the inclusive environment that exists at Marlboro fosters a feeling of belonging. "I have always felt like part of the community since the day I registered at Marlboro," said one student. "The size of the community plays a big part in my feeling comfortable and fitting in."

There is no real formula for students who qualify for Marlboro. Standardized test scores are considered, but a desire to design a major field of study and to follow a real passion in life is equally important. Admissions committees weigh on-campus interviews, recommendations, writing samples and an autobiographical sketch.

African-American students who want a unique college experience in which they can pursue a dream to explore a particular culture, works of art, history or the like, will benefit from the freedom and academic support Marlboro has to offer.

Evergreen State College
Olympia, Washington 98505
206-866-6000

Type: **4-year liberal arts**
Overall campus environment: **Cordial**
Total enrollment: **3,340**
African-American students: **133**

Graduate students: **116**
African-American graduate students: **2**
Percentage of applications accepted: **64%**
Average SAT/ACT score: **900/18**
Average SAT/ACT African-Americans: **900/18**
Special admissions programs: **N/R**
Percentage African-American graduates: **78%**
Percentage receiving financial aid: **50%**
Average amount of award: **N/A**
Percentage in ROTC programs: **N/A**
Number of faculty: **175**
Number of African-American faculty: **8**
Student/faculty ratio: **20 to 1**
Tuition: **$6,297**
Scholarship programs: **Cultural Diversity Scholarship, First People's Scholarship, Jackie Robinson Scholarship, Shauna May Scholarship**
Academic programs: **Multidisciplinary Studies in Environmental Studies, Expressive Arts, Knowledge and the Human Condition, Language and Culture, Management and the Public Interest, Native American Studies, Political Economy and Social Change, Science, Technology and Health, Center for the Study of Science and Human Values, Tacoma Program-Art of Leadership**
Most popular majors: **Environmental Studies, Sociology, Visual Arts, Psychology, Philosophy, Religion, Theology, Communications, Computer Science, Japanese (Language and Culture)**
Prominent African-American graduates: **N/R**
Prominent African-American faculty: **N/R**
African-American student organizations: **Umoja**
Administrative services and programs: **First People's Advising, Recruitment and Peer Support**

If obtaining a college degree through self-directed learning in a supportive environment is your ideal college experience, Evergreen State College may be the place for you. This highly rated liberal arts college sixty miles outside Seattle creates an unusual learning opportunity by empowering students to take a large role in their education. The curriculum moves from beginning to advanced work in a way that is consistent with individual learning style.

Everything about Evergreen is nontraditional, including the curriculum, class structure, grading system and the way in which you earn a degree. Students begin their education with a core of multidisciplinary coursework that strengthens basic communication, research and reasoning skills and gradually moves into the study of a major field of interest. Even then, learning continues through the exploration of a variety of subjects by a team of faculty representing different disciplines, and, finally, into more independent study, research and actual work in the major. Classes are generally taught in a seminar format, with an average of twenty students who through reading and discussion explore a specific topic. This collaborative approach to teaching and learning is one of the school's main attractions, as is its supportive and accessible faculty.

Evergreen is clearly successful in its efforts to establish a nontraditional, free-spirited educational environment, and it has attempted to use that same philosophy to create a culturally diverse campus. While minorities (or students of color, as they are called at Evergreen) represent a fair portion of the student population, African-American students are only about 4 percent of the students enrolled. The African-American faculty are very supportive of students; outside of their support, few campus organizations exist to meet African-American students' special needs. Because of this, most minority students tend to stick together. One student said, "I feel part of the community of students of color. I do not feel a part of the community at large, nor the ideals this college professes." The administration does support two organizations—Umoja, which promotes African-American culture and heritage, and First People's Advising, Recruitment and Peer Support which assists with the retention of students of color. But overall the administration believes that African-American students will join in the mainstream of college life.

For students who want a less traditional, more student-centered college environment, and can adjust to Evergreen's campus life, Evergreen has a lot to offer. The education students receive prepares them to be independent thinkers, strategic planners and sound decision-makers—skills that are required in most professional careers. In addition, more than half of Evergreen

students participate in one or more internships before graduation, compared to less than 2 percent nationwide. Students come
away from Evergreen with more than a degree, with an actual
working knowledge of their major field of interest, whether it is
designing computer data systems for a social service agency or
managing an advertising account.

Seattle University
Broadway and Madison
Seattle, Washington 98122
1-800-423-7123/206-296-5812

Type: **Comprehensive affiliated with Jesuit Order (Catholic)**
Overall campus environment: **Cordial**
Total enrollment: **4,600**
African-American students: **130**
Graduate students: **1,500**
African-American graduate students: **20**
Percentage of applications accepted: **65%**
Average SAT score: **950**
Average SAT African-Americans: **850**
Special admissions programs: **N/R**
Percentage of African-American graduates: **60% (graduating
on time)**
Percentage receiving financial aid: **90%**
Average amount of award: **$14,000**
Percentage in ROTC programs: **N/A**
Number of faculty: **230**
Number of African-American faculty: **2**
Student/faculty ratio: **20 to 1**
Tuition: **$11,510**
Scholarship programs: **Regents Awards**
Academic programs: **Science, Engineering, Nursing, Arts and
Sciences**
Most popular majors: **Diagnostic Ultrasound, Nursing,
Business, Engineering, Criminal Justice, International
Studies, Communications, Addiction Studies**
Prominent African-American graduates: **Elgin Baylor, former
NBA star; Norwood Brooks, Treasurer, City of Seattle; Quincy**

Jones, producer/musician; Dr. Donald Phelps, Chancellor,
Los Angeles Community College System; Emile Wilson,
Rhodes scholar
Prominent African-American faculty: **N/R**
African-American student organizations/activities: **The
Children's Literacy Tutoring Project, Rights of Passage
(R.O.P.), Central Area Motivation Program**
Administrative services and programs: **N/R**

Seattle University is a coed university of about 4,600 students
located in downtown Seattle. A fairly selective university with emphasis on teaching, Seattle University has strong academic programs in the liberal arts and sciences and business and
health-related fields. Besides a good academic record, it is recommended that students seeking admission to Seattle U have a
strong sense of self and of their culture, as well as an interest in
community service and leadership. Students will be called on to
use these skills, as many get involved in community or volunteer
work. The university has strong ties to Seattle's large African-
American community and its leaders. African-American students
are involved with the community in three primary projects including the Children's Literacy Project, the R.O.P. (Rights of Passage)
program for at-risk youth and the Central Area Motivation Program. The university also started a new mentoring project in the
fall of 1992 to help African-American students gain better access
to Seattle University alumni, staff and community leaders.

Although their numbers are small, African-American students
do well at Seattle U, with the university reporting more than 50
percent of those enrolled graduating and 90 proceeding to graduate school. Among its alumni are a number of highly successful
African-Americans, including producer and musician, Quincy
Jones, NBA legend Elgin Baylor and the school's only Rhodes
scholar. University officials attribute this success to the student
selection process, the strong emphasis on academics and the university's "inclusive policies," which encourage student participation in all organizations and events. However, not all students feel
that the university meets their needs. "With the lack of African-
American students, faculty, staff and diverse classes, I feel like my
education is incomplete and one-sided," said one student. "Faculty and administrators can be helpful if you make the effort to

approach them, but I do not feel comfortable doing so." Even students (as well as administrators) who are pleased with the university warn that a student must be outgoing and willing to ask for help as professors here do not "hold students' hands." Another student said, "Faculty and administrators are very helpful. Individuals do, however, have to make themselves known by networking and communicating with the right people."

Seattle U is a less traditional campus environment, largely because of its urban location. Freshmen are required to live on campus for the first year unless they are residents of the state and live with a parent or guardian. However, housing is also available in nearby communities. The university is affiliated with the Catholic Jesuit Order, but chapel attendance is not required, and less than half the students are Catholic.

The administration's attempts to encourage students to interact socially as well as academically regardless of race are admirable, and students seem to feel free to choose. However, group activities still tend to divide along racial lines. "I am not pressured to socialize only with African-American students, although I choose to do so because of a feeling of family I have with other African-Americans," said one student. The school has had racial incidents. Recently students protested an editorial in the student newspaper which depicted African-Americans in a stereotypical way. Like the rest of the country, Seattle U was affected by the aftermath of the verdict in the Rodney King beating trial in spring 1992, and it is believed that many white students were enlightened by events.

The small size of Seattle University, its urban location and strong academic programs are features which attract many students. But it is important that students considering Seattle University understand that they need to be focused, goal-oriented and assertive to succeed at this school.

Whitman College
345 Boyer Avenue
Walla Walla, Washington 99362
509-527-5176

Type: **4-year liberal arts**
Overall campus environment: **Conservative**

Total enrollment: **1,200**
African-American students: **15**
Graduate students: **0**
Percentage of applications accepted: **80%**
Average SAT score: **1150**
Average SAT African-Americans: **N/R**
Special admissions programs: **N/A**
Percentage of African-American graduates: **67%**
Percentage receiving financial aid: **100%**
Average amount of award: **$11,165**
Percentage in ROTC program: **0**
Number of faculty: **148**
Number of African-American faculty: **1**
Student/faculty ratio: **11 to 1**
Tuition: **$14,360**
Scholarship programs: **Whitman College Diversity Scholarship**
Academic programs: **31 degree programs in Anthropology, Art, Biology, Chemistry, Economics, English, Foreign Language and Literature, French, German, Spanish, Geology, History, Mathematics, Music, Philosophy, Physics, Politics, Psychology, Sociology, Theater**
Most popular majors: **English, History, Psychology, Economics, Biology**
Prominent African-American graduates: **N/R**
Prominent African-American faculty: **N/R**
African-American student organizations/activities: **Black Student Union, Black History Month**
Administrative services: **N/R**

Whitman College, a small liberal arts college of about 1,200 students, in many ways resembles a high-priced prep school. The overall environment is conservative, with students coming primarily from upper-middle-class backgrounds. There is little concern for politics, intercollegiate sports (almost none exist here) or issues of cultural diversity. Students come here primarily for the strong academics and the excellent and attentive faculty.

Whitman's academic program is based on a core curriculum and interdisciplinary courses which a student must complete in addition to the major field of study. Classes are small, with an average size of about twenty and a student-to-faculty ratio of 11 to 1. Freshmen may select from courses in the Origins of Modern Thought, Study of Classical Greece and the Survey of Great Works. There are also a senior colloquium and oral and written exams in a student's major field of study. The college offers thirty-one degree programs in traditional liberal arts subjects such as English, history, psychology, economics and biology, which are among the college's most popular majors. There is also a cooperative engineering program offered in conjunction with Cal Tech, Columbia University and Duke University. A master's-degree program in forestry and environmental science is also available at Duke. Students may take advantage of study abroad programs, including a special opportunity for selected students and alumni to teach in China. (If you have an interest in Asian culture, Whitman owns a multimillion-dollar Asian art collection, and has an Asian studies and history program.) In addition, students may participate in a Summer Fellows Program in conjunction with the University of Chicago Graduate School of Business.

Students are required to live on campus their first two years at Whitman, but housing is guaranteed for the entire four years. Besides the traditional residence houses, students may opt to live with a student whose native language is German, French, Spanish, Chinese or Japanese. Or they may decide to bunk with a student who has an interest in environmental issues, multiethnic issues or fine arts.

The minority community here is small, and African-American students represent about 1 percent of the student body. Besides the Black Student Union, there is little support specifically for African-Americans. The administration encourages all students to participate in all campus events and organizations. There is a small African-American community in Walla Walla, and students have some interaction through tutoring programs in local schools and through the churches in the community.

For the majority students here, Greek life dominates social activity. The town of Walla Walla (which means "water, water" to Native Americans from the region) is small and remote, so there is little social activity off campus. Those who enjoy the outdoors, however, will be pleased with the beautiful autumns, snowy winters and warm springs. Skiing is within an hour's drive and white-water rafting, backpacking and golf and tennis are all popular.

Whitman is an excellent college and its faculty are caring and attentive. However, need to know that you will be one of fewer than twenty African-American students on a campus far from a major city or town (Seattle and Portland are about 250 miles away). Although the college is open to students of all racial backgrounds, there are very few supports to help relieve the isolation that a student may feel. It is strongly recommended that students visit and talk with other African-American students as well as administrators to be sure Whitman is a good match.

St. Norbert College
Cultural Diversity Office
100 Grant Street
De Pere, Wisconsin
414-337-3005/1-800-236-4878

Type: **Liberal arts and sciences, affiliated with Catholic Church**
Overall campus environment: **Cordial**
Total enrollment: **1,877**
African-American students: **6**
Graduate students: **11**
African-American graduate students: **0**
Percentage of applications accepted: **90%**
Average SAT/ACT score: **1060/24**
Average SAT/ACT African-Americans: **N/A**
Special admissions programs: **N/A**
Percentage of African-American graduates: **N/A**
Percentage receiving financial aid: **100%**
Average amount of award: **$7,507**
Percentage in ROTC programs: **N/A**
Number of faculty: **149**
Number of African-American faculty: **0**
Student/faculty ratio: **15 to 1**
Tuition: **$10,730**
Scholarship programs: **Cultural Diversity Scholarship; Education Diversity Scholarship**
Academic programs: **More than 30 majors in liberal arts and sciences**
Most popular majors: **Business Administration,**

Communication, Accounting, International Business, International Studies
Prominent African-American faculty: **N/A**
Prominent African-American graduates: **N/A**
African-American student organizations/activities: **N/A**
Administrative services and programs: **Cultural Diversity Office, Intercultural Student Alliance, Intercultural Lounge, Faculty Mentor program**

St. Norbert is a small private liberal arts and sciences college affiliated with the Catholic Church. It is a highly rated institution and one that is fairly selective in its admissions process. The average student admitted to the college scores above 1000 on the SAT and 24 on the ACT. St. Norbert offers more than thirty major fields of study; its most popular majors are business and accounting, international business, education, communications and international studies. Almost all faculty hold doctoral degrees and many have published or done substantial research in their field. Although these accomplishments are important, the administration emphasizes teaching and prides itself on a student-to-faculty ratio of 15 to 1. Besides an accomplished faculty, St. Norbert offers an honors program, independent studies, an academic mastery program and a professional practice program in which students can get credit for internships.

Although chapel attendance is not mandatory, the college does require students to complete two religious heritage courses. The campus is fairly conservative and the majority of students live in the dorms. Students whose families do not live within commuting distance are required to live on campus.

Although African-Americans and other minorities represent a small proportion (about 2 percent total) of the student body, the administration makes efforts to accommodate student needs through its Cultural Diversity Office. Here staff and faculty provide academic counseling, mentoring and individual advising. Administrators combine these efforts with the Academic Mastery and other support programs to give students a leg up on academics. Students will also find support for their concerns through the Intercultural Student Alliance and Intercultural Lounge. In addition, the administration holds regular forums with student leaders and organizations to discuss concerns and to foster understanding among all cultural groups. The administration believes these efforts have been successful, and no racial incidents have occurred, to its knowledge, on campus.

St. Norbert has no African-American student organizations, and students are encouraged to participate in all activities and organizations. Perhaps the small number of African-American students on campus accounts for this fact; the college reports that fewer than ten African-American students were enrolled in 1992, and about the same number of Hispanic and Native American students were enrolled.

Being one of a handful of other minority students is a situation that potential students may want to consider carefully. A student who attends St. Norbert will need to have a strong sense of self, to be independent and to be able to cope with the isolated and small-town environment of Wisconsin without a great deal of peer support.

University of Wyoming
Box 3435
Laramie, Wyoming 82071-3435
307-766-5160

Type: **Public**
Overall campus environment: **Cordial—Western-style**
Total enrollment: **10,700**
African-American students: **102**
Graduate students: **1,580**
African-American graduate students: **N/R**
Percentage of applications accepted: **81%**
Average ACT score: **23**
Average ACT African-Americans: **N/R**
Special admissions programs: **Western Undergraduate Exchange Program**
Percentage of African-American graduates: **N/A**
Percentage receiving financial aid: **N/A**
Average amount of award: **$3,162**
Percentage in ROTC programs: **N/A**
Number of faculty: **831**
Number of African-American faculty: **N/R**

Student/faculty ratio: **19 to 1**
Tuition: **$1,300 in state/$4,498 out of state**
Scholarship programs: **Hurst Scholarships, University of Wyoming Minority Scholarships**
Academic programs: **More than 100 majors in 6 undergraduate Colleges, Agriculture, Arts and Sciences, Business, Education, Engineering, Health Sciences**
Most popular majors: **Education, Business Administration, Accounting, Psychology, Computer Science, Political Science, Molecular Biology, Animal Science, Communications, Pharmacy, Nursing, Electrical and Mechanical Engineering**
African-American student organizations/activities: **Association of Black Student Leaders, Black Greek organizations, Black History Month, Dr. Martin Luther King, Jr., Celebration**
Administrative services and programs: **Minority Student Affairs Office, Student Educational Opportunities, Tutorial Services**

If the name of this university conjures up thoughts of the Old West, cowboys and one-horse towns, you're not too far off. The University of Wyoming is a state-supported university. The largely untouched natural beauty of UW's campus reflects the entire state; and since it is the single university in the state it is often indulged like an only child.

Students are attracted to UW by its academic programs, which focus on the environment, technology and the sciences. This is no wonder, considering that Wyoming is probably one of the last bastions of real Western territory where students have access to a natural laboratory. Programs in agriculture, botany, physics, zoology and petroleum engineering are popular; the ecology department is highly rated. This is not the college to attend if you're interested in the high-profile world of journalism or public affairs; nor does it provide the broad base of a liberal arts program.

UW is in the small, isolated town of Laramie; the pace is slow and life revolves almost totally around the college campus. Social life off campus centers around the numerous bars that dot the area and offer special attractions nearly every night. On campus a strong fraternity and sorority presence dominates, and students who want any social life join them.

For African-American students social life is even more limited; aside from the two Black greek organizations on campus and the

Black Student Association, there's not much to do. "Being an African-American student at UW is rough," said a sophomore. "There are not many activities that cater to our interests and needs; and the student community is not as friendly as I had expected." The outdoorsy type will find the skiing, hiking, mountain climbing, riding and camping great.

Nearly 25 percent of students come from out of state as well as foreign countries, but the student body is largely from Wyoming. For many of these students, this is the first time they have interacted with African-Americans. To help all students adjust to a diverse campus, the administration has an ongoing educational program of panel discussions, seminars and workshops on ethnic diversity. The administration is concerned about its racial relations. Recently the university divested itself of all investments in South Africa.

Although the administration is concerned, it clearly has a lot of work to do before African-American students begin to feel a part of campus life here. "I feel like an outsider at times not only because there are so few African-American students here but also because white students seem unable to relate to me and so they avoid doing so," one student said. "There is also a tendency for African-Americans to separate themselves into small groups with little interaction with other students."

Students report that they are pleased with the academics and with a fairly responsive faculty. "The academic program at UW meets my academic goals and at an affordable price," said another student. "The faculty and administrators have been very helpful and I have enjoyed the opportunity to interact with other ethnic groups. This experience is truly going to have a lasting effect on my view of society."

If the Old West intrigues you and you're willing to make some sacrifices, UW's solid academic programs and the beauty of its setting can add up to an experience that can't be matched elsewhere.